FOR RECORD

To Ann
and
all who stood by me

BRIAN LENIHAN

BLACKWATER PRESS

Acknowledgements

My wife *Ann* and family - particularly my sons *Conor* and *Niall,* who put in long hours on the book.

My son *Brian* and *Esmonde Smith,* who were helpful at a difficult time.

Publishers Blackwater Press - particularly *John O'Connor,* Managing Director, who was also philosopher and friend.

Editors *Hilda O'Sullivan* and *John O'Connor.*

Philip Ryan for his expertise in design and layout.

Dr. Thomas P. O'Neill, Biographer of Eamon de Valera, whose help and guidance were invaluable.

Attic Press – publishers of *Emily O'Reilly's* book "Candidate", and O'Brien Press – publishers of *Fergus Finlay's* book "Mary Robinson", who kindly allowed me to use the benefit of their published researches on the Presidential Election.

Geraldine Kennedy and *Raymond Smith* for the use of their published researches into events covered in this book.

To *Eoghan Harris* and *Gay Byrne* for the use of their material.

To Adapt Marketing Ltd. (*John D. Walsh* and *Peter Griffin*) for their brilliant analysis of the Waterford constituency.

To *Bertie Ahern* T.D. Minister for Labour, my Director of Elections, and his campaign team, particularly *Niamh O'Connor, Michael Dawson, Sean Paul Mahon, Terry Shannon,* and *David Watson,* who did the tour with me everyday.

To the party workers and supporters of the Fianna Fáil organisation.

Finally, to all my friends, particularly in politics and the media, who helped me in so many ways, I am unable to enumerate here.

Printed in Ireland at the press of the publishers 1991
© Blackwater Press 1991. 8 Airton Road, Tallaght, Dublin 24.

ISBN 0 86121 362 9

Design and layout Philip Ryan

Special Acknowledgement: The appendix and extracts at pages 110, 139-144 are taken from a tape recording between Mr. James Duffy and myself made on 17th May 1990.

Contents

Foreword

"A POLITICAL NECESSITY"

So spoke General Mercier, French Minister for War, on the condemnation of Alfred Dreyfus for treason at a court-martial in France on 5th January 1895. Three years later, Émile Zola wrote his famous exposé "J'accuse", in which Dreyfus' innocence was clearly established. My dismissal from Government was also deemed to be a political necessity in spite of the injustice involved. I do not intend to accuse, but merely to establish the truth of my repeated statements during the Presidential election 1990, that I did not ring Áras an Uachtaráin on the evening of January 27th 1982, or speak to President Hillery in connection with the exercise of his powers under the Constitution, or on any other matter.

Of itself, the issue is not of great consequence. However, it was used extensively during the campaign to brand me as a liar, and was a major factor in my dismissal from Government, and my defeat in the election. I have also taken this opportunity to advance some views on the politics of our times, and the need for change evolving from the roots and mores of our people.

I have a long reputation of being honest in politics, and I wish to continue in public life on that basis. With William Shakespeare I say:

"He that filches from me my good name, robs me of that, which not enriches him, and makes me poor indeed."

(Othello Act 3 Scene 3)

I hope this explains why the book "For The Record" has been written.

Brian Lenihan
May 1st 1991

1

PRESIDENCY

When I was elected a member of the Senate in 1957 it was at a time when many of the founding fathers of modern Ireland were still active in politics. I became a member of the Fianna Fáil parliamentary party in which Seán Lemass, Seán McEntee, Dr. Jim Ryan, Seán Moylan and Frank Aiken were ministers and Eamon De Valera was Taoiseach. I felt that I was walking with history, that I was a link with the generation which had won our independence. That was a period when the perennial question of Northern Ireland was causing an acute problem. It is often forgotten that over 150,000 people attended the funeral of Seán South of Garryowen, and four Sinn Féin candidates were elected to the 1957 Dáil. I remember well the balanced leadership of Eamon De Valera as he guided the party through the difficulties of the emotions which many of us felt in that trying time. It was the lesson learned then that helped me and many others through later and even greater traumas and taught me to weigh the issue at stake and to look to long-term consequences when facing immediate problems.

Perhaps one of the greatest traumas in my time as a minister occurred on January 30th 1972. Thirteen people were killed in Derry that day and many more were wounded when the British army went berserk in the Bogside. It soon became known as "Bloody Sunday". At the following Tuesday's government meeting, I volunteered to represent the government at the funerals the next morning. The late Jerry Cronin from Mallow and David Andrews TD were among the deputies and friends who travelled by cavalcade from O'Connell Street the following morning. I said to Jack Lynch the day before that Derry would be safer than Dublin on the day. I was right - the British Embassy in Dublin went up in flames - and in Derry order was maintained by the citizens of the Bogside.

I met Fr. Ned Daly, the priest who had tended the dead and

dying, and I arranged for him to fly out to the United States where he told his story on American radio and television. I was Minister for Transport and Power then and was responsible for the Semi-State Bodies. Our people in the U.S., Seán White of C.I.E., Joe Malone of Bord Fáilte, and Tom Kennedy of Aer Lingus opened doors for Fr. Daly to tell his story of mass murder, and so the future Bishop of Derry pre-empted the British propaganda machine by getting the truth up front first. In rapid succession, we had the Widgery report, Direct Rule, the abolition of Stormont, the power-sharing Executive and Harold Wilson's abandonment of the Executive in the face of pressure. Tory Prime Minister Heath tried - his successor failed, but after Bloody Sunday things would thankfully never be the same again. Stormont was gone.

The years were to pass with no political solution, with continuing deaths and with the tragedy of the H-Block hunger strikes. The impact of these on the people of the north, on Anglo-Irish relations and on the politics of our state are matters of history. They are also matters of deep and abiding tragedy. The intransigence on all sides left the problems as pressing and as difficult to solve as the years passed. Perhaps the most interesting positive step taken towards meeting this great problem was the 1985 Anglo-Irish Agreement.

In any assessments of this arrangement, I feel that we have to note both its benefits and its shortcomings. It did not in any way provide a framework for a solution to the Northern question. Its aim was to provide a permanent structure for consultation between the government of the Republic of Ireland and that of the United Kingdom in which matters relating to Northern Ireland could be discussed. However, though the agreement was between the equally sovereign states, there was not an equality of position between the two. A particular example of that, which is very relevant, is the fact that under Article 8 of the agreement the joint conference could deal with matters of the administration of justice within the Republic but similar issues within the U.K. were excluded. Thus the whole position of the Guildford Four, the Maguires and the Birmingham Six were excluded from the Anglo-Irish conference even though they related to members of the nationalist community in the north.

Despite reservations on these and indeed other aspects of the agreement, it fell to me, as Minister for Foreign Affairs in 1987, to try to get the best possible benefit from the agreement. I was not able to raise the issues relating to Irish prisoners in Britain through the conference meetings, but I did deal directly with the then Home Secretary, Douglas Hurd, at several face to face meetings in London at which real progress was made. However, in regard to other matters I worked to the fullest extent possible as Co-Chairman of the Anglo-Irish Conference, with Tom King, the Secretary of State for Northern Ireland. The issue on which I concentrated was the need for equality of employment opportunity in the north. I am pleased that the Fair Employment legislation introduced by Mr. King for Northern Ireland owed much to my efforts from 1987 to 1989. The system is in place and resources can be made available to end job discrimination in Northern Ireland. It is now a matter of political will on the part of the British government to operate it.

Of course this is but a small step forward on the road to internal peace in Northern Ireland. It should help us to break down barriers between the divided communities for there can be no mutual trust without mutual justice. Any future developments must be built on that base. The future development of politics and of administration in Northern Ireland and of relations within the island of Ireland and between the neighbouring islands of Great Britain and Ireland are impossible to foretell, but within a European framework, it must be hoped that a broad vision can develop which will heal the wounds of ancient quarrels. With the Brooke initiative a major step has now been taken to agree on talks covering all aspects of the totality of relationships and I am hopeful of the eventual outcome.

In 1972, Dr. Patrick Hillery, as Minister for Foreign Affairs negotiated Ireland's entry into the Common Market and under his direction I co-ordinated the referendum campaign on behalf of Fianna Fáil. With Fine Gael support we secured an overwhelming national result of 83% in favour of entry. On January 1st, 1973, Ireland, along with Britain and Denmark, joined the European

Community. Dr. Hillery became our first Commissioner and Cearbhaill Ó Dálaigh our first Judge of the European Court. I succeeded Dr. Hillery as Foreign Minister. On January 15th I made the first address on behalf of Ireland to the Council of Ministers in Brussels in which I emphasised the need to develop "a comprehensive and effective regional policy", which became a reality in the establishment of European structural funds in 1988.

The 19th Dáil was dissolved and a general election took place on the 28th February. The Fine Gael-Labour electoral alliance was successful, and Liam Cosgrave succeeded Jack Lynch as Taoiseach. I was out as Minister for Foreign Affairs and what's more, I had lost my Dáil seat. I crawled out from under the wreckage and started to re-build. I ran for the Senate and enjoyed the country-wide tour, meeting the members of my electoral college, the councillors of Ireland. They turned up trumps - I headed the poll on the Industrial and Commercial Panel and became Opposition Leader in the Senate.

By May, I was looking forward to a sedentary summer when my old colleague, Erskine Childers, was selected unanimously as the Fianna Fáil candidate for the Presidency against a free-wheeling Tom O'Higgins, who had been campaigning for months and would be hard to beat. George Colley was Director of Elections, but Erskine insisted that I become his personal campaign manager. We were old family friends since he first won a Dáil seat for Athlone-Longford in 1938 and we understood each other well. My father used to nominate him in Longford-Westmeath and I stood with him on the ticket as a young candidate of 23 years in the 1954 general election. Childers had been Tánaiste and an exceptional Minister - a brilliant speaker with a fine intellect. Furthermore, he had great credentials across the spectrum, being the son of Erskine Childers, who was executed summarily in the Civil War, and was revered by De Valera. He was also a Protestant who was strongly opposed to violence of any kind.

With only a few weeks to go to polling day, we had a brainstorming session, and we came up with the concept of developing a positive role for the President within the framework of the Constitution. Erskine expanded on this theme in speeches throughout the country, and these were re-echoed by all the candidates in the 1990 election. He was very much the authentic pre-cursor in this respect. We devised a slogan which epitomised the man and his record - " A President for all the Nation". We used the Presidential colour scheme of St. Patrick's Blue and Gold. He was packed into a bus and began to tour the country. A wag christened the bus "Wanderly Wagon" after a children's television pro-gramme of the time. After the Dáil and Senate elections I had no money so I got a month's expenses, £400, in advance from Fianna Fáil– a hundred pounds a week to get a President elected! I hired the coach and Tom Stafford got the driver, Brendan Murphy, who I still see at funerals driving the Stafford limos. I remember it well - we set off from Clondalkin for the South, West and North West, winding up near polling day in the home counties of Louth and Meath. I worked on and off the coach, and between Fianna Fáil headquarters and country locations. Erskine made short inspira-tional speeches, all on the same themes, of community leader-ship, practical patriotism and an open Áras. It was great stuff. O'Higgins was tiring, Childers nosed ahead and won with 51.97% of the vote. He was inaugurated President, performed brilliantly, but died after just months in office on the 17th November 1974. Requiescat in pace.

After the election, Jack Lynch nominated me as Fianna Fáil leader in the European Parliament and I embarked on a new career in Strasbourg. It introduced me to the great European experience, which has changed our international role fundamen-tally. We established an alliance with the French Gaullists, which stands to this day. My good friend Christian de la Malene, a former Mayor of Paris, is now leader of the Group with Paddy Lalor as a Vice-President of the Parliament. The French connection has served Ireland well. It had been a hectic year, but an idea was born which only germinated years later. I would run for President some day. The year ended well - my only daughter, Anita, was born in November.

The real success over the 20 years since then has been our involvement in the European Community. We were expected to be just another vote for Britain, but in the event we have shown consistent community solidarity as against Britain's "go it alone" policy, which is only now being ditched after Mrs. Thatcher's departure. In the environment, agriculture, marine and fisheries facilities, infrastructural requirements, industrial, regional and social developments we have gained practical benefits, and given Community solidarity in return. Membership of the European Monetary Union and Political Union within a single market will help to stabilise the nation's financial and monetary position. Our political and international status has been greatly enhanced by our partnership within Europe.

We are now on the threshold of a comprehensive arrangement for collective European security from the Atlantic to the Urals under the CSCE process started in Helsinki in 1975, and inspired by Willy Brandt's policies of Ostpolitik and Détente. I remember the Madrid CSCE meeting in 1980 when the process nearly broke down. Herr Genscher, the German Foreign Minister, asked me, as a neutral, to negotiate between the Eastern and Western bloc countries to get a survival formula to enable the conference to proceed. We succeeded, and now 10 years later, the recent Paris conference has firmed up the new approach, which makes redundant the old NATO-Warsaw Pact defence strategies, and effectively ends the Cold War. Historically, the great achievement for Europe and the world has been the accelerating tandem of France and Germany, now strengthened by German unity. The resultant stability of Western and Central Europe will be extended hopefully into Eastern Europe and the Soviet Union. Hans Dietrich Genscher is the man who has done most to make this feasible over the years.

In domestic politics, negative factors tended to obtrude, particularly in the decade up to 1987. Garret Fitzgerald's infamous "flawed pedigree" speech about Charles Haughey on his nomination as Taoiseach in 1979 initiated a fashion of ugly and personalised politics which I thoroughly deplore. It was compounded by leadership "heaves" within Fianna Fáil, in which the late George Colley and Des O'Malley sought to unseat Charles Haughey on three occasions in the period between 1982 and 1983. I defended the leadership during these crises. As if to add to the acrimony and instability we had three general elections in 18 months, in which people developed a thorough detestation of politics and of politicians of all shapes and sizes.

The Fianna Fáil Government, elected in March 1987, helped to improve the atmosphere by concentrating on the practicalities of government. The right decisions were made in rectifying the national finances, taking the necessary but unpopular steps in regard to government spending and borrowing, promoting confidence and a climate for investment, while implementing the Anglo-Irish Agreement. The Taoiseach took account of the parliamentary arithmetic after the 1989 election and included two PDs in the cabinet but the government is essentially following the course successfully set in 1987.

2

ENTER MR. DUFFY

The general election of 1989 was, for me, the most extraordinary one which I ever fought. I fought it on the broad of my back thousands of miles away from my constituency. During early 1988, while I was Tánaiste and Minister for Foreign Affairs, I began to develop medical symptoms which weakened my constitution. Diabetes was diagnosed, and it was combined with a deterioration of the liver. Despite this I continued with my work in Foreign Affairs. I kept to a strict regime and lifestyle and was able to perform my duties for the following sixteen months. My mind was alert and clear. My body, however, was deteriorating. In late April 1989 I collapsed and my medical advisers in the Mater Hospital decided that I should be rushed as a last resort to the Mayo Clinic in the United States. Medical tests were carried out in the clinic and I was cleared for a liver transplant.

After the completion of the tests, I was sent to the Kahler Hotel across the way from the hospital where, I was told, I would be contacted as soon as a liver became available. There I waited for the call which might save my life. I remember vividly the last Sunday before my operation. It was hot and humid. I ruminated on a rock gazing at the waters of Lake Pepin off the Mississippi River near Rochester. It reminded me nostalgically of my childhood years by the shores of Lough Ree on the River Shannon. No liver was available and I was going downhill rapidly. Acites, a serious fluid swelling in the stomach, had set in and my diabetes was going haywire. I was dying and I knew it.

On Tuesday morning, the 23rd May, it happened, and in amazing circumstances. I got an emergency call to my hotel bedroom that a liver had suddenly become available. I was across the road and on the operating table within an hour. Fate had taken a hand. Another patient ahead of me on the waiting list was due to receive a liver transplant, but when they opened him up complications were discovered, which made it impossible to carry out the transplant. The organ would only last a matter of hours but it matched my requirements. Thanks be to God I was on hand. It was sheer good luck, and speed was of the essence. It was a six hour operation and a success.

On Thursday, only two days after the transplant operation, the Taoiseach called a general election. My last words of advice to Mr. Haughey before I left for Minnesota were not to go for an election. My instinct was that the public would regard an election as unnecessary and the mood could turn hostile towards the government if an election was called. However, the election went ahead and I was returned for the sixth consecutive term as a member for the Dublin West constituency. This time I topped the poll, securing over 11,000 first preference votes.

I was back in Dublin for the opening of the new Dáil on June 29th. The reception which I received in the Dáil chamber that day from parliamentary colleagues on all sides of the House was the most moving of my political career - opposition deputies were as generous in their welcome as my own colleagues. The 1989 general election result was traumatic for many people in Fianna Fáil. The problem for our party was that the election results suggested that we would have to enter into a coalition, and moreover the Dáil refused to give us a mandate/or a minority government.

Mr. Dukes offered a 50% participation in Government by Fine Gael, with Mr. Dukes as rotating Taoiseach. This was so obviously tongue in cheek that it was never a runner. Dick Spring and the Workers Party had decided to renege on any arrangement, and adopted a posture of isolating themselves on the Left, as they described it. So when Fine Gael, Labour and the Workers Party forfeited their responsibilities in regard to governing the country, the options open to us were limited. We could have ceased further efforts to form a government, in which event there would have been another General Election. This in my view would have been bad for the country particularly in terms of investment confidence. In practical terms the only real prospect of forming a government was an alliance with the PDs who numbered six, and would just give us the required majority. That was quite simply the parliamentary arithmetic, and the reality of the case.

However, many of our supporters considered single party government to be a core value of the party. In addition, there was the problem of how the party could enter into coalition with former Fianna Fáil colleagues who had broken party pledges, and who had not accepted clear-cut majority decisions given on several occasions. While I sympathised with those views, I realised that a duty fell to Fianna Fáil, as the party with the largest number of seats in the Dáil, to form a government. With that national interest in mind, I fully supported the formation of the new coalition. Of course, I had doubts about how it might work. The main danger, as I saw it, lay in how personalities, who had been so clearly unable to accept the obligations of collective responsibility several years previously, would now co-operate in government. This unsatisfactory side to our alignment with the PDs was to emerge during the presidential election campaign. The performance of the two PD cabinet ministers in that election will be dealt with at greater length in later chapters. Suffice to say at this stage, that the doubts I had about them, when they sought to seize the leadership of Fianna Fáil in the early 1980s, have only been re-inforced by my experience of them during the presidential election.

I took my place in the new Government as Tánaiste and Minister for Defence. The most urgent problem facing me in the Department of Defence was the whole question of pay and conditions in the Defence Forces. Since the foundation of the state no independent commission had ever examined these matters. Also, despite the fact that other state employees had, for forty years, enjoyed the benefits of conciliation and arbitration schemes in regard to salaries and conditions of work, the Defence Forces had no such system. Indeed, they were denied the right to form associations to negotiate on their behalf.

These issues had become matters of public controversy during the general election and the wives of soldiers were in the forefront of a campaign which certainly affected support for Fianna Fáil in army areas. My job was to try to resolve the difficulties. Within a month of my appointment as Minister for Defence, I established a commission, under the chairmanship of Mr. Dermot Gleeson S.C., to carry out a major review of the remuneration and conditions of service of the Defence Forces. Members of that commission represented employer, trade union and other interests, and they consulted very widely before they made their report. The range of the Commission's enquiries, and the fact that the commissioners met some 3,000 members of the Defence Forces and heard their views, did much to assuage the feelings which had been building up over a long period. It was remarkable that about one quarter of all the personnel of the Defence Forces actually met the commissioners.

The traditional view of a government referring an issue to a commission is that it is a way to shelve the problem. This was not my view. Nor was it that of the government. I gave every encouragement to people to use the process to present their views. However, I did not wish to see any delay in the presentation of the report. While the commission was sitting I personally involved myself with the second aspect of the problem – the issue of the right of military personnel to form and join a representative association. This aspect of the problem took a great amount of work. New legislation would be needed and it would have to be steered through the cabinet and the Dáil. At the same time, an ad hoc organisation was in existence within the army for some months before I came into office. It was a delicate task to bring in new structures but it was essential to the smooth running of our Defence Forces.

Sometimes great heat was generated. I was accused of "callous intentions", of "insulting the intelligence of members of the Defence Forces", and so on. In March and April 1990, I piloted the necessary legislation through the houses of the Oireachtas and, by May had the decks cleared for the election of representative associations in the Defence Forces. My sustained work on this issue won recognition from many members of the army. One very important group, as late as the 2nd November 1990, issued a statement recognising that I "was deeply and personally committed to the setting up of the representative association as a statutory body".

The importance of my activities in the resolution of these issues from July 1989 to the following summer was recognised by the commission in its report on pay and conditions. The Commission said that my success in this regard reduced its work to such an extent that what would have taken two to three years to investigate was speeded up, so that it was able to complete its report in one year. Indeed, by the late summer of 1990, all the outstanding issues leading to discontent in the Defence Forces had been resolved.

Throughout most of this period my health was improving. My medication was gradually reduced and my energy returned. By late 1989 colleagues began to suggest that I should be a candidate for the Presidency. As my workload increased I was perhaps overdoing things. Despite a ruptured Achilles tendon, which had my right leg in plaster, I went, with my wife Ann, to Washington DC for St. Patrick's Day. I met a number of Congressional leaders and visited President Bush for talks in the White House. At home, too, I was very active throughout March and April. The bill to provide for the establishment of associations representing the Defence Forces was circulated on 9th March. Over the following two months I steered the bill through the Dáil and Seanad in sessions that were hotly debated and contested. So heated were the parliamentary exchanges that the Government was forced to bring in closure motions to expedite the passage of the bill. All stages were difficult as opposition members tried to play on the worries and anxieties of those who were most concerned, the members of the army and their wives and families.

Around this time, a new medical problem surfaced. For some months my right leg had been in a plaster. After this plaster was removed, it gave way to a new and more serious problem which affected my muscular nervous system in the lower abdomen and both legs. It was a terrible period. The pain at night in particular was severe and I was literally unable to sleep for days on end, and even then only fitfully. As a result of this sleeplessness, I was put on pain killers and sleeping pills. The result of all this was that I had to go into the Mater for observations and tests on the 1st May. I stayed there for two weeks, coming out during the day to fulfil engagements in the Dáil and elsewhere.

In the period immediately preceding my interview with Mr. Jim Duffy on Thursday 17th May, I underwent my most serious medical setback since my liver transplant operation. In order to convey to the reader the sudden deterioration in my condition during that short period, which was indeed the only serious setback that I have had in the two years since my operation, I have decided to present my activities in the days leading to my meeting with Mr. Duffy in diary form.

Tuesday 1st May

I was admitted to the Mater Private Clinic for tests in connection with the pain in my legs and thighs and for general tests in connection with my liver and diabetes.

Wednesday 2nd May

When my doctors had carried out their tests they diagnosed me as suffering from diabetic amyotrophy, a neurological complaint more commonly known as neuropody. They wanted to confirm their diagnosis with a neurologist, and so an appointment was set up with a London specialist. My general health was slipping and the diabetes was going askew. My doctors feared that I was in danger of suffering a rejection of the liver, and so decided to carry out an immediate biopsy of the liver the following day.

Thursday 3rd May

This biopsy was carried out in the operation theatre of the Mater Hospital. A biopsy of the liver involves a surgical investigation of the liver under anaesthetic. The result of the biopsy confirmed what the doctors had already suspected. I was diagnosed as suffering an acute rejection of the liver. My transplant was in danger. When I had the transplant I was warned that I was at risk for a year after the operation. Here I was on the verge of rejection within a few weeks of the anniversary of getting the transplant.

Friday 4th May

Much against the advice of my doctors, I left the Mater Hospital to attend the opening of a new medical facility by Tony O'Reilly at the Central Remedial Clinic in Clontarf. I had promised Lady Valerie Goulding that I would be there and I did not want to let her down. In the afternoon I welcomed home troops from the Lebanon at Dublin Airport. From there I travelled to a night-time function organised by Fianna Fáil in Oranmore, County Galway. I stayed in Oranmore overnight.

Saturday 5th May

I did not return to the Mater until the following afternoon, and was in a state of exhaustion. I was severely reprimanded by my doctors for leaving the Mater at all during this period. Indeed the reader might find it strange that I should seem to have taken such obvious risks with my health. However since my illness began in early 1988 I refused to allow my workload to be lightened, except where it was absolutely necessary. I always found work a great therapy, and to keep going at it was part of my philosophy of life. One of the reasons for my rapid recovery from the liver transplant operation was this determination to stay at it. A more cautious patient would not have returned to the cut and thrust of Dáil Éireann a mere four weeks after such an enormous operation.

I was now put under serious medication, and the doctors began a programme involving the administration of massive doses of steroids.

Monday 7th May

I had an appointment to review the Army Cadets at the Curragh. I arrived for the ceremony at 2.45 p.m. After a few paces I nearly collapsed on the barrack square, right in front of the assembled cadets and troops. My right leg was refusing to function. After a few moments I regained control, and hobbled back to my seat. When I went back into the Mater that evening I was put under additional pain killers.

Thursday 10th May

I underwent a second biopsy of the liver. This biopsy showed my liver condition as having improved significantly. In order to keep my condition stable the heavy programme of medication was continued.

Saturday 12th May

Professor P.K. Thomas of the Department of Neurology at the Royal Hospital in London flew into Dublin to examine me. Professor Thomas was examining me in connection with the pains in my thighs and legs. He confirmed what the doctors at the Mater had already found, and diagnosed me as suffering from diabetic amyotrophy (neuropody) in addition to my other medical problems.

Neuropody involves a very painful deterioration of the muscular nervous system. Dr. Thomas recommended the administration of further medication to deal with this particular problem. This presented new problems for the doctors. They now had to deal with a combination of medical complaints that could only be met by a careful and balanced administration of what were powerful drugs. My doctors who treated me were obliged to protect the transplant in addition to treating the neuropody and diabetes, and to do so had to administer massive doses of steroids. These, while necessary in order to counteract my growing medical problems, did have toxic side effects of which I, as a layman, would have been unaware.

My wife Ann was naturally very keen that I should take a rest at this time and cancel all my ministerial engagements for the following few days. However I decided to push ahead.

On Saturday afternoon I went to Dublin Airport to receive home the remains of the late Cardinal Tomás O'Fiaich. Cardinal O'Fiaich had died unexpectedly of a sudden heart attack while on pilgrimage in Lourdes. He was a very good friend of mine for many years and I had huge admiration for him. He was not only a great Churchman, but a great Irishman. He was a man whose humanity and personal warmth transcended all barriers. I felt that I could not miss the return of his remains to Dublin.

Monday 14th May

I left hospital for the funeral of an old friend, Louis Brennan, in Donnybrook.

Tuesday 15th May

I went this day to the funeral of Cardinal O'Fiaich at Armagh Cathedral. Both myself and the Taoiseach, alongside political, religious and social leaders from both Britain and Ireland assembled in the Presbytery before Mass, and we then proceeded to walk in groups towards the cathedral a mere 100 yards away. I walked with my colleagues Albert Reynolds and Michael Woods. Suddenly, without any warning, my right leg buckled and I fell to the ground in full view of over a thousand people just short of the Cathedral steps. Albert and Michael helped me to my feet and up the steps. During Mass I was in great pain in my legs and right arm which I had injured in the fall.

Wednesday 16th May

I went into the Dáil chamber to represent the Taoiseach for the Order of Business at 10.30 a.m. I was in great pain and my arm was very swollen. I returned to the Mater and had myself examined there by Dr. Martin Walsh. He put my right arm into a plastercast with a sling to support my injured wrist. I was now put on more pain killers in addition to my other medications.

Thursday 17th May

I attended a government meeting in the morning but had to leave it early to host a lunch in Iveagh House for some Arab ambassadors. The Minister for Foreign Affairs, Gerry Collins, was out of the country and I was asked to stand in for him. In the afternoon my diary shows that I had an appointment with Mr. Jim Duffy at 3.30. The diary reads simply "3.30 - Jim Duffy."

I obviously kept my appointment with Mr. Duffy but I have no recollection of this meeting with him. The meeting was brought to my attention five months after it happened when my private secretary Brian Spain showed me a letter written to me from Mr. Duffy. In this letter, which was received in the Department of

Defence in mid-October, well after the election campaign had started, Mr. Duffy enclosed some innocuous quotes from his interview with me. He wanted me to approve or amend these quotes for his thesis. When Brian Spain showed me Mr. Duffy's letter I had no recollection of the meeting at all. I asked Spain where the meeting took place. He told me that the meeting took place in my office in the Dáil and that it went on for about forty minutes. I myself do not remember anything about the interview or what I may have said. At that stage the presidential election was in full flight, and I did not give very much thought to the matter.

Over 40 years, since I was a student myself, I have been generous with time in regard to students, and have given hundreds of such interviews. They are always confidential, and a text always comes back to be corrected, amended and finally approved, sometimes with quotes to be attributed or otherwise. Brian Spain tells me that the reason why Duffy got the interview was because of his connection with the U.C.D. Politics Department. These were his credentials and I knew nothing of him beforehand. I did not even recognise him when I saw him on the 6.01 Television News of 25th October when he released the excerpt from his taped interview with me. Brian Spain also says that Duffy pleaded with him over the telephone that he needed to conduct the interview urgently as he was completing his postgraduate thesis for immediate submission. Indeed Spain says that I had doubts about meeting him at the time and that the final arrangements were made to meet him only after Duffy telephoned Spain two or three times. According to Spain my reluctance to meet him was, of course, because of my illness.

It is interesting to note what Duffy had to tell Emily O'Reilly in her book *Candidate* about his meeting with me back in May. I quote directly from Ms. O'Reilly's book:

"Duffy arrived, late, to Leinster House, shortly after lunchtime on 17 May. Shown into Lenihan's office his first reaction was one of visible shock at Lenihan's appearance. Then it was Lenihan's turn to look alarmed as he noted Duffy's expression. He rushed to reassure him. I'm OK, he said, I'm not dying, don't worry. The medicine I'm on, he added, makes me look drawn. A few days ago, he added, he had slipped and fallen at the funeral of the late Cardinal O'Fiaich. As a result his wrist was swollen and bandaged. But he was perfectly fine, he continued, just carry on. But Lenihan was not telling the whole truth. He had just come through a nightmarish time in hospital, an event which he had concealed from all but his closest friends and family."

What went on at that meeting with Jim Duffy is by now known to almost everyone in the country. I told Duffy in the course of a forty minute taped discussion that on the night of the 27th January, 1982, I telephoned Áras an Uachtaráin and spoke to the President, Dr. Hillery. As this book will clearly demonstrate, what I told Mr. Duffy in this respect was untrue. Since I myself do not remember the meeting with Duffy my only explanation for telling him such rubbish is that my medical condition at the time was such that I was in a total state of confusion. I will allow readers to make up their own minds with the help of the report of my medical condition at the time which has been compiled by John R. Lennon, Consultant Gastroenterologist at the Mater Hospital and the Blackrock Clinic.

"Mr. Brian Lenihan was admitted on the 1st May 1990 because of agonising pain shooting down the front of both thighs. This had been increasing over three weeks prior to his admission and was associated with numbness and a feeling of hot and cold in his feet. There was marked weakness in his legs, particularly for climbing stairs or getting out of low chairs. The pain and weakness developed over the course of a few days. This pain and weakness is a well recognised neurological complication of diabetes called diabetic amyotrophy. The pain can be so severe as to cause the patient to commit suicide but it is always self limiting and tends to improve and disappear over the course of a year. This was confirmed by neurologist Dr. Hugh Staunton who because of the severity of the pain arranged for a consultation with Professor P.K. Thomas of the Department of Neurology, Royal Free Hospital, London. In Mr. Lenihan's case the pain and weakness was preventing walking, adding to the marked weakness that already existed because of the partially ruptured Achilles tendon, interfering with diabetic control.

"His liver function tests up to now had been satisfactory but his general health was not. He had failed to regain his muscle power and weight both of which really should have continued to improve since his liver transplant which took place on the 23rd May 1989. His diabetic control in the preceding months had been poor partly because he was driving himself unnecessarily hard at his work and was therefore taking irregular meals and perhaps not sticking to his diabetic regimen as he might. He was constantly being advised by both Dr. Firth and myself to take a short holiday, but he absolutely refused to make any compromise towards his general ill health.

"During the course of this admission (May 1990) liver function tests that were routinely carried out proved to be abnormal with liver enzymes (seven times above normal) and alkaline phosphates both grossly elevated, highly suggestive of acute rejection. It is of interest that he had no symptoms of acute liver disease. Liver biopsy carried out by Dr. John Crowe on 3rd May 1990 showed acute liver rejection (liver biopsy no. S932/90). He was commenced on massive dose of IV steroids on 5th May and given further doses of steroids.

"Repeat liver biopsy carried out by Dr. John Crowe on 10th May (liver biopsy no. 973/90) showed dramatic improvement and liver function tests returned to virtually normal.

"Immediately following the start of massive steroid treatment for his acute liver rejection, he insisted on leaving the hospital overnight to give a party political talk, and together with his previous refusal to follow medical advice concerning work reduction, was a particular worry in a man who had recently undergone liver transplantation, and who was ignoring the implications of rejection of his transplanted liver. High dose steroids are well known to cause a euphoric state and can cause confusion. I felt his behaviour and his chronic ill health, his poor nutrition, his poor diabetic control and massive steroid dosage on top of his chronic steroid medication would certainly explain his inappropriate behaviour."

Looking back on it all now, it strikes me as an extraordinary misfortune that Mr. Duffy should have chosen to enter my life at the only time since my operation two years ago when I was unfit to see or speak to anybody. Dr. John Lennon says that my behaviour for some time after my departure from hospital in mid-May was not normal and that I was confused. To quote Dr. Lennon's conclusion " my opinion at that stage was that Mr. Lenihan's general health and intellectual alertness would return to normal if Mr. Lenihan took some time away from work."

My recovery over the month of June was rapid and the summer recess gave me an opportunity to take a vacation. I went on a magnificent holiday with Ann and Anita in the South of France in late July and early August. I swam in a pool twice every day and rebuilt my muscles and my system generally. It was marvellous therapy and under a benign sun I enjoyed my first holiday for three years. I came back a new man and the Mater specialists gave me a glowing report. According to Dr. Lennon, "Mr. Lenihan improved considerably before his holiday in July but the three weeks in the south of France permitted him to regain a reasonable state of health and at last improve both mentally and physically to the level one had expected from a successful liver transplant."

Dr. Richard G. Firth, consultant Physician/Endocrinologist Mater Hospital, gave a written report on my medical condition to the Taoiseach in early September, which the Taoiseach had in his possession for the Fianna Fáil party meeting called to nominate a candidate for the Presidency.

The final paragraph of that report read "In summary therefore, I am able to state that the Tánaiste is in good general health. Obviously it is impossible to predict what the future holds in store for anybody but with a reasonable degree of common sense, routine medical follow up and in the absence of unreasonable demands upon his physical resources, he should be certainly fit enough to sustain an election campaign and go on to hopefully hold office."

3

SPECULATION AND NOMINATION

In December 1989 the newly launched Sunday Business Post newspaper conducted an opinion poll. The main focus of the poll was to find out who was the most popular successor to Mr. Haughey. At the time there had been a great deal of uncertainty about the Taoiseach's future. It was even being suggested that he would step down from the party leadership as soon as the country's six month Presidency of the European Community was over. That was due to begin in the new year and in the meantime newspaper pundits were indulging in their favourite pastime of speculation. There was still annoyance among Fianna Fáil activists around the country over the Coalition deal with the Progressive Democrats. Some branches of the organisation, particularly in Galway, were threatening to secede from Fianna Fáil. The presence of Bobby Molloy in the cabinet did little to help tempers in the Galway West constituency. The rumblings went on right through the autumn.

Anyway, the poll conducted by Lansdowne Market Research showed that the public rated me their first choice to succeed Mr. Haughey should there be a vacancy. The poll came both as a surprise and a welcome boost. My mind was far from contesting the leadership of Fianna Fáil but it was nice none the less to have such a public confirmation of my standing.

The most encouraging factor to come out of the Sunday Business Post opinion poll was that I was perceived to be the most capable minister in the Government. The poll results were all the more encouraging since my mind had already turned towards running for the Presidency.

People like the Government Press Secretary, P. J. Mara, were supportive of the notion that I should run for President. A number of other colleagues and advisors favoured the idea. Then

Mr. Haughey seemed to give it his own endorsement while speaking at the Cáirde Fáil function in the Burlington Hotel in December 1989, when he declared, "He (Brian Lenihan) will still be one of us whatever high office he is called to during the next decade." The audience jumped up from their seats to applaud. It was a happy occasion which marked Mr. Haughey's tenth year as party leader. The annual dinner dance was attended by a host of celebrities including the singer Chris de Burgh, Noel Pearson and actor Richard Harris.

My main reason for running for President was that I felt that I could do a reasonably good job in developing the potential of the office along the lines advocated, in his time, by Erskine Childers. The Defence portfolio represented a considerable challenge. However, I knew that once the task of restoring army morale was completed there would be little of consequence left to do, apart from overseeing the implementation of the reforms which, at that stage I was planning to introduce. Despite the newspaper speculation about a leadership race within Fianna Fáil, I felt Mr. Haughey would be there for some time, particularly if he managed to get through the six month Presidency of the European Community with a degree of success.

The next year would see my work largely completed in Defence and if there is one thing I do not enjoy, it is holding down a job for the sake of it. The Presidency at this stage in my political career, seemed both a realistic ambition and a serious challenge. In the run up to Christmas, a number of newspaper articles began to speculate that I might be the Fianna Fáil candidate for the office. As yet the matter was far from being determined so I simply told journalists who inquired, that if asked to stand, I would be honoured to serve.

At home, my wife Ann was working away on her book. It was to be an account of her experiences through my illness and subsequent liver transplant operation. After our return from America we were inundated with letters from people wondering how, as a family, we had managed to cope with such serious illness. Out of those letters Ann got the idea to write a book. Her objective was to help others who have to go through the trauma of a serious illness affecting a loved one. She also felt it would be good to give something back.

All of her proceeds from the book would go to the Kidney Transplant Foundation of Ireland. The Foundation's research work benefits all organ transplant patients. It was a very worthy project and in the early months of the new year took up a lot of time. She was helped in her task by the Irish Independent journalist Angela Phelan.

The publication date was set for Friday, March 30, and Ann arranged with her publishers for a book launch function in the Westbury Hotel on the same day. There was great interest in the book before it came out. As with any launch, publicity would be important. The publishers approached The Late Late Show about getting a mention for the book. Researchers from the programme were enthusiastic. At this stage all Ann hoped for was a few minutes to go on and promote the book. However, The Late Late Show had different ideas.

At lunch in the Westbury were many of our friends, members of the Government and naturally the media. Ann was quite nervous about the whole thing as it was the first time ever in her life she would be asked to make a speech. In fact, throughout my political career, she has tended to avoid interviews and that sort of thing. Up to the point where I walked on to the set of The Late Late Show later that evening, I was quite unaware of what they had in store. I had been deliberately given the impression that mine was just a walk on part. It was only when Ann and I arrived on the show that it dawned on me that this was going to be no ordinary Late Late. It took me some minutes to settle into the programme as it became clear this was more like an Irish version of the "This is Your Life" programme. The audience was packed with friends, relations and political colleagues who had given no indication over the previous few weeks of what was afoot. Later, there was to be simulated outrage from Fine Gael and others that the programme was a launch pad for my Presidential election hopes. Nothing could have been further from the truth.

As ever with these tribute style programmes, a lot of praise is heaped on the chosen subject, not all of it true. This programme was no exception but none the less enjoyable for that. The anecdotes from the audience, all of whom knew me well, were on the whole enjoyable. The programme was great entertainment with Brendan Shine, Louis Brown, Michael Woods and Ronnie Drew of the Dubliners all singing songs and Brendan Grace telling jokes.

Ronnie told a yarn which brought down a tumble of protest about the programme allegedly glorifying "stroke" politics. The fact that the story was not about me and had all the signs of sixties legend about it did not deter the critics. It was even cited by opposition deputies as proof positive of my bad character in the Dáil debate that preceded my dismissal from Government at the height of the Presidential election campaign.

Fine Gael went on the attack the day after the programme slamming RTE for being party political in their choice of subjects for the Late Late. At this stage, I was far from being a declared candidate for the Presidency. It was also conveniently forgotten that in the audience that night was former Fine Gael TD from Fermoy, Dick Barry, while former Labour minister Justin Keating put in an appearance as a panelist. Despite these carping attacks the programme was received well and the book "No Problem: To Mayo and Back" became a best seller.

Speculation about who the different parties would stand in the Presidential election intensified early in the new year. Before the Dáil returned from its Christmas recess, the Labour Leader Dick Spring gave an interview to RTE where he indicated that there should be an electoral contest for the position. If necessary he would stand himself, he told Shane Kenny of the "This Week" programme, to ensure there was an election. His statement that he might be a candidate was greeted with incredulity all round. However, it was clearly an attempt by him to head off the left wingers within his own party who were anxious to see Dr. Noel Browne become their standard bearer.

Since I was emerging as the front runner, media attention began to switch on to the possibility of a by-election in my own Dublin West constituency. It was pointed out by some commentators that Fianna Fáil had come a cropper there in the past. The by now famous Dublin West by-election of 1982, which followed the Taoiseach's appointment of Dick Burke as European Commissioner, was cited as an example. The names of Jim Tunney, the Chairman of the Fianna Fáil parliamentary party, and Minister for the Marine John Wilson were canvassed as possible alternative candidates. Wilson's main advantage at this stage seems to have been the fact that a by-election would be very easy to win in his Cavan-Monaghan constituency. For the moment, I dismissed much of this for what it was ... speculation.

Fine Gael were still floundering around for a candidate. Alan Dukes, perhaps to his subsequent undoing, told his party's Ard Fheis early in March that they would be putting a candidate of substance into the field. It was generally assumed from his tone that this would be former Taoiseach Garret Fitzgerald. However, Fitzgerald moved quickly to dismiss suggestions that he might run. An air of unreality hung over Fine Gael with many in the party assuming, wrongly as it turned out, that if things got desperate either Fitzgerald or Peter Barry would run.

Interestingly enough, in another poll conducted by the Sunday Business Post at the end of May 1990, I got 40% support as against 26% for Garret Fitzgerald and 18% for Mary Robinson. Commenting on the poll, the Post said that when the 16% "don't knows" made up their minds, I would be well on my way to securing the 50% needed to get elected in later counts.

At one point, former Fine Gael minister John Boland urged the party to select John Kelly, the former minister, constitutional lawyer and previously deputy for Dublin South. At the time I thought it would have been wonderful to face Kelly in a Presidential contest. We were close friends and his death this year was a great loss to the country. He and I had engaged in civilised debate across the floor of Dáil Éireann down the years. He was a man of great intellect and I am sure that had he run for the Presidency, it would have been a clean fight.

The position of the PDs on the election was as yet unclear. I expected, perhaps somewhat naively, that they would, at worst, maintain a stance of benevolent neutrality towards my candidature. I had served with both Bobby Molloy and Dessie O'Malley in a variety of governments under both Jack Lynch and Charlie Haughey. Though not involved in any immediate way in the negotiations to form the current coalition government, I moved quickly to cool tempers within Fianna Fáil over the deal. In an interview with the Sunday Business Post around mid April I spoke highly of both men and their contribution to the government's success. As a matter of record, I remain the only member of the government to speak of them in such praiseworthy tones. In the end they settled for a position of "neutrality" before the election campaign. How neutral their behaviour was had yet to be seen.

My collapse at the late Cardinal O'Fiaich's funeral in Armagh seems to have triggered a fresh wave of doubts at leadership level in Fianna Fáil. This, coupled with the fear of a by-election defeat in Dublin West, persuaded the Taoiseach Mr. Haughey to cast around for other potential candidates. This was done secretly and without consulting me. Leinster House is a small place and before long the newspapers were claiming informal approaches had been made to the Fine Gael Chief Whip, Jim Higgins, about an agreed candidate for the Park. Initially, I viewed these revelations with a degree of suspicion, feeling that perhaps Fine Gael were mischief making. Subsequently, I discovered that there were in fact approaches made by the government Chief Whip Vincent

Brady. After my appearance on The Late Late Show, Brady raised the matter with his opposite number in his office at Leinster House. Brady apparently asked the Fine Gael deputy would his party consider the possibility of an agreed candidate. Jim Higgins said he had taken it that Brian Lenihan would be the Fianna Fáil candidate and that his selection was a foregone conclusion at this point. Brady replied that this was not quite the case. He also suggested that either T. K. Whittaker or the SDLP leader John Hume might make suitable agreed candidates without having an election.

This move by Vincent Brady had clearly taken Fine Gael off-guard. Jim Higgins inquired about the nature of the approach to which Brady replied "somewhere between personal and semi-official". Despite Fianna Fáil denials the whole approach seems to have been bungled and badly thought out from the start. At the end of April, Labour had formally adopted Mary Robinson as their candidate for the office so attempts to have an agreed candidate were far removed from reality. Added to that, Brady's concerns about a by-election in Dublin West were entirely ill-founded.

Back in 1982 we went for a by-election in the constituency on a worthwhile gamble to give some stability to the government. At the time we were surviving from week to week on a slender one vote margin and that was the vote of Independent TD for Dublin Central Tony Gregory. However, the figures were not right for a by-election victory. In fact in the earlier February general election, Fine Gael had got a marginally bigger percentage share (42.5%) of the vote than Fianna Fáil. When transfers came into the reckoning it would have been a daunting task. Fianna Fáil lost the by-election with all the damage to the government that that entailed. The appointment of Dick Burke to the European Commission in Brussels was depicted by the newspapers as "the stroke that failed".

The circumstances in 1990 were entirely better for a Fianna Fáil by-election win. While the Fianna Fáil vote stood as it was eight years ago the Fine Gael share had plummeted to just 24.6%. This would make it very difficult for Fine Gael to win as they would be dependent on a very high level of transfers from the Workers Party and others.

As the Dáil faced into the summer recess, Fianna Fáil made its first move towards the selection of a candidate. With one candidate, Mary Robinson, already in the field it was time to set a date for the nomination. That date was set for September 17. With that definite news I settled into the Dáil recess. Ann, my daughter Anita and I spent a three week holiday in the south of France, one of the most enjoyable we've had together. It was my first time to holiday there. Based at Antibes we made a few visits around the surrounding countryside spending a few days in Monaco and across the Italian border in San Remo. I swam a lot and felt fitter than I ever have been on returning to Ireland in early August.

In the week before the parliamentary party meeting that I expected would nominate me, John Wilson suddenly dropped his bombshell. In a letter to Fianna Fáil TDs he set out why he too would be seeking the nomination to run. Taken at face value it came as a surprise. Throughout the summer and now into the autumn, I had been led to believe that my nomination would be unanimous, so much so, that Fianna Fáil headquarters in Mount Street had gone to the trouble of having me photographed with Ann for the election posters. There had also been visits to Carr Communications to receive advice on how I should present myself as a candidate to the media. Initially, I was disappointed to see that my nomination was going to be contested. Frankly, it caught me unawares. John Wilson had given me no intimation that he was interested, though it has to be pointed out, that earlier in the year, at the Fianna Fáil Ard Fheis in the RDS, he told John Bowman of RTE that he would not need much persuading to throw his hat into the ring. At the time his comments were not followed up and given the due prominence by the papers that they then deserved.

John Wilson and I have been colleagues and good friends all

our political lives. Like me he had spanned the Jack Lynch period in Fianna Fáil and survived to serve under Mr. Haughey. His candidature rang alarm bells among some of my closest supporters. Here was a fellow member of the cabinet writing to TDs and ringing backbenchers in a bid to secure the nomination. The more suspicious of my supporters felt that Mr. Haughey was behind the Wilson gambit. For them it was a very public confirmation of Mr. Haughey's professed doubts. Ironically the Wilson bid for the nomination managed to attract both a strong regional support as well as the support of those discontented with the current leadership at the top of the party. Numbered among his supporters were a few junior ministers anxious to move up the ladder. I decided to press ahead and look around for suitable people to both nominate and second me at the parliamentary party meeting. I first thought of Albert Reynolds but he was anxious not to offend Wilson who occupies a neighbouring constituency to his own in Longford-Westmeath. The Wilson challenge caused embarrassment all round for ministers, since both he and I were in the current government. In the end Bertie Ahern and Padraig Flynn agreed to nominate and second me respectively.

The contest, if it can be called that, was a good natured one. Unfortunately some TDs did not see it that way. A number of them rang me, clearly annoyed at what they saw as Wilson's attempt to spoil my candidature. There were other deputies of course who were uneasy about the possibility of a by-election in Dublin West and how this would affect the Government's position in the Dáil. Again it was necessary to reassure them that the current situation in the constituency was quite different to that which obtained back in 1982. The vote was on a Monday and up to the Saturday I had hardly spoken to a single deputy. Wilson had sent letters and in some cases rung individual deputies twice. The contest was making great copy for the newspapers but I wanted to check out how real the challenge would be. Some newspapers were openly suggesting it was all part of an attempt by John Wilson to get the vacant Tánaiste slot once I was installed in the Park. I made a few calls to deputies I regarded as important, including some named in the newspapers as supporting Wilson. Some of the latter were apologetic but stated they had to support him because of their geographic proximity to the Cavan man. The upshot of these and other calls was that things would be all right.

There was one rather farcical moment on the Friday before the actual vote when I went on a visit as Minister for Defence to open a new barracks in Cavan. John Wilson was there as local TD and the media were out in force. After the ceremony was completed we both retreated to different rooms where we were interviewed separately by RTE's Seán O'Rourke. The meeting at Leinster House the next Monday was an emotional one. It was uppermost in many deputies minds that this could in fact be my last appearance at the parliamentary party. Before the voting got underway, Mr. Haughey pointed to a folder in front of him and indicated to the meeting that he had independently sought the advice of my doctors on my medical condition. They had, he told the meeting, assured him that Brian Lenihan was well up to the rigours of a Presidential campaign. When deputies cast their vote I won by 54 votes to 19. Later, as happened when De Valera ran for the office, I was photographed with the entire parliamentary party on the steps of the plinth at Leinster House. Finally I was the party's choice to run for the Presidency.

4

HARRIS – SPEAK

The position of President within the Irish constitution is largely symbolic. The inclusion of the office within the 1937 constitution was to highlight the transition to an essentially republican form of Government, though the country was not to become a republic, in the formal sense, until 1948. Though conferred with few powers, the office became a focus for heated discussion during the Dáil debate on the new constitution. At the time, Fine Gael suspected that the new office would be subverted by Eamon De Valera and somehow enable him to gain a dictatorial presence over national life. Like most parliamentary accusations it owed more to hyperbole than any study of the President's actual powers which are limited in the extreme. His two most important powers are to refer Bills passed by the Oireachtas to the Supreme Court for a decision on their compatibility with the constitution, and secondly, to refuse to dissolve Dáil Éireann on the advice of a Taoiseach who has ceased to retain the support of a majority in Dáil Éireann. The exercise of the latter power by President Hillery in 1982 was to become a source of considerable controversy during the Presidential campaign of 1990.

It is basically a non-political office with the serving President acting as a focus for national unity in addition to representing the country abroad. At a practical level the limited powers enjoyed by a sitting President are thrown into relief by the fact that every public statement issued by him or her must be cleared with the Government beforehand. Over the years different Presidents have evolved their own sense of what the office means by imposing their own personality or style on the job at hand.

At the first formal press conference following nomination by Fianna Fáil, I outlined my own vision of the office. It was my firm belief, facing into the campaign, that it would be wrong to create false expectations in the public mind about what the office could achieve. There had not been an election for the office for seventeen years and, to a certain extent, a whole generation had grown up unaware of the issues involved. To this extent the campaign would inevitably involve a secondary debate about the relevance of the office itself, quite apart from the merits of the different candidates seeking election. If elected, I saw my role as encouraging community groups, civic spirit and the multitude of voluntary bodies that are helping people in our society, sometimes without any formal recognition. As a former Minister for Foreign Affairs I was keenly aware of how the President could help the government of the day as a kind of roving ambassador overseas. It was my intention to try, with the co-operation of the government, to sell this country as a place to invest in when on visits to foreign countries.

The Fianna Fáil party electoral machine swung into action as soon as I was selected. Ann and I were photographed for the purposes of campaign literature. Outdoor advertising had been pre-booked and would feature Ann and me with the slogan **"The People's President"**. The intention was that I would travel around the country on coach, train and helicopter. The use of helicopters was a particular benefit since it cut down on time wastage in what was a very, very busy country-wide tour. Apart from the six counties, it would cover all the main urban centres as well as every county in Ireland. Newspaper hype had it that Fianna Fáil were spending some £1.2 million on the campaign. In fact, the original budget was for around the £600,000 mark. Understandably, given the controversy generated by the campaign, this budget was exceeded and about a million pounds was spent overall. Some £500,000 came in to party headquarters by way of donations. This was much less, naturally enough, than would normally come in if it was a general election.

In September, Fianna Fáil commissioned qualitative research by the company Behaviour & Attitudes. The marketing research company's study explored voter perceptions at national and local level and what bearing these would have on the campaign. In addition to this, the qualitative research looked at how their sample group viewed the Presidency and the different candidates on offer.

The research threw up a general attitude that the Presidency was not held in high regard. The fact that the office was uncontested since 1973 seems to have confirmed the view that politicians themselves did not rate it too highly in their list of priorities. The public perception of President Hillery seems to have suffered as a result of this general impression with respondents viewing his tenure at Áras an Uachtaráin as low key. "In summary then, there is a general feeling that the role of the President is limited and not a particularly demanding one. At the same time, there is a feeling that the President might take extra functions upon himself usefully. In many respects, these are linked to the area of social and voluntary activity, involvement in "good causes", environmental issues, architectural heritage and a general sense of pride in the community," read the report.

When it came to the other candidates the report showed that Mary Robinson was making quite an impact, probably reflecting the fact that she had been campaigning since the summer and was therefore first into the race. The role of the office was being questioned and "Mary Robinson is seen to have taken a lead in making the definition of the role of President an issue in the campaign".

Even at this early stage, Fine Gael's Austin Currie was being seen as an "Outsider" both in terms of his origin and the campaign itself. The fact that he was not clearly the party's first choice seemed to be damaging him as well as a perception that he had not "served his time" in southern politics. Mrs. Robinson, according to the market research, was a much more familiar figure in Dublin and among middle class voters. This view seems to have been confirmed by research conducted for the Robinson campaign. Her affiliation with both Labour and the Workers Party was seen as a disadvantage. However, the Fianna Fáil research showed there was a growing perception that she looked the part. Fine Gael commissioned a London-based research company to do work on the campaign. This involved qualitative work both during the summer and in the autumn when Currie became their candidate. It showed a high level of apathy about the office and the election itself. Currie, according to this research, had a high degree of name recognition among voters but unfortunately little else was known about him beyond that.

The research on our side threw up one other name that did feature highly with voters. This was that of Carmencita Hederman. According to the research, she was widely admired for her successful period as Dublin's Lord Mayor.

Undoubtedly she was helped by the coincidence of her stay at the Mansion House with Dublin's millennium celebrations. That said, her appeal was quite strong outside Dublin according to the research. A strong parallel was drawn among those interviewed between the role of Lord Mayor and the Presidency in the country as a whole. It always bewildered me that Fine Gael did not consider her as a candidate more seriously. After all, when both Garret Fitzgerald and Peter Barry refused to run, they were bound to be in trouble. Rather than casting around for a candidate, Alan Dukes could very easily have stood Mrs. Hederman as a non-political candidate for the office. If she had fared poorly it would not have rebounded so badly on him.

It was unfortunate for Fine Gael that from the outset the whole issue of Alan Dukes' continued leadership became inextricably bound up with the party's performance in the Presidential election. It is clear that Currie, initially at least, was unwilling to stand. In fact, the day he admitted publicly that he would be prepared to run, he was featured in the Dublin Tribune newspaper saying he would not be and that he wanted to concentrate on strengthening his foothold in the Dublin West constituency. The interview was obviously conducted and written before the last vital days when he changed his mind, though it would be wrong to assume his name was not canvassed within Fine Gael before this time.

"Some people including Garret Fitzgerald had been promoting Currie since early in the new year. The idea had been floated at senior levels in the party," according to Joe Kenny, then General Secretary of Fine Gael. When he did accept the offer to run, it is understood he also approached John Bruton to see what his attitude to the candidacy would be. Bruton was openly being talked about at this stage as a successor to Dukes should the Presidential election go wrong. As things turned out Bruton did become the unanimous choice of the parliamentary party when Fine Gael polled poorly in the election.

What made the internal leadership struggle in the party so unfortunate was that it meant the Presidential campaign would not simply be about putting their best foot forward but rather a backdrop to the settling of scores within Fine Gael. At one level you had the party leadership desperate for at least second place, if not outright victory. At another level, arguably, there were people in Fine Gael who were afraid that too good a performance by Austin Currie might only serve to bolster the current leadership. It would seem that the only thing that managed to unite them was a common desire to stop Fianna Fáil. That there were now two wings in Fine Gael was made abundantly clear in a front page article in the Irish Press shortly after Fine Gael appointed members of their front bench to run the campaign. The article claimed that Seán Barrett, Michael Noonan, Jim Mitchell and Senator Maurice Manning had been plotting to change the leadership and that they would move after the Presidential campaign. The article also maintained that some weeks previously the same four had given Alan Dukes an ultimatum to find a candidate quickly or face the consequences. All four men denied the existence of a plot as outlined in the article. However, the story was given a certain credence at Leinster House and there was undoubtedly unease within the party about the search for a viable candidate. The other intriguing revelation in the story was the suggestion that Garret Fitzgerald, if not against Dukes, was ambivalent about his continued stewardship of the party. If true, it would be remarkable, since he was always identified as Dukes' main backer when it came to the party leadership in the first place. I write all this to give the reader a sense of the collective mind of Fine Gael as it faced into the campaign.

The Robinson campaign, on the surface at least, had none of the difficulties confronting Fine Gael. They had formally selected her as candidate as far back as 26 April. This gave her time to familiarise herself with issues and to travel extensively around the country. Her selection was not without its problems. The left in the party, symbolised by deputies like Michael D. Higgins and

Emmet Stagg, favoured the selection of Dr. Noel Browne. Browne was Minister for Health in the inter-party coalition government from 1948 to 1951 and is widely credited for his courage in taking on tuberculosis, then a major cause of death in Ireland in a much more visible way than heart disease is today. It is not widely known that Browne joined Fianna Fáil after the collapse of Clann na Poblachta, the party to which he then belonged. While in Fianna Fáil I served with him on an Education policy sub-committee of the national executive. I worked closely with him then and admired him greatly. When the Labour Party leader, Dick Spring, emerged from a meeting in early April saying he had received the authority of the parliamentary party to invite Mary Robinson to become a candidate, this was disputed by Emmet Stagg. It all served to create an impression of division about the matter to the public but it proved to be a storm in a teacup. However, the damaging public row at the outset of the campaign seems to have left a certain distrust of the party in the candidate's own mind. Underneath the surface there seemed to be other tensions and these are well documented in Fergus Finlay's book on the campaign. Finlay is the Labour Party press officer based in Leinster House.

Another source of tension was the hidden involvement of Eoghan Harris in the Robinson campaign. Harris, a former producer in RTE, had previously been a close advisor to the Workers Party leader Prionsais De Rossa until he split from the party in a dispute between the hardliners and those who favoured a more social democratic direction for the future. Though Finlay denies Harris exercised a "Svengali" influence over the campaign, he does seem to have had quite an effect. As far back as 6 April he wrote to Mary Robinson outlining how the campaign should be run. Harris was putting his own professional services at the disposal of the campaign. Needless to say Mrs. Robinson took him up on his offer. Much of what subsequently became both the Robinson image and the Robinson campaign is set out in his document to her.

He wrote to her in the following terms:

"Dear Mary,

Congratulations on taking up the Presidential challenge with determination. As a long time admirer of yours - especially on the issue of pluralism and Northern Ireland - I wish you all the best.

I want to give you some practical help. What I do is deal with mass media. For the past ten years my small media group created the 'image' of the Workers Party. Given the party's past it should be clear that I would have to be the best in the business ...."

Harris is, it has to be acknowledged, a genius when it comes to the televisual presentation of political candidates. His packaging of Prionsais De Rossa for the European Parliament elections of 1989 should serve as a salutary lesson to all political rivals. For the moment it is worth quoting from that letter written to Mary Robinson, when winning the Presidential election must have been very much an outside bet.

Here are some quotations from that letter:

"Mary Robinson's current image is one of integrity and intellect - but this is somewhat discounted by cool and competence, which sometimes come across as aloofness in a country which paradoxically values both cool and the common touch, each in its own place. The Parnell factor, the mixture of aloofness and affection is the ideal for candidates for public office in Ireland."

This quotation very much marks out at an early stage the path which the candidate ultimately took:

"Mary must visit community clinics - but clinics which are full of fight-back. One of the classic errors of the hard left is not to understand a simple piece of psychology: ordinary people are full of pity - but they hate whiners. So Mary should visit the Rape Crisis centres - but stress the positive. She must visit mental hospitals - but where we see things done so well that we don't grudge a call for more cash."

There was also advice on the sort of people needed on the Robinson campaign team:

"I tell you all this because you have some hard choices to make and one of them is not to listen to every Tom, Dick and Harry - and especially Dublin 4 dicks. On your team you need some who are racy, of the soil, who have a feel for Catholic cultural mores, who are at home at a noisy Fine Gael function, who could watch a hurling match with relish and know who Packy Bonner is."

In a part of the letter entitled "The Psychology of a Campaign" he gets around to dealing with hazards of the election:

"Lenihan has not the stamina for a campaign, by which I mean a fighting, moving attack, over a large geographical area. He will falter and be seen to falter. He will be forced into helicopters - which are not democratic as a bus is - and he will be forced to fight from Dublin. And this will be noticed by the media - when we bring it to their notice. Then it will become a proverb of the campaign 'Ah Brian is past it ...'. This is tough but this is politics."

At this stage, I, like most of the population, was unaware that this man, once of the hard left, was about to steer Mrs. Robinson steadily towards the middle of the road.

Who could have guessed then that the same Eoghan Harris would, within a few short months of the Presidential election, end up working for Fine Gael.

I would like to finish this chapter by presenting profiles of my two opponents in the election.

Mary Robinson (née Bourke)

Born: May 1944, Ballina, Co. Mayo

Married: Nicholas Robinson, two sons and one daughter

Education: Mount Anville, Trinity College Dublin, Kings Inns, Harvard University.

Academic qualifications: 1st Class Honours Legal Science, L.L.M., called to bar 1967, Masters of Law 1968.

Mary Robinson's biggest achievements up to her victory in the Presidential election were in the areas of academic and constitutional law. At the age of 25 she was appointed Reid Professor of Law at Trinity College Dublin. She was the youngest ever to hold down such a senior academic post. In fact throughout her academic career she was to win scholarships and get first class honours in every degree exam she sat. There was little, either in her formal education or upbringing, that would suggest her later radicalism as a lawyer and member of the senate.

As Fergus Finlay puts it in his book on the Presidential election: "Mary had been raised in an atmosphere where there were no major questions to ask. Her parents were both doctors, and the family was a comfortable one, well-known in Ballina and the surrounding countryside. It was a sheltered, somewhat patrician upbringing. Both her parents were doctors and she, along with her brothers, was educated privately. Her period spent in Harvard seems to have changed her outlook", according to Finlay. "She was there during the period of student protest over the war in Vietnam and the spread of the civil rights movement around the United States".

Running as an almost unknown candidate for the Senate in 1969 she was elected for Trinity. The result was against the odds and all the more remarkable given that she became the first Catholic to be elected as a Senator from Trinity. The college would still have been staunchly Protestant in its ethos. In fact her own parents sought permission from the local Bishop in Mayo in order to enrol her at Trinity in the first place. In the Senate she soon gained a reputation as something of a radical putting forward her own legislation widening the availability of contraceptives. A Government Bill published shortly after hers was defeated when the then Taoiseach Liam Cosgrave and one of his ministers, Dick Burke voted against their own legislation.

Other electoral outings for Mary Robinson were less successful than at Trinity though she did manage to get elected to Dublin Corporation. Both of her attempts to get elected to the Dáil ended in failure. She ran first in her own area of Rathmines in 1977 but the Labour Party was not at its most popular at this stage. She ran again, but this time in my own constituency of Dublin West, in the general election of 1981. She polled less than two thousand votes and was out-polled by the H-Block's Hunger Strike candidate. She was seen as belonging to the left-wing of Labour that was, in the early 70s and later again in the 80s, unhappy about the party's participation in coalition with Fine Gael. "I am a socialist - the task now is to build the socialist movement. We want banks nationalised and building land controlled," she said after becoming a senator. As a lawyer she took a good number of cases in the area of constitutional law. She also specialised in European law. Some of the more notable cases which she took include the De Burca case in 1976, which challenged the jury system as discriminating against women, and the Wood Quay case in 1978, which managed to establish the Dublin site as a national monument and allowed archaeological excavation work to continue before building work on the civic offices began.

Many admire her most for her persistent championing of a number of social causes and in particular her constant support of the travelling community, all too often at the receiving end of prejudice in our society. In politics, she was active as an alternate member of the New Ireland Forum, which held its deliberations in 1983 and attempted to reach a consensus among nationalists about the way forward in Northern Ireland. Ironically, Northern Ireland was to be the principal reason for her parting with the

Labour Party just two years later. She resigned from the party in 1985 because she opposed the Anglo-Irish agreement which she felt would only alienate unionists further. She then began to concentrate on her legal practice. In the general election of 1989 she dropped out of politics and did not stand for election for the Senate at TCD. She was the Irish winner of the European of the Year award the previous year.

Austin Currie

Born: October 1939, Coalisland,
Co. Tyrone
Married: Anita Lynch, 3 daughters
and 2 sons
Education: Edondork Primary School,
St. Patrick's Academy Grammar
School, Queen's University Belfast
Academic qualifications: B.A. (Hons.) Politics and History,
1963. Research fellow Trinity
College Dublin 1976.

Austin Currie is most easily remembered for his part in the explosion of the Civil Rights campaign in the North of Ireland in the late 1960s. He and others campaigned hard for equal opportunities for the nationalist population in the north, which at that time was subjected to a welter of discrimination in what was, not inaptly known as an "Orange state". His occupation of a council house in Caledon in County Armagh in 1968 began the challenge for equal rights. Four years previously he had been elected to the Stormont parliament at a by-election in east Tyrone.

He was, at the age of just 24, the youngest member elected for Stormont. He was re-elected as a nationalist member, unopposed, in the subsequent general election in 1965. His occupation of the house at Caledon, in protest over its allocation to a young Protestant woman when local Catholic families were denied housing in the area, shot him to national prominence. It effectively began the Civil Rights movement and ushered in a new era in the six counties, where Catholics were no longer prepared to accept their status as second class citizens. Later, Currie was to organise the first Civil Rights march from Coalisland to Dungannon. He was re-elected yet again to Stormont in 1969.

He was instrumental, along with five other members of the Stormont parliament, in setting up the Social Democrats and Labour Party which then went on to become the accepted voice of constitutional nationalists in the north. He was strongly supportive of the then leader of the SDLP Gerry (now Lord) Fitt. Something of a maverick, he often remained at odds with the current leader John Hume. In the 1979 general election, Currie, in spite of advice to the contrary from his own party, stood against the sitting nationalist MP Frank Maguire in the Fermanagh-South Tyrone constituency. It was an unpopular move and led to both condemnation from the SDLP as well as opening him to the accusation that he was splitting the nationalist vote. In the event this fear was unfounded and Maguire was re-elected. During the brief Sunningdale power sharing administration Austin Currie served as Minister for Housing, Planning and Local Government. He has, like many other politicians in the North, suffered because of the absence of a proper form of administration there since then. With seats at Westminster all too scarce, remaining on in politics in the north can be a soul destroying business. All the more so, given that Austin Currie had been touched in a very personal way by the violence in the north. His wife was the subject of a horrible attack, the details of which would be far too painful to record here. In 1983 Austin Currie served as part of the SDLP delegation to the New Ireland Forum. A year later he was made a special advisor to the European Commissioner Peter Sutherland. From this time he became quite close to Fine Gael, as many in the SDLP did in the lead up to the signing of the Anglo-Irish Agreement in 1985. Within the SDLP he has been seen as more pro-devolution than most. In 1988 he participated in the failed Duisberg talks with unionist politicians. The discussions in a hotel in West Germany were aimed at trying to set up a framework for talks between the political parties in the north. It seems to have put Currie further out on a limb in relation to his own party leadership.

Few could begrudge Austin Currie the opportunity to enter southern politics when invited to stand for election in Dublin West in 1989. Many have dropped out of politics in the north in the past. Northerners have often made a great contribution to politics in the south. Seán McEntee is the best example from the past.

THE EOGHAN HARRIS LETTER

15 Trafalgar Tce.,
Monkstown,
Co. Dublin.
6 April 1990

Dear Mary,

Congratulations on taking up the Presidential challenge with determination. As a long time admirer of yours - especially on the issue of pluralism and Northern Ireland - I wish you all the best.

I want to give you some practical help. What I do is deal with mass media. For the past ten years my small media group created the 'image' of the Workers Party. Given the party's past it should be clear that I would have to be the best in the business, which quite simply I am, not because I understand media, but because I understand the political framework in which media must work – something Saatchi and Saatchi got wrong for Fianna Fáil last election.

One of the reasons I did well for the Workers Party was because I was given control from the centre. I had no Committees with coercive power to change 'lines'. This was critical. You need the same control. Media messers are ten a penny. Most are wrong. You have to have a tiny team, a clear strategy, and stick to it.

The hard decisions come first. What I call Beecher's Brook. Your Beecher's is divorce and abortion. Get it right and you can beat Lenihan in my view. Get it wrong, or worse, mess around, and you are dead.

Let me give you a model of what I mean:

The 1989 General Election and European Election was a classic media campaign by the Workers Party. The Beecher's Brook decision was to accept the 'market' - a decision made as far back as 1989 April Ardfheis for which I wrote De Rossa's U-turn speech. The election media campaign kept up that modernising momentum, from stylish 'summary' television broadcasts that eschewed socialist jargon in favour of populist lines like 'Our motto is - if it works pay it properly!' right down to the 'green' subtext of the slogan 'A Breath of Fresh Air' and the smoky 'fashion' photos of De Rossa.

Let me stress that the 'dialectics' of the poster photo were critical. Any fool can think up a green slogan. The political point of the poster was that the Pigeon House chimneys were belching smoke in the background - a signal that we were not Dublin 4 green loonies, that we could live with generating stations, that we accepted that some smoke is part of the working life of a modern city. In political terms it had a gritty appeal to workers while holding down the 'green' vote.

This poster, this subliminal signal that we lived in the real world, is what I mean by a political media campaign. All these details are critical. It was critical that De Rossa should wear his jacket slung over his shoulder. That's why he, a relatively unknown leader of three months, headed the poll in Dublin. You can't do that without a brilliant media campaign.

A media campaign must be a marriage of content and form. De Rossa's 1989 Ardfheis speech calling for acceptance of the market was no more and no less important than my other contributions such as the slogan 'A Breath of Fresh Air', or the decision to use Mike Bunn - a 'fashion' photographer in trade terms but known to me as a 'nature' photographer too. And I had to fight off messers on Election committees who wanted to take out a TV broadcast line of mine: 'We're not dogmatic socialists, we're democratic socialists' because 10 days before Tienamen Square I believed Deng would use force. I was right. If I did not understand politics, if I was just a media 'technician' that vital line would have been left out. Or again I fought for the line 'Our motto is - if it works pay it properly' because it moved forward to welcome entrepreneurial activity rather than just begrudgingly accepting it à la Michael D. Higgins & Co. Half measures are fatal in media matters.

I tell you all this because you have some hard choices to make and one of them is not to listen to every Tom, Dick and Harry - and especially Dublin 4 dicks. On your team you need some who are racy of the soil, who have a feel for Catholic cultural mores, who are at home at a noisy Fine Gael function, who could watch a hurling match with relish and know who Packy Bonner is.

My view is that you can win the campaign, or come so close as to give you a famous political victory, by presenting yourself as a democratic rather than liberal candidate, and never as a liberal left candidate.

Politically you have huge ground to make up. You must secure the entire Fine Gael vote - which you can't do unless you deal with the Distortion issue (Divorce and Abortion). You need to split the Fianna Fáil vote - which you can do by pulling their progressive women voters away by a bravura campaign. You need Labour/ Dublin 4/Divorce/Abortion/Rape Crisis/Incest and all that like a hole in the head. You have that.

Right now you have a whole country to win. This does not mean compromising your principles. But it does mean accepting that every morning we invent a new world. In politics you need to put previous political personas aside and start fresh. People like fresh starts.

Finally in offering you practical help I want to make my status clear. I will not be going back to the Workers Party, or joining Labour, or any other party. The media team - which left the WP with me - means to devote itself to single issue campaigns on progressive issues such as Peace & Northern Ireland. We are happy to do what we can and meet you wherever you like.

On an upbeat note I met Paul Durcan for a political chat today. He asked me what I thought of you. I said what I thought. He was pleased because he said he had written to you supportively. I thought it a good omen.

Eoghan Harris

A PRESIDENT FOR ALL THE PEOPLE

The makings of Mary Robinson's media campaign, the essence of which is to understand the importance of a preposition.

Take the word 'for' above.

There is a difference between 'A President of All the People' and 'A President for All the People'. The difference is that the first one is Dublin 4 and do gooding and the second is democratic.

There is no need to talk down. But the mark of a democrat is to seek out the 'fors'.

The first mark of a 'for' person is a sense of humour. You must be serious enough not to take yourself solemnly.

From first to last you must set out to enjoy this campaign. And be seen to enjoy it.

And why not? This is a 'Discover Ireland' trip. Every so often we have to get to know our changing country all over again.

Go out in that spirit of adventure and zest and the sheer energy will enthuse the electorate. That's something Lenihan can't match. Sheer energy and stamina. So hit the road ...

Warning: Do Not Pass Beyond This Point

Every campaign has two Beechers Brooks for some reason. One is always political. The other is always personal.

The personal issue is an easy jump. You have a plummy Dublin 4 lawyery image. You can fix that easy enough and the rest of my notes are about how to fix it.

The political fence in the Presidential race is the Divorce and Abortion issue. Call it the Distortion issue. Call the problem voter Carmel Murphy.

Carmel Murphy is a bank manager's wife, Cork bourgeoisie, Jack Lynch voter, progressive, but a Catholic in the Cork sense. She says: "I'd vote for Mary Robinson only for her position on abortion". Now you can't mess around with this. Either you deal with it up front or it's no use even starting the campaign. What you have here is a Jack Kennedy problem - and of course a John F. Kennedy solution too.

Your very first Press Conference must deal with Distortion in a frank and firm fashion as follows: "Now I want to make something clear. Everybody knows my position on divorce and abortion. But that was Mary Robinson's position. As President I will fully accept the views of the electorate expressed at the Referenda. On this I compare my position to John F. Kennedy - As President of Ireland I represent the views of the people of Ireland. On every issue. Including divorce and abortion. As President my private views don't count ..."

You must say that every chance you get for a whole week and then you will never have to say it again. If you don't say it first, and without fidgets, and without fiddling you are a non-runner in this race.

Do it right and you get Carmel Murphy's vote.

President Mary Robinson - Images of Integrity

Mary Robinson is cool and competent. But she needs a warmer image. The common touch. That's about it.

Television, as ever, is what counts. This time more than ever. Paradoxically Mary's image of integrity, which comes with the Irish Times so to speak, can come across as a cold, Garret Fitzgerald 'mission to explain' persona which is death at the polls. Explaining things is fine for Dublin 4, but a problem nationally. Alan Dukes is still struggling with his cold fish image. Fine Gael never seems to grasp that intellect is intimidating, so they continue to lack the common touch.

Mary Robinson's current image is one of integrity and intellect - but this is somewhat discounted by cool and competence which sometimes come across as aloofness in a country which paradoxically values both cool and the common touch, each in its own place. The Parnell factor, the mixture of aloofness and affection is the ideal for candidates for public office in Ireland.

Television can warm up Mary's persona without compromising her three basic strengths: character, calm and competence. But we need cool, not cold.

This has nothing to do with what she says. It is a problem of 'form' not content. Mary needs more 'policies' like a hole in the head. Mary is articulate enough as it is. Now she needs more 'silences'. She needs to be seen listening, what Meryl Streep calls 'listening and thinking and letting them see you do it'.

What Mary now needs most of all is for the plain people of Ireland to like her as much as they respect her.

Mary's image of integrity and intellect can be taken as given, they are part of her received image. Any classic picture of her in classic clothes conveys this.

To this must be added a strong 'feminine' factor. Simply stated her image must be softened - caring and compassion must be added to competence and cool, and her image needs much larger doses of the latter.

Start with her non-intellectual and 'character' strengths. She looks good. She looks like she could look soft and caring - when she's off duty so to speak.

This is the subtext of any media campaign for Mary:

Mary must come across as a person who would make a great President. Dublin 4 subtext question: Why? Because she has the brains for it. Plain People subtext: Why? Because she has the beauty for it, she'd make us look good. General subtext question: Tell us why? Because she's the kind of competent, compassionate, caring and attractive woman we would like our wife/daughter/sister/mother/girlfriend to be if we are men and the kind of woman we want to be if we are women - and remember women's images of the ideal are also reflections of how men view that ideal too.

For women Mary should be the kind of woman they want to be; for men the kind of woman they would like to be seen with in public; or to talk with in private.

But Mary must listen twice as much as she talks!

The Twin Prongs of A Presidential Campaign:

The twin prongs of a campaign should be posters and photo-opportunities. The posters should be presidential. The photo moments - which are always aimed at television first - should be strongly feminine and stress her informal and democratic instincts.

This contrast must be pointed by dress and deportment - presidential posters with classic clothes; photo-tv ops in summery dresses, casual raincoats, slung bags, etc.

The Big Posters:

Mary cool but casual with Áras an Uachtaráin in background. This should be a Mike Bunn picture - cool and misty colours, classic but contemporary - distant aloof house, nature opaque and misty - but the woman foreground is warm, definite, composed and caring. She lights the picture - and keep the slogans stylish too. People hate gloomy slogans.

Slogans:

This House Needs a Woman's Touch , You'll never see me in a top hat, No problem (Just that and picture).

The Purpose of the Photo/TV Ops:

There is no need to fake anything. Mary Robinson has a strong track record on women's issues. What's needed is to take the 'issue' out of these issues and put people back at the centre. Put aside the 'mission to explain', the over-articulation of 'problems' in terms of precedent and procedure, the L & H boredom of summoning up previous malpractices of Fianna Fáil (what I call in RTE training courses The Fatal Tyranny of Fine Gael Fact) and instead talk about moving on.

But not just talk - for television you must really move...

Mary must be seen on the move, meeting the right people, almost always with a caring dimension, which is not the same as a Michael D. Higgins 'pity the poor whores' dimension. Nobody ever won an election on pity. Only by promising an end to the need for it.

Mary must visit community clinics - but clinics which are full of fight-back. One of the classic errors of the hard left is not to understand a simple piece of psychology: ordinary people are full of pity - but they hate whiners. So Mary should visit Rape Crisis centres - but stress the positive. She must visit mental hospitals - but where we see things done so well that we don't grudge a call for more cash. She must visit the disabled - but disabled on the move, disabled who are fighting back, the Gene Lambert type, fighters and full of hope, only needing a figurehead, a President who is not afraid to be seen with people in need, but people who need hope as well as hard cash.

General Aims:

Posters and Photo Ops do different - and this must be faced - dialectically contradictory jobs. This contradiction is in my view the dialectical secret of making use of mass media. The posters aim is to create confidence in her ability and authority to do the job. The photo-ops aim is paradoxically almost to contradict this by softening the way she goes about it, by creating confidence, not so much in her 'macho' ability to see it through but to give people a subliminal signal that she would not be rigid about the rules as a man would, that she would not hesitate to break Presidential rectitude to pick up a crying child. So while it must convey that she can do the job it must also convey that she would do it with compassion - simply stated we must never forget she is a woman.

The Purpose of the Posters:

The large 'presidential' posters, shown on billboards, have three main aims: 1. To convey competence and command respect. 2. To break down male prejudices about a woman's competence for the top job. 3. To reassure women by conveying that 'their' candidate looks like she can do the job. The poster pictures therefore should show Mary in classic suits and cool blouses of the type she wears so well. She should pose with a touch of formality in 'constitutional' or 'national' settings such as the Phoenix Park, Dublin skylines, Airports (Knock or Shannon) to catch international subtext, Leinster House (Seanad); the Four Courts and most importantly a timeless 'environmental' setting such as a lake or forest park scene - but devoid of specific connotations of IFA rurality or specific place. These settings are meant to stress the subtext of integrity, constitutional suitability, competence, authority, sensitivity to 'green' issues but without 'rural' reverberations of the sort that messed Dukes up before.

Particularly Mary should visit three kinds of places:

1. Clean high tech factories of all sorts (to break down the Dublin 4 image that machines are messy - the thing that put Thatcher ahead of Michael Foot who died in suburbia). 2. Sports Complexes in schools and towns (to develop an active outdoor image to discount the 'law library' look), these should be sports places where the 'new' games like Basketball and 'girls' games like

athletics and gymnastics are performed so as to have lots of girls and boys around her who are in sharp clothes like shorts and sneakers and not in sweaty, macho clothes like rugger buggers and GAA geriatrics. (Basketball is a huge working class game in Cork; Gurranabraher is an ideal tour area for TV). Finally 3. Hospitals and clinics, demanding that the grotty places be brought up to the level of Blackrock clinic. Don't go on about facilities (it's boring Garret factual gudge, they know it, they want it dealt with from a new angle) but DO go on about what bothers them more - how they are dealt with in a human sense; the delays, the lack of communication, need for reassurance, throwing people out of mental homes back on their relatives. This is as much a 'fact' as any health statistic. And the subtext slogan here is: A President Who Listens.

Final Warning:

Facts are tyrants on television which is about feelings about facts. In an important sense television is a woman. It deals with feelings. Which is where we deal with right and wrong. Which is why people put feelings first. And why television is so powerful in politics. Thirty years empirical evidence tells us that television loves feeling, hates fact. Television corrects Western worship of the macho 'fact'.

Clothes:

Pictures, especially television pictures, determine modern voting. Clothes are critical. You cannot spend too much on good clothes. Classy and classless clothes that speak softly. Ian Galvin at Browne Thomas has a gift for clothes for cameras. Take his advice and don't blink at the bill. It is money well spent.

Final Word of Advice:

Whenever a camera points at you - think hard about a real problem. Focus on it. Nod imperceptibly as you solve it. Let them see you do it …

The Crucial Constituency:

Munster is the one to win. This is fertile territory for you. Michael Collins Powell ran a brilliant campaign here for Tom O' Higgins years ago and that feeling against Fianna Fáil under Haughey is there. Cox tapped into it again last year. You must spend twice as long in Munster. You must conjure up the Jack Lynch factor in Cork by hitting Blackpool. Go into Béal na mBláth and Bandon and Michael Collins country. Clonmel, Cashel, and all these towns are worth investing time in. Munster can make all difference to what your final tally looks like.

Campaign slogan:

"A President for All the People"

Campaign Logos:

You need distinctive, attractive 'European' colour systems for posters and logos. Colour is critical. Think of the way Peter Manelson used the red rose in Britain. You need a 'feminine' but strong colour system, preferably 'Italian' style with a typography designed by a graphic artist with a feel for that kind of 'soft' political attack. I know some. But this is what costs. Like clothes it's worth it. Campaign Songs: For TV and Radio a gentle version of the 'Zoological Gardens' song. For cars with speaker systems there should be a version of 'Mrs. Robinson' with a few new simple lyrics. Nobody really remembers its risque film connotations and if they did it would be a plus. What you need is kids on the street singing 'Hey Mrs. Robinson', and then going dum de di 'President Mrs. Robinson, dum di dee ...' and if you got that you could go and count your surplus before the poll.

TV and Radio Broadcasts:

Like this. Gentle rollicking version of 'Did you ever go up to the Phoenix Park' or whatever. Pictures of you looking Presidential in a Paul Costello suit at Law Library, Dáil, National Library, Collins statue Cork, Galway City, Airports, Dublin Castle. All intercut with summery pix of you in coat and scarves, moving around streets, schools, clinics, smiling, shaking hands, listening a lot, nodding a lot, and above all surrounded by people. No commentary. Just a few lines at the end from a very male voice. 'Mary Robinson. A President for all the people. A President we can all be proud of. A President for today and tomorrow ...'

Newspapers:

I put this after 'clothes' to make a point. Newspaper press releases have no effect on a modern election. The function of a press release is mainly to keep the pot boiling, to authenticate what you say for Seán Duignan on 'Six O One' and in 'Today's statement by Presidential candidate Mary Robinson calling for a European curriculum was welcomed by Mr Jack Sweeney of the DFEWSD CUT TO SOF Sweeney. Newspapers have two important functions: 1. To follow the Presidential tour with feature articles. 2. To offer codes of cultural conduct. You do not need anybody to read what you say. But it is critical in what paper your picture appears most often. The very fact that you are in the Sunday Independent reassures devout Catholics even if they never read a word. Contrariwise if you appear in colour on the Sunday Tribune more than once Carmel Murphy will see it on the stand and mark you down as a Dublin 4 Tribunal type (Remember the Tribune has a tiny circulation, and its covers are a cultural code for a certain kind of lefty, trendy and indeed designer Provo type). Sunday newspapers matter more than weeklies. The newspaper you need every week is the Sunday Independent with its million readers - and whose endorsement reassures everybody you are not anti-Catholic. Vital too is the Sunday Press to pull in the Jack Lynch and populist vote. And it goes without saying that you have to crack the Sunday World which is a paper I respect because it is what it is and has no Provo messing and always delivers good features to me. The Irish Times you have - and a poisoned chalice it can be too. Mind the Irish Press whose journalists have much better politics (i.e. they are not Provo hush puppies like many in the IT) and the Irish Independent. Further you need to nurse selected papers such as the Southern Star by personally phoning the editors and stroking them. The Southern Star will set out to destroy you unless you remind them of a Fine Gael dimension. From that you can deduce that you need a Fine Gael godfather, in short you need the imprimatur of Garret Fitzgerald.

The Campaign Bus:

This election will be won by the Pat Cox factor. I mean you get into a bus on day one and you stay in it, hitting town after town, at a steady remorseless pace, running Lenihan ragged, like Sheridan going down the Shenandoah valley, leaving nothing but scorched earth behind for Lenihan.

People and Photos:
Mary Robinson has a cool image. It is critical that she is almost never pictured alone on walkabouts. She needs to be mobbed by people, crowded by people, pressing flesh all the time.

The Psychology of a Campaign:
Lenihan has not the stamina for a campaign, by which I mean a fighting, moving attack, over a large geographical area. He will falter and be seen to falter. He will be forced into helicopters - which are not democratic as a bus is - and he will be forced to fight from Dublin. And this will be noticed by the media - when we bring it to their notice. Then it will become a proverb of the campaign 'Ah Brian is past it...' This is tough but this is politics. Conversely the physical and emotional strains on Mary Robinson will be enormous. She needs total time off, total support systems at home, total freedom to take off in a bus and do nothing day in day out but listen to people who want to touch her. This is no fun but it is bearable if there is nothing else demanding your attention. Mary doesn't need a big team, two will do, and then pack the bus with locals. Having a detailed itinerary, not stinting on good hotels, making sure of good telephone communications and faxes - which are now everywhere - will make it a lot easier. This kind of campaign needs a special kind of logistical backup. Headquarters is on the bus. What Dublin does is to plan ahead and keep speeches coming ...

The Secret of Listening:
Whenever a camera is pointed at you - which is almost all the time - remember the Streep secret. Suppose somebody is going on and on. Focus on some problem in your head - say you set out to colour co-ordinate the dreary room you're in. Now nod imperceptibly as you solve the problem. Let them see you solve it. Of course it's easier if somebody is telling you a real problem. Think about how you would solve it as you listen. Let them see you think.

Live The Moment:
Human contact is very wearing as we all know. In this campaign it's vital. Best to 'live the moment'. In other words go forward to meet the stress rather than dodging away from it.

Humour:

A sense of fun is critical in an Irish election. Because Lenihan has it you need to do something about that side of your image. Nobody says you should jump around. But a nice line in dry humour and a bouncing bonhomie will do fine. People must see that you are serious enough about this not to take yourself too solemnly. Here's a test. Given that the odds are against you. Given that the Irish people love a fighter, love grace under pressure. Given that they like a sense of fun. How do you convey spunk, a sense of fun and lose Lenihan in two words? Well first time a reporter asks you about your chances you look at them levelly and say blandly: 'No problem'. (Funk this and it's no go. Without some fun it's not on).

The Surprise Factor:

Surprise is the key to victory. Everybody will expect Mary Robinson to run a dignified losers campaign. What they will not expect and what the public will delight in is if Mary Robinson runs a barnstorming, bus-pounding, no holds barred, will to win, old style political campaign that leaves Lenihan panting.

That will take enormous energy. Mary has that energy.

What's needed now is the will to win.

5

OPENING SHOTS

It will surprise some today if I tell of the exact circumstances that brought me first into politics. In a way it has all the appearances of an accident. My father was a businessman in Athlone and Chairman of the Westmeath County Council. The key TD in the constituency was the late M. J. Kennedy, an old IRA man and lifelong friend of Eamon De Valera. He knew my father well and one day, as the general election of 1954 was approaching, Joe, as he was known, visited our home. At this stage the election hadn't even been called but Kennedy was already thinking what candidates to run. Chatting to my father he told him frankly that he felt an election was imminent. They discussed the constituency and then Kennedy pointed to me and said he wanted me to stand. I was a bit surprised having only recently qualified to practice as a barrister. Up to that moment I had been active in the party but for the most part I would probably be better known as a soccer player.

My only worry initially was whether I could get through the Fianna Fáil selection convention. Kennedy was a bachelor from Castlepollard and a devoted republican all his life. As a founder member he knew the party well, and just told me to show up on the day.

Nowadays conventions are a different matter. Kennedy ruled the organisation, and was admired because of his involvement in the IRA and the struggle for independence. He was also an enlightened man who could see beyond himself, and saw the need for more young people in the party. He and Seán Lemass learnt their politics as they conducted a guerrilla war against British rule in Ireland. Later, in the sixties, politics and politicians were to become more glamourised than they had been before this. To a large extent the escapades of myself, the late Donogh O'Malley and Charlie Haughey have been mythologised beyond the mundane reality of a society that was quite simply modernising. The times were changing but perhaps not as quickly as many then undoubtedly imagined. Still, at the age of 23, I was the unanimous choice to be the fourth runner alongside Joe Kennedy, the late Erskine Childers and the late Frank Carter in the five seat constituency of Longford-Westmeath.

Childers never found it easy to hold on to his seat. Longford-Westmeath was just one of several constituencies he represented in his long political life, eventually finding stability in Monaghan. Joe Kennedy was not enamoured with Childers. To a certain extent his sponsorship of my candidature was directed at Childers.

As the campaign got underway it was clear I was doing much better than was intended for a candidate who was meant to act as a sweeper. Word began to trickle back to Fianna Fáil headquarters that Childers might be in danger. De Valera had always been very protective of Childers because of his father who had been executed during the civil war for his anti-treaty stance. Joe Kennedy got a call from the "Chief" and was told to make sure Childers did not lose his seat. It was typical of Kennedy that in the last week of the campaign he canvassed his own home town of Castlepollard telling the people to vote for Childers. He had a consummate knowledge of the proportional representation system, and knew exactly how many votes Childers needed to be safe. Needless to add Childers retained his seat.

I mention all this to give the reader a sense of the discipline and loyalty of these men who had soldiered through tough times together. It is often forgotten the influence men like Kennedy and others had on young people like myself who were just starting out in politics at this time. Far too often myself, Charlie Haughey and Donogh O'Malley are presented by people writing of that period as brash "new men" anxious to throw off what had gone before.

I, for one, had a great admiration for Lemass and the others who had fought and worked for our freedom.

The opening shots of the Presidential campaign in 1990 were a far cry from my first outing as a candidate. At that time, campaigns were fought on the traditional basis of the door-to-door canvass, the after Mass meetings and speeches from public platforms around the constituency. The battleground in 1990 was to be on the newspapers, television and radio. The contrast between the electorate then and now could not be greater. The Ireland that Seán Lemass ushered in was slightly gauche in its modernity. What became very clear to me during the Presidential campaign was the extent to which our country had gained in self-confidence, become comfortable with progress.

The first real encounter of the campaign was on the RTE programme "Saturday View". Rodney Rice hosted the programme which went out live on 22 September. I have appeared on this programme a number of times in the past and it is rarely bad-tempered. It is one of those jovial magazine-type programmes where politicos and journalists bounce around the issues of the preceding week. Naturally the politicians try to score points but it never really becomes a bad-tempered debate. All three prospective candidates for the Presidency were there on this particular Saturday. Each of us in turn set out our vision of the office and explained why we were best suited for the job. The debate became more tense with both Austin Currie and Mary Robinson combining to claim that I was unsuitable to occupy the post as President. Their reasons were to become more familiar as the campaign rolled on. The argument, when everything else was boiled down, amounted to the suggestion that, because of my loyalty to the Taoiseach, Mr. Haughey, over the years, I could not conduct myself with the required independence as an occupant of the office of President. It was to be a charge rich with irony later in the campaign when I was dismissed from the Government by the Taoiseach Mr. Haughey despite his entreaty that I resign.

It was a niggardly suggestion but both of them pursued it with abandon. As ever with allegations of this kind nothing is precisely spelled out but the allegation itself was constantly repeated. I quickly dismissed the charge as a smear. I repeated that if elected I would swear an oath to uphold the Constitution, and that was exactly as I should do.

The programme, while of no great significance, did give a taster for what was to come. Back at home in Castleknock I was perturbed at the tactics being employed by Currie and Robinson. "Saturday View" was a sneak preview of what would turn out to be a very dirty campaign. In a way it was to be expected since I was so far ahead in the opinion polls before even a shot was fired. Perhaps both opponents felt that I had to be taken down a bit. I was a little concerned that if the campaign took on the features of a mud-slinging contest it would only serve to damage the office of President in the public mind. It was my fear then that it would be difficult for the winner to remain above politics if political controversies were generated during the election. It was, to my mind at least, to the benefit of all that the campaign should be seen to be cleanly fought so that whoever won the contest could enjoy the confidence of the whole country without bitterness or rancour about the result.

The other candidates did not see things this way. They were both, to a large extent, new to the highly charged atmosphere of a national campaign and, coming from behind in the opinion polls, were ready to take more risks. The allegation that I could not be an independent President always struck me as slightly ludicrous. In a way the charge was so ludicrous that it was difficult to handle and deal with head on. All the more difficult since I have always regarded loyalty as a virtue to be praised rather than impugned. Anyone who has looked at my political career, even in the most perfunctory way, would know that I have never been beholden to anybody. In that career I have served under three different Taoisigh. In the 1980s I became identified in the public mind as a Haughey loyalist, or at the very least, the man sent onto the television when he was in trouble. His arrival to the leadership of Fianna Fáil in 1979 was not without its difficulties. There were constant challenges to his authority from within the party by a recalcitrant group of deputies who found it difficult to accept that the late George Colley had been beaten in the leadership contest following Jack Lynch's premature withdrawal from political life.

I felt duty bound to support Mr. Haughey during this period. I had refused to express an opinion publicly on whom I had supported in the original contest between him and George Colley. I must say that I liked both men. I decided not to take part in the leadership contest. It was an unruly affair sandwiched into two quick days in order to give George Colley, the then favourite to succeed, maximum advantage. When Haughey was banished from the government after the Arms Trial, I had maintained our friendship of years. Other members of the Government had not done so, partly out of fear. Haughey was an outcast of kinds within Fianna Fáil in the seventies. Even when restored to the cabinet in 1977, it was considered infra dig by those in authority to be seen fraternising with him. This never bothered me. One of the saddest things that I witnessed in my political life was an occasion when Mr. Haughey, then Minister for Health, was sick in the Mater Hospital. Though in hospital for some time, just one other colleague from government, apart from myself, bothered to visit him and that was Michael O'Kennedy. The bitterness from the Arms Trial ran deep.

To my mind, the public challenges to Mr. Haughey's leadership in the early eighties were in a way an extension of the divisions opened up by the Arms Trial. I did not believe at any stage that the challenges were being mounted for any other reason than naked political ambition on the part of those who had lost out in the 1979 leadership battle. If there were any tangible differences in how the party should be run they were only grafted on afterwards as a justification for the actual power bid. A grave disservice to this country was done in that period of uncertainty. It was then that difficult problems facing the nation needed to be tackled but instead, the public were treated to the spectacle of a party constantly at war with itself. Firm government was the first casualty in this dispute. In this sense the eventual departure of Des O'Malley and others from the party was a welcome development.

My support for Mr. Haughey at this time had good precedent to back it up. I have always been committed to the leader of the party once elected. In the aftermath of the Arms Trial, I was one of the strongest supporters, along with Paddy Hillery, of the then Taoiseach Jack Lynch. The extent of that support can be gauged by a lingering distrust of me, in the immediate aftermath of the 1979 contest, among certain members of the Haughey camp. This suspicion had been exacerbated by my refusal to become committed to either side in the contest. This belief of loyalty to the party leader is based on the sound rational principle that our political system of parliamentary government requires a stable party system. In Ireland and in most European countries, the government or executive power is drawn from parliament, whereas in the United States the executive is elected for a fixed period and is quite independent of the legislative arm of government. In the US, the President is elected directly by the people and is the head of the executive branch, so there is no need for a strict party system. This is not the case in Ireland or most European countries where governments depend on stable support in parliament to get on with the business of the nation.

Prior to his resignation in December 1979, Jack Lynch's leadership was under threat on several fronts. The 1977 Government was in difficulty amid an atmosphere of industrial unrest and two damaging by-election defeats in his native Cork. Added to that he was being encouraged to step down early by George Colley who felt the timing was right for his own challenge. I advised Jack Lynch to stay on and ride the political storm out and urged him on at least two occasions not to step down. He had a clear majority in the Dáil and strong backing in the parliamentry party. Despite isolated disquiet in the party he had the overwhelming support of deputies if it was put to the test. I also knew that any subsequent leadership battle would be both bitter and divisive, which unfortunately proved to be the case. However, Jack had his own personal reasons for bowing out.

Therefore, I found the allegation that I would not be sufficiently independent to fulfil the office of President very annoying during the campaign in 1990. I have always been on friendly terms with opposition deputies in Leinster House. Though I had political differences with the former Taoiseach, Liam Cosgrave, over the years the fact that he was Fine Gael never prevented us from being good friends. That this question of independence was to become a central plank in Fine Gael's campaign was evident from the start. At the official launch of their campaign Austin Currie was to declare: "It is difficult to see how the habits of loyalty to Mr. Haughey for half a lifetime will be abandoned by Mr. Lenihan if elected President." Warming to his theme Currie then went on to state that after the 1989 General Election when Mr. Haughey failed to be elected Taoiseach by the Dáil and refused to resign, even though required to do so by the Constitution, Mr. Lenihan, his Tánaiste, did not demur. In fact the truth is quite the opposite. I, along with Albert Reynolds and Gerry Collins, was among the first ministers to advise Mr. Haughey to tender his formal resignation to the President on that occasion. This matter is well documented in Shane Kenny's book on the 1989 general election *Go Dance on Somebody Else's Grave.*

It struck me at this point in the campaign that many of these allegations were falling on deaf ears. Anyway, I have never been one to make personalised attacks on opponents and I did not intend to start now by responding in kind to either Austin Currie or Mary Robinson. The only ominous reminder of the controversy yet to come in the campaign was Currie's assertion that I had "at the behest of Mr. Haughey" phoned Áras an Uachtaráin back in 1982. At the time it hardly made the front page of any newspaper but it is interesting to note that Austin Currie quoted, by way of evidence to back up his assertion, an article written in the Irish Times by Jim Duffy on 27 September. It could be that his citing of the Duffy article was coincidence. If it was coincidence then it belongs to a series of such coincidences which I intend to deal with in a later chapter.

Jim Duffy, the research student from University College Dublin, had written a series of articles on the Presidency for the newspaper as this was the area of his MA thesis. When these articles appeared, my campaign was in full swing and I did not in fact read them. It is often thought by members of the public that politicians spend all of their time reading newspapers. For me at least this is not the case. Looking back on those articles by Duffy they assume a critical importance though it did not ring any alarm bells at the time. The critical factor was that, unknown to me, Jim Duffy had already set out on a path which would see him confuse his role as an academic engaged in research and his occasional role as a writer for the Irish Times.

For the record, he wrote in the Irish Times of September 27:

"In this instance, the President in his "absolute discretion" could have refused the request, forcing the Taoiseach's resignation. Dr. Fitzgerald's trip to the Park was delayed, however, until the Secretary to the President, who was not in Áras an Uachtaráin, could be located. In the delay, the Fianna Fáil leader, Mr. Haughey called an emergency front bench meeting. A press release was issued in which he indicated that he was "available for consultation" with the President. To hammer home the point, a series of phone calls was made by him, and at his insistence, by Brian Lenihan and Sylvester Barret, two close friends of Dr. Hillery. The President angrily rejected all such pressure and, having judged the issue, granted Dr. Fitzgerald the dissolution."

The rhetorical question was posed by political opponents when the crisis came, why did I not rebut the contents of this article at the time. The simple answer is I didn't see it until it was pointed out to me much later. In any event throughout my political life I have never bothered to go about correcting the factual inaccuracies about me in newspaper articles or complaining to the media about coverage. It is something of a fool's errand to do so, the act of a political Don Quixote. The downside of this is that sometimes things are written about people in public life which, if left unchallenged, become accepted as true. A good example of this kind of thing has been a consistent claim by Vincent Browne, Editor of the Sunday Tribune, that back in 1979, I voted for the late George Colley. I had a lot of time for George but I voted for Haughey not Colley on the grounds of greater ability. Until now, I have kept the matter of who I voted for then to myself.

The whole thrust of my refusal to get involved in the 1979 leadership conflict was that I was happy I could work with either man. I already knew, and have pointed out here, that the contest would prove to be both close and divisive. In this situation I felt that someone who had not been identified too closely with either side in the leadership battle would be an asset to the party in the aftermath.

Apart from the media interviews it was quickly time to hit the road and get on the campaign trail. A very gruelling campaign schedule had been drawn up by Fianna Fáil headquarters. My wife Ann was a bit apprehensive but I didn't mind. Our three week holiday in the south of France over the summer had seen me get a lot of exercise. I swam twice a day and began to put back on a lot of muscle tissue which I'd lost before the liver transplant operation. Losing that weight had given me a rather cadaverous look but when I came back from France I felt marvellous. My doctors at the Mater gave me a glowing medical report. The busy life of being a government minister does not lend itself to getting exercise on any kind of a regular basis. It is always the intention to take exercise but inevitably the constant round of meetings gets in the way. While the last thing deputies ever want is an election, it is one of the few times they get some exercise. I've always loved campaigning and meeting people. Meeting people is the one thing that redeems public life of the petty intrigue that can so often, unfortunately, be part of it. Parliaments can also become cosy clubs where, gradually over time, the members become separated from reality. Elections bring us down to earth again.

Our first stop on the trail was at the Ballinasloe Horse Fair where I was due to present prizes. There was to be a trip into Galway city and then back for a tour of the Galway East constituency finishing that night with a rally in Loughrea. It was to be a busy day. At Ballinasloe we were swarmed with well-wishers and familiar faces too from the neighbouring constituency of Roscommon where I'd first served as a TD. All the same it was a day for horses, not politics. The fair is taken very seriously by those who attend. When I arrived in the enclosure at the crucial stage of the premier competition there was hardly any reaction from the crowd. The Irish Press journalist, Jimmy Walsh, was to joke that sometimes even horses were more important than entrants in a presidential race. Later that evening and despite the rain we were lead through Loughrea by a piped band who accompanied us in from the outskirts of the town. In the darkness, people came out and stood in their doorways to wave and wish me well. Then it was on to the Temperance Hall for the first rally of the campaign. That night Ann and I stayed with our old friends Maureen and Brendan O'Callaghan in Athlone. We had no inkling then of the dramatic circumstances of our next stay there some four weeks later.

The next day I stopped off in St. Patrick's College, Maynooth for the first of a series of visits to the universities. Both the Director

of Elections Bertie Ahern and my sister Mary O'Rourke were un-
enthusiastic about visiting the third level institutions. They feared
the possibility of stage-managed student protest which might lead
to bad publicity in the national press. I, however, thought differ-
ently and insisted that we get to as many of the third level
institutions as possible. Over the years I have frequently made a
point of accepting invitations to speak in debates organised by
student societies of one kind and another. They were always good
fun and the heckling a bit of a challenge. I once had the audacity,
as some saw it, to show up at Trinity College as Minister for
Education at the height of the student protest movement. An
angry mob of students had gathered and, with little or no security,
I was forced to make my exit from the college via a toilet window
near Trinity's front gate. During the campaign it was comforting
to note that today's students are not nearly as radical as in those
heady days in the 1960s! I was received courteously in all of the
colleges that I visited. It's always a particular pleasure to visit the
former N.I.H.E., now Dublin City University, the establishment of
which, along with Limerick, I was responsible for all those years
ago.

To give an idea of how hectic the schedule was in the first week
alone, I went to and from various centres around the country:
Galway, Cork, Mullingar, Longford, Carrick-on-Shannon, Boyle,
Sligo and finally finishing up with the Fianna Fáil commemoration to Wolfe Tone in Bodenstown, County Kildare. If there was
proof enough that my health wasn't a problem it was there in that
busy schedule. Yet my health, as I'd expected, would be raised in
one form or another before the campaign was out. On week one
there was a ripple of controversy when the Government Press
Secretary, P.J. Mara, told an inquiring journalist from the Sunday
Tribune, looking for a medical statement from my doctors, that
they had "fuck all" right to know about Mr. Lenihan's health. The
only people to raise it publicly, apart from this newspaper, were
Garret Fitzgerald and later Jim Kemmy, who, at one of Mary
Robinson's press conferences in Limerick said my health was an
issue on the doorsteps. Mrs. Robinson would not be drawn on the
matter when asked.

At national level, the first week was dominated by a series of mini controversies surrounding the arrangements for television coverage of the campaign. The first was a rather minor business about whether RTE should cover, as they normally do, the annual Jacobs Award which I had been previously invited to present. The programme was to go out before I had formally handed in my nomination papers. RTE were afraid of accusations of bias in the manner in which they were covering all three candidates and so decided not to cover it. In the end I pulled out of the awards ceremony rather than deprive the sponsors, Jacobs, of their valuable publicity. I felt RTE were being a little fastidious about their impartiality ruling, and a number of my ministerial colleagues felt this was deliberate due to their continuing anger about the controversial Broadcasting Act put through the Dáil the previous summer. Despite that, I found RTE's coverage of the campaign reasonably balanced in the circumstances of what turned out to be a highly charged campaign. The other controversy about coverage concerned the number of occasions all three would appear. Both Labour and Fine Gael claimed that Fianna Fáil were trying to restrict their air time by limiting my appearances. Austin Currie claimed I was running away from debate.

This culminated in a rather ridiculous press release from Mrs. Robinson where she claimed I lacked "street cred" for turning down an opportunity to appear with her and Austin Currie on the light entertainment programme, Nighthawks. She compared me to an ageing movie queen who, like Gretta Garbo, wanted to be alone. In a more unusual interview with the rock magazine Hot Press that same week she used words like "shit" in reply to questions. But this has apparently become the norm in Hot Press interviews.

Her Hot Press interview proved to be the first real controversy of the campaign for quite other reasons. Whether in fact it was a genuine controversy remains to be seen, particularly in the light of Eoghan Harris's belief quoted in Chapter 4, that it was important that she deal with the divorce and abortion issues, or as he calls it "distortion issues", early in the campaign. In his letter to her at the beginning of the campaign, Harris suggested that her stance on social issues might become something of a bugbear if not tackled correctly. The interview question which caused the greatest furore concerned her apparent willingness to open a condom stall in the Virgin Megastore if elected President.

The magazine quoted Mrs. Robinson as saying. "Yes. This is a very young country and I think it would be very helpful to have a President who was in touch with what young people are doing". In a subsequent RTE interview she denied that she would open such a stall, saying she had been either misquoted or misunderstood. She said she would never be involved in the promotion of contraception outside the law. In a later interview with the Irish Times she insisted she had been misinterpreted and that in fact she had been referring to the first part of the question, but said that she often answered yes to a question, meaning that she understood what was being asked. The editor of Hot Press, Niall Stokes, stood over the controversial interview and released a tape-recording of the relevant parts to the media.

Mrs. Robinson also said in the interview that, as a democrat, she didn't think the President should be going off at a tangent from the democratic representative Government.

"However," she added "and it is a big however, there is no constitutional restraint on what I do outside of official functions. As a President directly elected by the people of Ireland, I will have the most democratic job in the country. I'll be able to look Charlie Haughey in the eye and tell him to back off." This remark evoked a response from the Taoiseach Mr. Haughey who, at the Bodenstown commemoration described as "dangerous nonsense" suggestions that the President should take on some new kind of executive role. He said that any attempt to bring the role of the President into the political arena could undermine the democratic process in this country, adding that the Presidency should "be above politics". Mrs. Robinson responded to the Taoiseach by accusing him of "mischief-making", claiming he had misrepresented her views. Fine Gael's John Bruton also criticised the interview suggesting that Mrs. Robinson believed the President should be a generator of controversy. Austin Currie followed up by calling on her to withdraw those of her proposals which were unconstitutional, illegal or divisive. I did not get involved in the controversy.

At this stage Lady Luck favoured Mrs. Robinson in the shape of an Irish Times opinion poll which apparently showed her rating unaffected by the whole controversy and that she was forging ahead of Fine Gael's Austin Currie. The interviews for the poll were, for the most part, conducted before the actual controversy had sunk in and it managed to give her a well needed help over the whole business. The view began to form in the media that she was largely unscathed by the Hot Press debacle.

With just one week gone in the campaign, things had yet to get going in earnest. The controversy over the Hot Press interview had heightened interest but so far left Mrs. Robinson unaffected in the polls. My rating in the polls was slipping back a bit but that was to be expected since I had started from such a strong position. There would be a few key media appearances before the campaign was over, and I felt I could get over these without suffering any further loss in the polls.

6

QUESTIONS AND ANSWERS

The remainder of the campaign that led up to the by now famous RTE Questions and Answers programme passed without any great incident. My country-wide tour was continuing and the reception was warm wherever I went. I remember one day in County Tipperary with Deputy Noel Davern. We left Thurles in the morning by coach, and travelled to Killenaule, with Ballingarry nearby, where Smith O'Brien rallied miners and small farmers in the Young Ireland uprising of 1848. On to Mullinahone and fictional Knocknagow – the home of Tipperary and Fenian writer, Charles Kickham, through the Vale of Anner at the foot of Sliabh Na mBan, through Grangemockler of Big Sycamore and de Brún memory, and then to the lovely Suir Valley and Carrick-on-Suir, where we held a meeting in Seán Kelly Square, which is dedicated to our cycling hero. This is the country of great athletes, hammer-throwers and hurlers – the Davins, Dr. Pat O'Callaghan of Olympic fame, and legendary hurler Mick Roche. It is the heartland of the Fenians and the GAA. On to Clonmel and a fantastic welcome in the Dinny Lacey Hall with the Comeraghs on the left, and the Nire Valley beyond where Frank Aiken brought the Civil War to an end. From Clonmel to Cahir, nestling in the Knockmealdowns, past the Galtees and the Glen of Aherlow to Tipperary town with its memories of Breen, Treacey, Hogan, Lacey, the Fitzpatrick and the Barlow brothers, a small band of men who started the War of Independence on their own. Through Bansha where Canon Hayes began the Muintir Na Tíre movement that gave confidence to rural Ireland, and on to Cashel of the Kings. It was a day that evoked the roots, traditions and history of an Ireland that has maintained its vitality and will survive in the years ahead.

However, there were increasing signs of desperation in the Fine Gael campaign. With Austin Currie trailing Mrs. Robinson the party were apparently thinking of changing their tactics. Part of their problem seemed to be that they could not make up their mind whether to make a virtue of Currie's northern background or play it down. There were also newspaper reports that they were going to steer away from their negative tactics of attacking the other candidates. If this was the case the next fortnight was to show little sign of it.

Fine Gael began to attack Mrs. Robinson for her affiliation with the left wing parties. The party's finance spokesman, Michael Noonan, claimed that the Workers Party would portray support for Mrs. Robinson as a mandate for socialist policies. Jim Mitchell, the director of elections, said a transfer deal might not be on because he saw her support from the Workers Party as a liability. The former Taoiseach, Garret Fitzgerald, was then wheeled out to express his reservations about both myself and Mary Robinson in relation to the Anglo-Irish Agreement.

Fitzgerald intoned that the election of either Mary Robinson or Brian Lenihan would "give the wrong impression in the north and to British opinion as both of us had opposed the signing of the Anglo-Irish Agreement back in 1985". The Labour party, participants at the time in signing the accord, dismissed his intervention as "totally unworthy of him". It was a most undignified attack for a former Taoiseach to make but by no means his last intervention in the campaign. The allegation itself was not taken seriously, given that I was, at the moment, part of a government that was vigorously defending the Anglo-Irish Accord and operating it in close co-operation with the British government. At the first meeting of the new government elected in 1987, I had pressed for full acceptance of the Anglo-Irish agreement, so that we could make it work to the maximum extent. As Minister for Foreign Affairs for the following two years, I proceeded to implement it. As Co-Chairman of the Conference, I built up a relationship of trust with the then Northern Secretary Tom King. In particular, I pushed hard for the new Fair Employment legislation in the north and raised other issues of concern to the nationalist community.

Later on in the campaign, Austin Currie proposed that the other two candidates join him in signing a peace pledge on the north. The pledge was to form the basis for a subsequent peace referendum in which the people of the southern state would be asked to declare that the use of violence for political ends was contrary to their wishes. The pledge also would state that the unity of Ireland would only come about with the agreement of a majority of people in the north. It was an odd kind of initiative in the middle of a Presidential election campaign. It was hardly an appropriate time to begin such a move and even more so, I felt, at a period when the sensitive "talks about talks" process was continuing under the guidance of the Northern Secretary Peter Brooke. He, along with the government here and the parties in the north, was trying to find a way of breaking the political impasse in the north. It was all a bit of a surprise and frankly it struck me as a pretty poor form of gimmick to resuscitate a campaign. Mary Robinson's reaction was that while she had no objection in principle to the proposal, she did not see what its relevance was in the course of a presidential campaign. All too often here in the south, we become obsessed with the idea of noble gestures rather than solid action on the north.

On Monday, 22 October, I was scheduled to appear on the Questions and Answers programme out at Montrose. It was one of a number of set-piece television appearances agreed at the beginning of the campaign. While there had been some initial haggling with the opposition parties and of course RTE, it was finally agreed that all three candidates would appear separately on the programme. There had already been one occasion where all three of us had participated together in a radio programme at the outset of the campaign. A further two were planned before polling day. The first, on the Thursday before polling, was a three way debate between the candidates organised by Today Tonight. Then the following evening all three would be interviewed by Gay Byrne on The Late Late Show. The candidates' spouses were also going to be in the Late Late studio to be interviewed.

My diary had been deliberately left clear of any country tours for the days of all of these television interviews including the Questions and Answers programme. Advice on how I should present myself on television was given by Carr Communications who had been retained for that purpose for the duration of the campaign. I paid a visit to them before going on that night.

I had no particular worry about the programme as I'd appeared on it before and knew the format. It is an enjoyable programme. The programme has attracted controversy in the past. Some years back, the programme was attacked by the former Fine Gael Minister Gemma Hussey. She claimed that it was being packed with members of Sinn Féin from week to week. While she may have gone overboard, the programme makers did have to adjust the format to prevent members of that party from infiltrating the audience. Their presence among the studio audience was made all the more sensitive for RTE because of Section 31 of the Broadcasting Act which forbids any interview with members of Sinn Féin and other organisations proscribed by law. According to Peter Feeney, Editor of Current Affairs at the station, members of that organisation were turning up on their audience list, and then, after the programme, were announcing either to RTE personnel or to the newspapers that they had yet again broken Section 31.

It now means that they have to check all members of the audience more thoroughly beforehand, lest they be open to the charge of breaking the law. Members of different interest groups, whose area is currently topical, are given tickets to attend, and if politicians are appearing, they too are given a number of tickets for their activists.

One of the chief changes introduced by the Sinn Féin efforts to infiltrate, is that the programme no longer goes out live, so that if there is a breach of Section 31 it can be edited out before transmission. RTE were, according to Peter Feeney, because of the election, taking extra precautions in relation to who got on the show. They were, he said, conscious of the fact that a party, simply by writing in and asking for tickets, could pack the audience during the critical election period. The programme makers went back to lists of applicants who had asked for tickets well before the campaign began. Because of the need to provide balanced coverage during an election period, Peter Feeney was taking a more active role in overseeing individual programmes throughout the campaign.

Up to this, it was understood that the directors of election for each of the candidates would appear on the programme when other candidates were the guests. So from the week before, Fianna Fáil believed that Fine Gael's Jim Mitchell would be appearing the night I was on. At 4 pm. on the day the programme was to go out, Fine Gael rang RTE to say that Mitchell would not be going on and that instead former Taoiseach Garret Fitzgerald would appear. "It was sometime between 5 pm. and 6 pm. before Jim Sherwin, the Editor of the programme, got to find out," says Feeney.

"We were actually surprised. From our point of view it was a bonus. He was a former Taoiseach and it would make for lively television," says the RTE man. It would be two days later before he would find out how lively it had actually been. Fine Gael subsequently claimed the last minute switching of their panelist was not as deliberate as some have been led to believe. The reasons advanced by them for the move are, that it was felt that a more heavyweight figure was needed to tackle me and that Garret's status as former Taoiseach would direct attention away from me on the night. Whatever the strategic logic of these arguments they sit uneasily with the facts.

That evening before the programme, Garret Fitzgerald issued a statement to the media, about the night of 27 January 1982 and the allegation that senior people in Fianna Fáil rang Áras an Uachtaráin, when he said the following:

"When I arrived at Áras an Uachtarán about 2 hours after my Dáil defeat, I found that the President had been besieged by phone calls from senior Fianna Fáil T.D.s demanding that he refuse me a dissolution of the Dáil and require my resignation as a preliminary to inviting the Fianna Fáil leader, C.J. Haughey, to seek Dáil support for nomination as Taoiseach without an election. As I recall it, the most persistent of those callers was the present presidential candidate Brian Lenihan."

This has been subsequently taken to indicate that Garret Fitzgerald either had prior knowledge of what was coming up or was at the very least signalling his intention of raising the matter on the programme. That evening at 5 pm., at their party headquarters in Mount Street, Dublin, a number of Fine Gael activists had been briefed by the director of elections Jim Mitchell. All of them were to take the party's allocation of tickets in the audience that night. The late substitution of Garret and his statement delivered that evening have been the focus of controversy. Incredibly the former Taoiseach was to claim in a later Dáil debate that he was unaware of the statement issued in his name.

"On returning home late on Monday night after the Questions and Answers programme, I was interviewed by a journalist from RTE who started to ask me why I had accused Brian Lenihan of ringing that night. When I denied that I had done so on the programme, she drew my attention to the fact that the speech I had prepared several weeks earlier before Brian Lenihan had made his denials had been issued by Fine Gael, of which I had until then been quite unaware. That was my involvement. No plot - no trap."

The question must be asked why did Garret Fitzgerald feel the need to deny he had accused me of ringing Áras an Uachtaráin back in 1982 that night after the programme, when he had clearly set out to accuse me of exactly that some weeks before when he wrote the speech? Either he was not sure of his allegation about me or hadn't in fact written the speech circulated by the Fine Gael press office. The latter would be difficult to believe were it not for the fact that he himself claims he was unaware that the speech was being circulated on the evening of Questions and Answers.

It is of course possible that he may have been a little confused by his late inclusion in the programme line up that night. It was only on the Sunday that Fine Gael had managed to make contact with him in Venice to ask him to return to Dublin in order to participate in the programme. He had been attending a meeting with the European members of the Trilateral Commission in the Italian city. The Commission is a large think-tank body that brings together an influential mixture of politicians and businessmen from Europe, America and Japan. The Left here in Ireland have tended to depict it in rather sinister tones but it has in the past included among its number Labour politicians including the current President Mary Robinson.

The original idea behind the Commission seems to have been

the integration of the then emerging economic power of Japan into the western bloc of nations. Its funding came initially from the American millionaire David Rockefeller.

There were two formal sessions planned for the Saturday and the Sunday. The Italian Foreign Minister Gianni De Michelis addressed the gathering on the Friday since his was the host country for the gathering. Fianna Fáil's Liam Lawlor is also a member of the Trilateral Commission and attended their sessions in Venice. He confirms that Garret got the urgent call to come back to Dublin on the Sunday. "It would be generally expected of him to stay on. After all, it is only a two day session really," says Liam. He also points out that Garret tends to be a pretty assiduous attender of the Trilateral's meetings.

Anyway, I arrived at Montrose for the programme accompanied by director of elections Bertie Ahern, my son Conor and Niamh O'Connor from the Fianna Fáil press office. As usual we were shown up to the hospitality unit where those not participating directly in the programme can watch the show. I went off to get the make-up put on as is customary in RTE. The other panelists were the Irish Times journalist Nuala O'Faolain and Michael D. Higgins from the Labour Party, both seemed fine. We all sat together in the hospitality room before the programme began. Peter White from the Fine Gael press office was there. Peter White's presence with the former Taoiseach makes Garret's assertion that he was unaware of the speech put out by the Fine Gael press office even harder to understand. Garret seemed a little fidgety as we sat and waited. None of us had any particular objection to the line up of guests.

It is not generally known by viewers that the panelists get to look at the questions before the show. The audience are invited in early and asked to write down questions they would like to ask. From these a number are selected and the presenter tries to get through them all. On this night, there were nine questions down but generally there is an opportunity for members of the audience to get in questions that don't appear on the list shown to the panelists. There was nothing unpredictable in the questions. Bertie Ahern cast his eyes up to heaven at some of them. His feeling was that none of the Fianna Fáil activists in the audience had got their questions selected. He recognised one of the names, that of Billy Stamp, as being a member of Fine Gael. My son Conor recognised the name of Terry Murphy, a member of Fine Gael, who had been in school with him. However, I was not unduly alarmed and, having appeared on the programme before, I knew that some of our activists would get in during the programme. In the event they did as I'd expected. The only interesting point at this stage is that the question that asked me directly about the events of 1982 came from Brian Murphy and that was not on the list.

Murphy was also a member of a key Fine Gael campaign committee which reported directly to Jim Mitchell, the director of elections. The committee exercised a monitoring role on behalf of the director of elections to ensure that his wishes were being carried out. Murphy was, as we shall later see, a good friend of the UCD MA researcher Jim Duffy.

There was some initial discussion of the listed questions by all of us before we went down to the studio. The first question came from Billy Stamp on a quotation from De Valera that seemed to imply that he did not want a party political person to occupy the post of President. When replying to this Garret Fitzgerald broadened out the discussion to talk about the serious constitutional question that had arisen over the last three to four general elections where there had been an inconclusive result with no party having a clear majority in the Dáil. He said that this meant that there were constitutional difficulties and near crises, and he linked this to the President's power to refuse a dissolution of the Dáil. Garret then tried to raise the issue of the dissolution back in 1982.

At this point John Bowman interrupted him saying, "I don't want you to proceed on that Garret Fitzgerald because we have a specific question on that point later." After more discussion of a general nature the presenter moved on to the next questioner who asked the panel whether it was right for the media and newspapers to inquire into the health, financial and personal records of candidates for the presidency. It related to a request made by the Sunday Tribune to see my medical records, referred to in the previous chapter. At the time, the Government's Press Secretary, P. J. Mara, told the Sunday Tribune in no uncertain terms that they were not entitled to have access to my medical records.

Garret said of the Press Secretary's reply: "It had the unfortunate effect of casting a doubt on the very issue he was presumably trying to remove from the scene." Warming to his task Garret suggested that this kind of reply and this kind of language should not be used. John Bowman had before this spoken about a medical report that Mr. Haughey had referred to when Fianna Fáil were selecting me as a candidate. "Why didn't he furnish the report?", said Garret referring to the Government Press Secretary's refusal to facilitate the Sunday Tribune. "I would have thought it better from your point of view," added Garret.

His clumsy attempt to raise the question of my health was incomprehensible because he, in his original reply to the questioner in the audience, had started by stating that he felt that in the United States the intrusiveness on these matters can be extreme. Gerry Moriarty, writing in the Irish Press, was to remark that the former Taoiseach's efforts to raise my health as an issue were "macabre and distasteful".

Later, the issue of phone calls to Áras an Uachtaráin back in 1982 came up as I was explaining that the power the President enjoys to refuse a dissolution has never actually been exercised:

Bowman: Brian Lenihan on this question, the discretionary powers of the President in such circumstances. What's your view?

Brian: Well in my view, it has happened heretofore, that a dissolution is granted when that is sought by the Taoiseach from the President. Now, I know there is provision there in which the President may not do so, may not grant a dissolution and may seek... That provision is there, that option is there. It has never been exercised by an Irish President heretofore.

Garret: Why the ... phone calls to try to force him to exercise it?

Brian: That's fictional, Garret.

Garret: It is not fictional, excuse me, I was in Áras an Uachtaráin when those phone calls came through and I know how many there were.

Later on, Brian Murphy, the Fine Gael activist referred to earlier, asked me directly did I make any phone calls back in 1982, to which I replied: "No I didn't at all. That never happened. I want to assure you that never happened."

The discussion then went on to consider the precise circumstance in which a President could refuse to give a dissolution to a requesting Taoiseach. That debate became quite heated with Garret questioning my knowledge of the constitution.

I had merely pointed out that it would only be in the most extreme of circumstances that a President would refuse to give a dissolution. To illustrate this I stated that it would only be in some anarchic situation, as I saw it, where this power could be used. Garret seized on this and tried to exploit the phrase anarchic to claim that I knew nothing about the constitution. The audience were becoming more restive and clapping a lot at different comments when Garret said:

Garret: It seems to me that eight phone calls were made by people who imitated the voices of the leaders of the opposition.

This assertion moves the goalposts along quite a bit in that it seemed to imply not only that he was in the Áras when the contentious calls came through but that he heard the voices. Later he would explain that this remark was entirely facetious on his part.

Over the next few days the former Taoiseach was to give a number of confusing and contradictory interviews where he seemed to be advancing and then backtracking again. For the purposes of simplicity and rather than confuse matters I have arranged these quite different assertions by him into four different categories, Garret 1, 2, 3 and 4. I have resisted the temptation of including a Garret 5 version - since it is a final closing position of a kind which will be dealt with separately.

Here is each version, only paraphrasing where the exact quote has been quoted already, but encapsulating what Garret said at the time:

Garret 1: This is his speech delivered by the Fine Gael Press Office apparently without his knowledge. This one claims that when he arrived at the Áras he found that the President had been "besieged" with telephone calls from senior Fianna Fáil people urging Dr. Hillery not to grant a dissolution.

Garret 2: This is the version given later on Monday evening on Questions and Answers. Here the difference is that Garret, rather than finding there have been calls when he arrives at the Áras, is actually in the Áras when they ring through.

Garret 3: This is the version which Garret gave on the Tuesday for the lunchtime news in which, in his own words, he corrected the version he had given on Questions and Answers the night before. This version claims as follows:

"I am not saying I was in the building; I am saying that my recollection is that I was told these telephone calls were made possibly before I arrived."

In this version he is denying being in the building (the Áras). So in Garret 1 he finds out about the calls on arrival at the Áras, in Garret 2 he finds out when he is actually in the Áras, and now in Garret 3 he finds out that the calls were possibly made before he arrived in the Áras. The novel feature in Garret 3 is the studied ambiguity, i.e. he was told the calls were "possibly" made before he arrived in the Áras.

Garret 4: This version was given in the course of an interview lasting eight minutes with Gay Byrne on the radio the Thursday after Questions and Answers. The interview is probably the most confusing of all. The nub of it, when Gay puts it to Garret that he claimed he was in Áras when the phone calls came through, is Garret's reply:

"Yes I was because some had come before I was there and whether all of them or not, I don't know, only what I was told."

The interesting thing with Garret 4 is that now he is saying that he believes that calls came through while he was in the Áras, but some came through before he was there. However, he refuses to say who told him this, and where he was told this. The full text of the Gay Byrne interview is at the end of this chapter for those who are interested. The point is that it is implicit in that interview that somebody in the Áras told him there had been calls. When Gay asked Garret who told him, Garret said he could not say. He would only say that he was told there were calls and given a number of names.

There is this wonderful line near the end of the interview when Gay Byrne thanks Garret for ringing up the show to which the former Taoiseach replies with unintended irony:

"I'm glad to get the chance to clarify it, because it's extraordinary the misconceptions that are around."

In a further effort he tried to clear up misunderstandings about his various versions of events when he spoke in the Dáil confidence debate. Here, a full nine days after Questions and Answers, he formally withdrew for the first time what he had said on the programme that night. He said in the Dáil:

"To this Brian Lenihan replied, "That's fictional, Garret." I called back on the spur of the moment "It is not fictional - excuse me - I was in Áras an Uachtaráin when those phone calls came through and I know how many there were." I should have said that "I was in Áras an Uachtaráin the night those phone calls came through ...""

On paper the difference does not seem enormous. But the factual situation is that his original assertion on Questions and Answers gave huge credence to the notion that I had phoned the Áras to force the President to exercise his power to refuse a dissolution. In his final version in the Dáil he admits, at last unambiguously, that he was not in fact in the Áras when the phone calls were made. However, it was too late, the damage had been done. The full impact of national television was used by Garret Fitzgerald to make a statement that was quite wrong. There were over 400,000 people watching Questions and Answers that night, and none of the subsequent hedging by Fitzgerald could undo the damage done by him.

His final position therefore was:

"... when I arrived at the Áras there had been a number of calls, and when I left I was told there had been eight and I was told who made them, and among the names mentioned was Deputy Lenihan. That is all I know on the subject."

Here he is ambivalent yet again about where and how exactly he learnt there had been calls. It is still unclear whether he learnt about the phone calls while leaving the precincts of Áras an Uachtaráin itself, or, crucially, when he had left it altogether and returned to the rumour-filled atmosphere of Leinster House.

By Thursday of the next week, I too was wondering about the misconceptions that were around. One week after that interview I was facing dismissal from Government after 33 years in public life. In the Dáil debate on that Thursday, Dr. John O'Connell TD was to defend me and point to an action by the then Taoiseach, Garret Fitzgerald, back in 1982 after the general election which followed the dissolution.

I quote directly from the official report of the Dáil:

"I can remember many of the events of 1982 vividly. When Deputy Fitzgerald failed in that election he made vain attempts to cobble together a Government but was spurned by both the Workers Party and the Independents. It was then that he phoned me as I was outgoing Ceann Comhairle and asked if he could see me. He was prepared to come to my house if necessary at any time during the night. In the event, I saw him the following morning at 8.30 am., some hours before the new Dáil was due to meet. Do you know what Deputy Fitzgerald proposed? I will tell you what he proposed - that I refuse to go forward as Ceann Comhairle, on the basis that with my refusal to take the Chair, the Dáil could not convene, there being no one else willing to take over as Ceann Comhairle, and such an impasse would necessitate another election. In no uncertain terms, I made it clear to Deputy Fitzgerald that his proposal was a grossly irresponsible one, with all the dangers to democracy that this would entail, that terminated our discussion. But I want to ask Deputy Fitzgerald now, did he contact the President that night? I think he should clarify that matter today."

If Garret Fitzgerald had succeeded in this amazing manoeuvre, it would have resulted in a constitutional crisis. After the general election of February 1982, Fianna Fáil secured 81 seats, Fine Gael 63, Labour 15, Sinn Féin the Workers' Party 3, Independents 4 (Neil Blaney, Jim Kemmy, Tony Gregory and Dr. John O'Connell, the outgoing Ceann Comhairle). The Coalition parties, along with Jim Kemmy, had 79 votes, while Fianna Fáil with Neil Blaney's vote could count on 82 votes. Though one short of an overall majority, Fianna Fáil were clearly in the dominant position in the Dáil. The country had swung in our favour with our vote rising from 45.3% to 47.3%. The electorate had clearly spoken and it was up to us in Leinster House to form a Government in some way. What Fitzgerald was proposing would prevent the result of the election from being implemented. In short, he was trying to plunge the country into another general election and all the instability that that would involve.

If that was the extent to which Fitzgerald was prepared to go to get power it says a lot for his concern for the constitutional proprieties. With this one approach to the Ceann Comhairle of Dáil Éireann, he displayed more naked greed for power than any man with a flawed pedigree. If ever there was an example of GUBU politics, this was it.

That night, after I left the Questions and Answers programme on RTE, I was happy with my performance. Some of those with me and watching the programme felt I had left a hostage to fortune by using the "anarchic" metaphor to explain the circumstances when I would consider it proper to refuse a dissolution. Indeed Mrs. Robinson was to attack me the next day on this exact point. Bertie Ahern felt I had done well. None of our people had given a moment's notice to my replies about the events of 1982. Jim Duffy's tape was to change all of that.

GAY BYRNE SHOW

INTERVIEW WITH DR. GARRET FITZGERALD

Programme *Gay Byrne Show, Station RTE Radio 1*
Subject *Interview with Dr. Garret Fitzgerald*
Date & Time *25/10/'90 – 9.15 a.m.*
Our Ref *S.H. 25/10/'90*
Duration *8 minutes 40 seconds*

Gay Byrne Now Dr. Garret Fitzgerald, good morning to you Sir?

Garret Fitzgerald Good Morning Gay

Gay Byrne Now, you've been told by somebody that I said something?

Garret Fitzgerald I did, I heard you said that, somewhere you had read or heard that I had allegedly heard phone calls in the Áras and recognised voices. I don't know who invited that or where it came from, I've never said anything of the kind in my life. I've only said one thing which has been published frequently over the last eight years, which is that when I went to the Áras, I was told there had been phone calls, putting pressure on the President, and then before leaving I was told they'd had eight such calls and among the callers was Brian Lenihan. That's all I've ever said on the subject and I don't know why there's such a fuss about it, it's not news, sure that was published in the Sunday Tribune by Geraldine Kennedy, a week later. It was in a book by Raymond Smith about me, it was in ... the Government Fianna Fáil sources, it was published by a research student, Jim Duffy, in the Irish Times some months ago and the only new thing is that Brian Lenihan has suddenly decided at this stage to deny it, although it had previously been confirmed.

Gay Byrne Well, he wouldn't have denied it if he hadn't been asked about it, if it hadn't been brought up by somebody or other at this time. But to get back to the original point Garret, the reason I said what I said was, that you did say to Brian Lenihan on Questions and Answers, to the effect that somebody rang the Áras who made a very good imitation of you, or who sounded very like you, you said to Brian Lenihan.

Garret Fitzgerald Ah, I said nothing of the kind. At the end of this thing … it is an extraordinary denial by him, I said so jocosely … well in that case, if it's denied the calls were made, there must have been eight people ringing up making very good imitations of voices of Leaders of Fianna Fáil, obviously to convince people there, that they were them, that's a jocose remark for God's sake, it's extraordinary an Irish politician can't make a joke.

Gay Byrne Well, you find that in radio and television too Garret, you're not alone, unfortunately there are people out there who don't have a sense of humour, but the net result for you is, that a great number of people decided that when you said, there must have been somebody doing a very good imitation of you, that you actually had overheard the voice …

Garret Fitzgerald I never said that, I never said of me.

Gay Byrne No of him, you were talking to Brian Lenihan on Questions and Answers?

Garret Fitzgerald Nor did I say Brian Lenihan, I never mentioned Brian Lenihan ringing up on that programme, by the way, that also is a miss. He had made a denial and I didn't raise the issue, it was raised in the audience, not by me.

Gay Byrne And you are saying that you did not say on Questions and Answers, that it must have been somebody doing a very good imitation of you Brian?

Garret Fitzgerald I say that and you'll see the transcript in the Irish Times and what I raised is the issue ... I was raising the issue of the Constitutional role of the President, explaining that it was important. And annexed with that, I was saying what was happening in '82 and I said Brian, you'll recall the business of the phone calls. Somebody in the audience asked Brian about it and he denied it. The denial, which is not the first one, he denied it before that, is the only new evidence to the whole story. It's been published over and over again. I don't know what the fuss is about, but it is surprising that after all these years, he should decide to deny something which ... has hitherto been said without denial.

Gay Byrne Well I can only tell you that the ... a lot of people got the ... interpreted what you said on Questions and Answers, the implication of that was, that you were there yourself when the calls came through, the call or calls came through?

Garret Fitzgerald I made it clear on every broadcast I've been on that I was there, I was told the calls had been made and that when I left I was told there were eight calls including, among them Brian Lenihan. That's the only thing I have ever said on this subject, I've been extremely careful because I am concerned, always to stay rigidly, and completely to the truth and nothing else. I gather the Taoiseach has been calling me a liar in the Dáil today, but that's par for the course with him I suppose.

Gay Byrne So you were not in Áras when the phone calls ... yourself, you were not there when the calls came through?

Garret Fitzgerald I made it clear again and again when asked, on television yesterday, half the country saw me at lunchtime, I said that when I arrived, there had been calls, I was told, when I left I was told there had been eight calls, including among the callers Brian Lenihan ...

Gay Byrne When you left ...

Garret Fitzgerald And as regards when they .. whether they all occurred before I arrived, or whether some occurred before I arrived and some while I was there, I admit I don't know, I only know what I was told.

Gay Byrne But you say that it was when you left Áras An Uachtaráin that you were told this?

Garret Fitzgerald When I arrived I was told there had been calls, putting pressure on the President, and when I left I was told there had been eight calls, including amongst the callers Brian Lenihan.

Gay Byrne But you didn't see anybody taking a call and you didn't hear anybody taking a call, you weren't a witness to the calls?

Garret Fitzgerald No I never suggested that in my life ...

Gay Byrne Oh I know that, I know that, I'm only trying to clear my own mind on it ...

Garret Fitzgerald Well I'll be glad to clear your mind and some other people's minds as well.

Gay Byrne Indeed. That's the object ...

Garret Fitzgerald That's an extraordinary misconception, but the crucial point is, this belated denial and whether this denial stands up or not, that is the only question at issue at this stage.

Gay Byrne But Garret, just before that ... when you say you were told there had been calls, when you were leaving, were you told that inside the house or on the doorstep or afterwards, or when you were in the car or wherever?

Garret Fitzgerald If I say I was told in Áras an Uachtaráin, I mean in Áras an Uachtaráin.

Gay Byrne In Áras an Uachtaráin?

Garret Fitzgerald Yes.

Gay Byrne Both when you arrived and when you were going.

Garret Fitzgerald Yes, that's right, yes.

Gay Byrne You were told in Áras an Uachtaráin, I see.

Garret Fitzgerald Yes.

Gay Byrne And you're not prepared to tell anybody, who told you?

Garret Fitzgerald No, I think it would be improper to go beyond that point.

Gay Byrne Why would that be so, Garret?

Garret Fitzgerald Well, I just think that one should try to keep the Presidency out of controversy. Unfortunately in this issue, it has come into controversy, because this story which has run for eight years, has suddenly been denied, and that has brought the issue into controversy. It was never in controversy before now, for eight years, but suddenly this extraordinary denial has made the matter controversial. I don't think the President should be dragged into controversy in any way we can avoid.

Gay Byrne Well, who brought it up now at this time, on this occasion? It certainly wasn't Brian Lenihan brought it up, I mean it was somebody else from your side brought it up, or from Austin Currie's side, or whoever.

Garret Fitzgerald The issue has been there and undenied until now. Apparently Brian Lenihan denied it, it was in the Irish Times about a fortnight ago, and somebody in the audience shouted that denial. And he repeated the denial, which I think is something he now has to face, the consequences of that.

Gay Byrne You said in fact, on the tape on .. we've got the tape of the show Questions and Answers, and what you said was, "I was in Áras an Uachtaráin when those phone calls came through."

Garret Fitzgerald Yes.

Gay Byrne That's what you said, I was in Áras an Uachtaráin when those phone calls came through.

Garret Fitzgerald Yes, I was because ... some had come before I was there and whether all of them came then or not, I don't know, only what I was told.

Gay Byrne You only know what you were told, I see, I see.

Garret Fitzgerald That's right, yes.

Gay Byrne It would appear to me, from people who heard you on Questions and Answers, it would appear to me that this is rather back-tracking ...

Garret Fitzgerald No, no, I'm not back-tracking at all. I'm making it quite clear, those calls were made, I was told about those calls, at the time, and I was told that one of the calls was Brian Lenihan. I've never said anything beyond that, because I only speak from my own personal knowledge. If there is other evidence, that's for other people to deal with.

Gay Byrne So where do we go from here in this whole controversy Garret, do you reckon? I mean if ... somebody has brought it up, it wasn't Brian Lenihan, he's denied that it ever happened.

Garret Fitzgerald Well, his denial in the Irish Times a fortnight ago and repeated denials since then, has raised a difficult issue of credibility because it is something that had not been denied previously, and it's a matter which has to be sorted out. At this stage the Irish Times have corroborative evidence. It's a matter for them to decide what further action they want to take in the matter. All I can do is, I can't go back on what I have said in the past, whenever I've been asked on the subject, and I've really repeated what I've always said.

Gay Byrne Well, I can only tell you that the perception of it is, that you, that people believe that you said a great deal more than you are now saying.

Garret Fitzgerald No, I ... well actually, well, I can't help the perception. I said what I've said now and I said it, indeed I produced a script of a speech on the role of the Presidency, which was published, but ... released several weeks ago, that was published the other day, and on the programme however I specifically didn't raise the question to Brian Lenihan, because he had denied it and I didn't want to get into, I did, you didn't, I did, you didn't, type of argument. No point in that. That's why I spoke of the phone calls being made, but did not raise the question of his making it, and I'm not going back on that. I just thought there wasn't much point in a Questions and Answers programme to get into that kind of dialogue, so I decided there was no point in pressing that issue again. But the fact is, that is what I was told.

Gay Byrne But the nub is, that you were told that people rang Áras an Uachtaráin.

Garret Fitzgerald Yes.

Gay Byrne You were told?

Garret Fitzgerald Eight calls, by the time I left.

Gay Byrne Yes, and you are not prepared to disclose the identity of the person who told you?

Garret Fitzgerald No.

Gay Byrne Okay, all right Garret, thank you very much ...

Garret Fitzgerald I'm glad to get the chance to clarify it, because it's extraordinary the misconceptions that are around.

Gay Byrne Indeed, indeed.

Garret Fitzgerald But I think the question now is the question
of credibility that has to be determined.

Gay Byrne Indeed. Okay thank you very much indeed,
God bless, goodbye. That was Doctor Garret
Fitzgerald.

7

FLASHBACK TO JANUARY 27TH 1982

On the 27th January 1982, John Bruton, then Minister for Finance, presented his budget on behalf of Dr. Garret Fitzgerald's first coalition government. This government had been elected in June of 1981. The result of that election had been inconclusive. The election gave Fianna Fáil 78 seats, Fine Gael 65 seats, Labour 15 seats, and Others 6 seats. With Fine Gael and Labour set to go into coalition together the balance of power lay with the six uncommitted deputies. These were Neil Blaney (Independent Fianna Fáil), Dr. Noel Browne (Independent Socialist), Jim Kemmy (Democratic Socialist), Seán Dublin Bay Loftus (Independent), Dr. John O'Connell (then Independent) and Joe Sherlock (then Sinn Féin, the Workers' Party). When the Dáil assembled, Dr. O'Connell was unanimously elected Ceann Comhairle, and Dr. Fitzgerald was elected Taoiseach at the head of a Fine Gael/ Labour coalition. This government was two short of an overall majority and thus depended for its survival on the support of at least some of the deputies who were not committed to Fianna Fáil or the Coalition parties.

It was generally assumed in political and media circles that the budget would be successfully voted through the Dáil as the government seemed to have the safe support of at least Noel Browne and Jim Kemmy. However, as the division bells rang for the first vote on the budget there was a mounting sense of excitement in the corridors of Leinster House. As deputies assembled in the Dáil chamber it became clear that all was not well with the government. There was the somewhat astonishing sight of the Taoiseach Dr. Garret Fitzgerald pleading on his knees with Jim Kemmy not to vote against the government. Kemmy shook his head and in the first division voted alongside Neil Blaney, Seán Dublin Bay Loftus, Joe Sherlock and the 78 Fianna Fáil deputies. As is traditional in parliamentary votes, the Chief Whip for the winning side brings the result to the Chair. This time it was the then Opposition Whip, Ray Burke, who gleefully carried the result to the Ceann Comhairle. The Government had been defeated by 82 votes to 81. It was an unprecedented situation - it was the first time in the history of the state that a Government was defeated on a budget resolution. The essence of running a Government is to carry the annual financial resolutions - otherwise all confidence disappears and the Government must go. This was the case here.

Dr. Fitzgerald immediately announced that as a result of the vote he was going to the President to seek a dissolution of the Dáil. The Dáil adjourned pending his return from the Phoenix Park. It was 8.16 pm. There was chaos in Leinster House. The Government went into emergency session. Politicians, pressmen and officials were in a tizzy. The public gallery, corridors, restaurants and bars were crowded with an over-spill of members of the public. It was one of those crazy nights.

Mr. Haughey, then of course Leader of the Opposition, called a meeting of the Fianna Fáil front bench immediately after the Dáil vote. The various members of the front bench were hustled together by our Whip Ray Burke. The meeting took place in the opposition leader's conference room on the fifth floor in Leinster House. It must have taken several minutes to assemble all the members of the front bench, but we can safely say that the meeting had got underway before 8.30. We sat around the usual rectangular table. Charles Haughey presided at the meeting with the late George Colley, then Deputy Leader and Spokesman on Energy, sitting to his left, and Ray Burke on his right. Apart from myself the other members present were (in alphabetical order) Sylvester Barrett (Spokesman on Defence), Gerry Collins (Foreign Affairs), Ger Connolly (Environment), Sean Doherty (Justice), Gene Fitzgerald (Labour), Mark Killilea (Posts & Telegraphs), Ray MacSharry (Agriculture), the late Seán Moore (Social Welfare), Dr. Martin O'Donoghue (Finance), Des O'Malley (Industry & Commerce), Paddy Power (Fisheries & Forestry), Albert Reynolds (Transport & Communications), John Wilson (Education) and Dr. Michael Woods (Health).

Mr. Haughey informed the meeting of the President's discretion under the Constitution to refuse to dissolve the Dáil where the Taoiseach has lost the confidence of the Dáil. Mr. Haughey felt that because of the numerical situation in the Dáil the possibility arose of the President exercising his powers under the Constitution, which would facilitate the nomination of a new Taoiseach by the Dáil without the need for a general election. It must be remembered that the unprecedented nature of the situation meant that no guidelines existed as to how it should be handled apart from the relevant clause in the Constitution, which reads:

"The President may in his absolute discretion refuse to dissolve Dáil Éireann on the advice of a Taoiseach who has ceased to retain the support of a majority in Dáil Éireann."

The discussion centred on this constitutional point. I had sat beside Dr. Hillery at every Government meeting for eight years from 1964 to 1972 and was naturally asked for my opinion. I gave my view that he would not exercise his option to refuse dissolution, but would grant the Taoiseach's request. Mark Killilea, now Member of the European Parliament, remembers vividly what I said, and recalls me saying that "we wouldn't get anywhere with Hillery". Then and now I believe that the President was correct to dissolve the Dáil on the advice of the Taoiseach. Furthermore, I was doubtful that Fianna Fáil had enough support among the independents to cobble together a government should the President have exercised this power. It was, at any rate, innate in President Hillery's cautious nature to act as he did.

Having said all that, there was nothing objectionable or sinister in opening up to the President the possibility of exercising his discretion to refuse to dissolve the Dáil, and this was the view taken by the Fianna Fáil front bench. After all, it was and remains an executive option open to the President, which may be exercised without reference to anybody else, in his or her absolute discretion. The front bench made a collective decision, and unanimously agreed on a statement to be issued by Charles Haughey as follows:

"It is a matter for the President to consider the situation which has arisen now that the Taoiseach has ceased to retain the support of the majority in Dáil Éireann. I am available for consultation by the President should he so wish." This statement is a matter of public record.

The discussion ended in a matter of minutes, but before we rose from the table Charles Haughey suggested that Dr. Hillery should be rung in order to explain the reasons for our statement. Mr. Haughey was anxious that, out of courtesy to the President, he should not first learn of our statement on the television news at 9 o'clock. He nodded at me - he has a habit of making requests by nodding his head instead of actually saying anything. I shook my head and indicated that I was not prepared to make the phone call. It wasn't that I saw anything objectionable in ringing the Áras to explain our position, but simply that I regarded it as a futile enterprise in view of the opinion I had just expressed at the meeting. Ger Connolly, now Junior Minister for the Environment, is very specific in his recollection of the meeting. He says that he remembers me being requested to make the phone call, and that I refused, saying to the meeting that "I am not the man for the job".

Mr. Haughey then nodded to Sylvie Barrett. Sylvie was an obvious choice as he was Dr. Hillery's former constituency colleague and a fellow Clareman. Sylvie agreed to ring the President's office. There is a difference of opinion as to whether Sylvie made the phone call from a telephone on Haughey's desk in another part of the conference room where the meeting took place, or whether he left the room altogether to phone the Áras. I myself originally believed that Barrett got up from the table and made the call from an office desk in another part of the room. Ger Connolly also thinks that Barrett rang from a phone in another part of the room. Connolly remembers Barrett making two such calls and informing the meeting that he could not get through to the President. Mark Killilea, on the other hand, says that Barrett left the room to make the phone call. Killilea also insists that when he left the room he was accompanied by Dessie O'Malley. This fits in with O'Malley's own story that he had left before the calls were actually made. He was there, however, when the decision was made to inform the President of the front bench decision. O'Malley's early departure would seem to indicate that he knows less about the phone calls than any other member of the front bench. Killilea says that Barrett then returned to tell us that he had failed to get through. Both Killilea and Connolly are therefore agreed that Sylvie informed the meeting that he had failed to get through to the President. He told us that the Duty Officer in Áras an Uachtaráin who took the call said that the President was not available.

What I remember about the evening's events is confirmed by other members of the Fianna Fáil front bench. Ray MacSharry, now European Commissioner for Agriculture, Albert Reynolds, now Finance Minister, Gerry Collins, now Minister for Foreign Affairs, Ray Burke, now Minister for Justice, Gene Fitzgerald, now a Member of the European Parliament, along with Connolly and Killilea, are all very emphatic that Sylvie Barrett rang the Áras and that I had nothing to do with making any phone calls. In fact, they all agree that there was no need for anyone else to ring, and that everybody present knew what was going on. MacSharry, Fitzgerald, Reynolds, Collins, Burke, Killilea and Connolly agree that there was nothing sinister in what was done. Barrett was simply asked by Haughey to explain the reasons behind our statement. Ray Burke and Albert Reynolds remember how natural it was that Barrett should be asked to make the call as one Clareman to another. Gerry Collins distinctly remembers the late George Colley voicing support at the meeting for Mr. Haughey's proposal that the Áras be contacted.

John Wilson, now Tánaiste and Minister for the Marine, Dr. Michael Woods, now Minister for Social Welfare, Paddy Power, now retired from the Dáil, and Seán Doherty, now Cathaoirleach of the Seanad, were also present at the meeting. While none of these are very specific in their recollection of events, they do agree with the general thrust of what I remember about the meeting and its aftermath. They all agree that Sylvie Barrett was asked to phone the Áras, and having done so reported back to the meeting. All agree that I did not make any phone calls.

Dr. Martin O'Donoghue was then the Fianna Fáil spokesman on Finance. As such, he had spoken in the Dáil earlier on the budget and of course was also present at the front bench meeting when the decision was made to issue a statement to ring the Áras and inform the President of our position.

Quite clearly the evidence of Sylvie Barrett is crucial on settling any uncertainties in this matter. His is the only direct evidence. During the presidential election, after the Irish Times published their story on Wednesday, October 24th, stating that they had corroborative evidence that I had telephoned President Hillery in an effort to persuade him not to dissolve the Dáil, I rang Sylvester Barrett, now retired from the Dáil, at his home in Ennis, County Clare, to confirm my recollection of events. I asked Sylvie straight out whether I was correct in saying that I did not ring the Áras. Sylvie replied emphatically that I did not ring. Since the election I have spoken again to Sylvie to discuss these events in greater detail. Sylvie confirms that he was asked by Mr. Haughey to ring the President to inform him of the statement that the front bench had issued and of the party's availability to form a new government with the support of some independents. Sylvie Barrett says that he got up from the table and left the room to make the call from an office across the corridor. He made the call and spoke to the Duty Officer in the Áras who informed him that the President was not available. Barrett explained that he was ringing on behalf of the front bench to inform the President that Mr. Haughey was available to form an alternative government. He says that he then returned to the conference room and informed the meeting that he could not get through to the President. Barrett says that he is certain that he rang two or three times that evening and he may have used my name. Perhaps this is where the misunderstanding has arisen. He is also absolutely certain that I did not ring.

Barrett is very emphatic on another aspect of the evening's proceedings. He says that because of all the commotion during the presidential election the impression was created that there was someting improper in the approaches that were made to the President. He points out that Fine Gael and Garret Fitzgerald alleged that Fianna Fáil was in some way attempting to pressurise the President. Mr. Barrett wishes to set the record straight on this point. He rang merely to inform the President of the decision made by the front bench and to say that Mr. Haughey could form a viable, alternative government. He is insistent that from a constitutional point of view this was perfectly in order. As a former member of the European Parliament he draws attention to the regular practice in other continental countries where the President or Head of State acts as an honest broker in the formation of new governments without recourse to a general election.

Everyone to whom I have spoken and who attended the front bench meeting that night says that the matter was entirely above board and straightforward. They are also agreed that Dessie O'Malley attended the meeting and did not make any objection to the statement that was issued in Mr. Haughey's name. Mr. O'Malley, on an RTE radio programme during the presidential election, said that "to the best of my knowledge a number of people rang Áras an Uachtaráin that night" and that that number could include Brian Lenihan. Mr. O'Malley's position then was that he did not know whether I made a phone call as he had left the meeting before the calls were made: "I wasn't present when the actual calls were made - I couldn't put my hand on a bible and say." More recently in an interview with the Irish Times Mr. O'Malley stated that he understands "other calls were made apart from Sylvie Barrett" and that Brian Lenihan was one of those who called. I do not know how Mr. O'Malley can be prepared to repeat this "understanding" of his in public. He was the first member of the front bench to leave the meeting and as such is the least qualified to comment. Mr. O'Malley is the only member of the Fianna Fáil front bench who is labouring under this misunderstanding and I can only suggest that he should consult with Sylvie Barrett on the matter.

When the meeting was over, I drifted out of the room and into the nearby Fianna Fáil Parliamentary Party room where the dissolution of the Dáil was being anticipated and election arrangements were already underway. There I bumped into Dr. Brian Hillery, then Senator and now Dáil deputy for Dun Laoghaire. Brian recalls that I remarked that Sylvie Barrett was trying to get through to his cousin President Hillery on the dissolution position.

It was now approaching 9 o'clock. I went downstairs to the Dáil bar, and remained there for a long and crowded evening in which gossip, rumour and story - fact and fiction - about the vote, the dissolution and the prospective election gathered momentum. The main speculation concerned the powers of the President in relation to the dissolution of the Dáil. Albert Reynolds and Ray Burke specifically remember being in my company in the bar that evening. Meanwhile, Sylvie Barrett joined us for a drink, and mentioned that he had tried several times to get through to the President, but had failed to get past the Duty Officer at the Áras. Sylvie remembers being in my company for the rest of the evening. That was the end of the matter as far as I was concerned. I had not made any phone call, and indeed I had advised against the whole idea in the first place. My memory was sufficiently strong to prompt me, nearly nine years later, to ring Sylvie Barrett to confirm my recollection.

It is clear that Sylvie Barrett was not the only person to have rung Áras an Uachtaráin that night. Other politicians, journalists and even members of the public have all been mentioned as trying to get in contact with the President. Raymond Smith, in his book *Garret : The Enigma,* published in 1985, recalls how Fianna Fáil was not the only group involved in the behind-the-scenes moves that night. "I remember that leading journalists, including respected political correspondents, were speculating on the powers of the President under the Constitution in the situation that had suddenly arisen. Journalists even rang Áras an Uachtaráin trying to get some direction on the question but again there was no direct contact with the President."

It is also clear that Independent Fianna Fáil deputy, Neil Blaney, was involved in attempts to contact the President that night. Mr. Blaney outlined the nature of his involvement in a speech in the Dáil during the recent election. In that speech Blaney recalled how he "was imbued with the idea that night that, in order for the President to have such an opportunity" (i.e. to use his prerogative to call on the then Leader of the Opposition to form a Government without an election) "he had to be made aware of the fact that there was a majority other than the outgoing Government to create a new Government". Mr. Blaney said that he was convinced that if there was an alternative to holding a general election, the President should be so informed. Mr. Blaney also described the extent of his involvement in the endeavours to get in touch with the President.

"Furthermore I was involved in that, with how many others I do not know... I have tried to fill the gaps; I cannot and I do not make any excuse for that - it happened eight years ago." Blaney went on to recall that "I and those with whom I had been in contact with - I cannot recall even one person - did get on to the Presidency, to Áras an Uachtaráin, and that we were not told of his non-availability. My recollection is that he was not there, that he was downtown at some show or other ... The information that there was available an alternative Government within the confines of the then membership of this House was left with whoever took the telephone call in Áras an Uachtaráin to be passed on to the President when he returned."

When kindly helping me with my research for this book Neil Blaney did not dismiss as untrue some additional information put forward by Raymond Smith concerning his involvement in the phone calls to Áras an Uachtaráin that night. Blaney quite naturally does not remember the exact details of what went on over nine years ago, and so he cannot rule out the possibility that what Smith had to say about his involvement may be accurate. According to Raymond Smith, Neil Blaney rang Garret Fitzgerald's direct telephone line that night to say: "I am glad you took my advice." The call was allegedly taken by Fitzgerald's Assistant Private Secretary. As Fitzgerald had had no contact with the Donegal deputy that night, he interpreted Blaney's call as having been put through erroneously to the Taoiseach's office (a number he would have had from the time Charles Haughey was Taoiseach) instead of to Mr. Haughey's office as Leader of the Opposition. From this Fitzgerald is convinced that Neil Blaney advised Haughey to contact the President and that he may even have been the originator of the moves by Fianna Fáil to inform the President of his prerogative to refuse to dissolve the Dáil. Raymond Smith is more reticent in his interpretation of Blaney's moves, pointing out that there is ample evidence to show that, without any prompting from Neil Blaney, Fianna Fáil would have moved anyway.

Whatever the impact of Blaney's suggestion to Mr. Haughey it does seem clear that Blaney must have spoken to Haughey at some stage in the evening on the matter. Emily O'Reilly, in her book *Candidate,* refers to a later report in the Sunday Press, where a spokesperson for Neil Blaney stated that, at a meeting with Mr. Haughey on the night in question, Mr. Blaney discussed with the Opposition leader the fact that the President had a right under the Constitution to call in the leader of the Opposition and attempt to form an alternative Government. According to the Sunday Press report "the leader of the Opposition was quite amenable to Mr. Blaney's proposals even to the extent of forming a National Government for six months."

Another politician who contacted the Áras that evening was the Independent deputy Seán Dublin Bay Loftus. Mr. Loftus has also helped me in my research for this book. His recollection of the evening's events is very specific as he believes that he was the first politician to ring Áras an Uachtaráin after the Dáil vote. When he rang the Áras he was told that the President was not available. He then spent some time speaking to the Army officer, explaining the position to him. Mr. Loftus felt very strongly that an election could be prevented and a new government could be voted into office by the Dáil if the President exercised his power not to dissolve the Dáil. Mr. Loftus felt that it was perfectly above board for him to ring the Áras. His only objective was to "put the President in the picture". He asked the Army officer to convey his views to the President. Mr. Loftus is highly critical of the impression that was created during the recent election that there was something improper about attempting to contact the President. He is of the opinion that a President, before taking his decision, would need to be informed as to whether a possibility of forming an alternative government existed. He makes the valid point that it would be absurd to suggest that the only source of such information and advice available to the President should be a defeated Taoiseach. Mr. Loftus contacted the Áras on his own initiative as he was prepared to support the formation of a new Government. He felt so strongly about all of this that he followed up his telephone call with a telegram to the President setting out his views. He deplores any suggestion that this idea to approach the President represented pressure of any kind. During the presidential election, Mr. Loftus issued a statement after the tapes controversy broke saying that he phoned the Áras back in 1982. However, the only newspaper in which this statement was published was the Cork Examiner on Monday 29th October.

Another name which has been linked to phone calls to Áras an Uachtaráin on the 27th January 1982, is that of the present Taoiseach, Charles Haughey. After the front bench meeting, Mr. Haughey remained in his office on the fifth floor in Leinster House. There he met Kildare TD Charlie McCreevy who, although a member of Fianna Fáil, had been expelled from the Fianna Fáil Parliamentary Party shortly beforehand for publicly criticising the party leadership. Haughey told McCreevy at their meeting that attempts were being made to contact the President to ask him not to dissolve the Dáil but to call on the Fianna Fáil leader instead to form a Government.

The nature of Mr. Haughey's involvement in these attempts to contact the President has been the subject of considerable speculation. All that I know about his involvement is what I witnessed myself at first hand at the front bench meeting and immediately afterwards. During the recent election all three of the opposition leaders were to claim in the Dáil that on the night of 27th January 1982, Mr. Haughey threatened to interfere in the future career of an Army officer on duty in Áras an Uachtaráin who refused to put a telephone call from Mr. Haughey through to the President. Such intimidation, if it occurred, would constitute a breach of the provisions of the Defence Act, 1954, and the Offences Against the State Act, 1939. The Labour Leader, Dick Spring, called on the Government to institute an enquiry by the Gardai into the matter.

The Workers' Party Leader, Proinsias de Rossa, went so far as to name the army officer involved in this alleged incident. "It has been reported that as a result of this incident the President subsequently took steps to protect Captain Barbour and spoke to the then Chief of Staff, Lieutenant General Hogan, about the matter."

Mr. Haughey has denied these allegations in the most trenchant terms possible. This is what he said in the Dáil in response to the allegations.

"My father was a distinguished Army officer until he left the Defence Forces through ill health. I have been an officer of the Defence Forces. I was brought up to believe in the integrity of our Defence Forces and the Army and I have the highest respect for them. I would never have insulted an Army officer of our Defence Forces in any way, and I never will."

I know no more about these allegations than what has been said in the Dáil.

Prior to the release of the Duffy tape, it was the accepted wisdom in some political and media circles that I had put through telephone calls to Áras an Uachtaráin on the night of the 27th January, 1982. It is, therefore, of the utmost importance to explore why this story gained credence. Geraldine Kennedy was the first to report the story as political correspondent for the Sunday Tribune shortly after the event on February 7th 1982. I quote, "three telephone calls were made to Áras an Uachtaráin by Mr. Haughey between the time that the Coalition Budget was defeated and the Dáil was dissolved. Two other calls at least were received from Mr. Brian Lenihan and Mr. Sylvie Barrett. They did not speak to Dr. Hillery. Her account was the only newspaper report of the incident at the time. Indeed, media coverage of the incident was so scant that the phone calls to the Áras were never raised as an issue in the ensuing general election. Raymond Smith in his book *Garret: The Enigma* refers to the phone calls to the Áras. He states that "my information is that Brian Lenihan rang at least twice while Sylvester Barrett also rang - and there were phone calls also from Charles Haughey."

The third source for the story is a political one - Dr. Garret Fitzgerald. As the Taoiseach of the day, Fitzgerald was the only politician to visit Áras an Uachtaráin that night. It therefore becomes important to retrace Dr. Fitzgerald's steps on that evening. When the budget was defeated in the Dáil vote at 8.16 pm., Dr. Fitzgerald, as I have already mentioned, announced that he would go to the President to seek a dissolution of the Dáil. Instead of doing so, however, he summoned an emergency meeting of the government. For some reason Dr. Fitzgerald did not go to the Áras until after 10 pm., and it was not until 11 pm. that he returned to Dáil Éireann to make the announcement that the President had dissolved the Dáil. The formal dissolution of the Dáil is carried out by Proclamation under the Presidential seal, signed by the President and countersigned by the Taoiseach. In normal circumstances it would be expected that the Taoiseach would go immediately from the Dáil to the Áras to make his request for a dissolution.

Garret Fitzgerald puts forward quite an elaborate explanation for his delay. This explanation is recorded in Raymond Smith's book. Garret says that he had presumed after the defeat of the Government in the budget vote that he would be going to Áras an Uachtaráin immediately. However, Michael Ó hOdhráin, Secretary to the President, happened to be at a play in the Peacock Theatre at the time. Someone was sent down to the Peacock where Ó hOdhráin was sought out and informed of the situation. According to Fitzgerald he was impatient to get on with it and, because of the frenzied atmosphere in Leinster House, set out for the Phoenix Park even though word had already reached him over his car phone that the papers were not ready for signing. He then waited outside the zoo until these papers, apparently following in another car, had caught up with him.

Mr. Ó hOdhráin's account of what happened that evening makes it quite clear that he was not in any way responsible for Dr. Fitzgerald's delay in arriving at the Áras. In a letter written to the Irish Times on his behalf by his solicitors during the presidential election, Mr. Ó hOdhráin states that although he had finished his work for the day and had gone to the Peacock Theatre with his wife, he had, because of the situation in Dáil Éireann at that time, left a note in Áras an Uachtaráin, in the Department of the Taoiseach and at his home of where he could be contacted. Having been duly contacted at the Peacock, he immediately returned to the Áras where he arrived at 8.45 pm. Mr. Ó hOdhráin's letter draws attention to the fact that Dr. Fitzgerald did not arrive at the Áras until 10 pm.

Of greater interest are the various claims that Dr. Fitzgerald was to make about what actually did happen when he eventually arrived at the Áras. As we have already seen, he was to claim during the election that he was in Áras an Uachtaráin when the phone calls came through, and he knew how many were made. This is quite simply not the case. The phone calls to the Áras were all made well before Dr. Fitzgerald arrived at the Áras. Fitzgerald was received by the President in the Áras after 10 pm, in the usual reception room where there has never been a telephone.

Dr. Fitzgerald, however, was to revise his claim, saying subsequently that although he may not have been in the Áras when the phone calls came through, he learnt from someone in the Áras that I had been among the phone callers to the Áras that night. Dr. Fitzgerald refuses to name this source and is very uncertain in his recollection of whether this information was passed on to him when he arrived at the Áras, or whether it was passed on when he left the Áras. Indeed Dr. Fitzgerald's recollection of all the details of what went on in the Áras that night is most unclear. I have already dealt with the uncertainties arising out of what he had to say on all these points in the previous chapter. For present purposes, it is sufficient to note that I am prepared to accept that it is possible that Dr. Fitzgerald may have heard from someone in Áras an Uachtaráin that I was among the callers to the Áras that night. However, if such is the case, Dr. Fitzgerald's informant was mistaken. What Dr. Fitzgerald may have heard was most probably hearsay and, in any case, was simply incorrect. It does not accord with the memory of those who were around me that night. Nor does it tie in with my own memory.

It is, of course, possible that my name became linked into the litany of calls that were made that night, and that my name was used or mentioned by one of the callers. I believe that an error was made somewhere along the line. It would have been generally known that I was friendly with Dr. Hillery and for that reason a caller may have believed that it was advantageous to mention my name. I want to make it clear, however, that I did not make a phone call to the Áras on that night, and furthermore I did not authorise anyone to use my name or ring on my behalf.

In that part of my taped interview with Mr. Jim Duffy which he released to the media during the campaign, I stated that I was among the callers to President Hillery, and that I got through to the President and spoke to him. I quote directly from the tape.

Duffy: And did any of the calls get through to the President?
Lenihan: Oh yeah, I mean I got through to him. I remember
            talking to him and he wanted us to lay off. There was no
doubt about it in his mind...

This extract from the tape is totally untrue, because I did not talk to Dr. Hillery on the night in question, and he has confirmed this to me. The only person who took phone calls in the Áras that night was the Duty Officer, and I did not ring or speak to him. If he received a call purporting to be from me, it was an inadvertence on the part of the caller, or it was done without my authority.

In fact, the tape on this matter is complete rubbish, and it should have been known to be such by the Irish Times and Mr. Duffy when they presented their excerpt from the tape at the press conference in the Westbury Hotel on 25th October 1990. Irish Times correspondent and former TD, Geraldine Kennedy, referred two days later in the Irish Times of 27th October to her article of February 7th 1982 in the Sunday Tribune, which I have already quoted in this chapter, in which she stated, "They (Haughey, Barrett, Lenihan) did not speak to Dr. Hillery". Did the Irish Times check with their own correspondent, Geraldine Kennedy, before they issued the tape on the telephone calls at the press conference?

However, this rubbish was hugely damaging to me, transmitted as it was to millions of people in the following days. The vast majority of those who heard the tape accepted it in good faith as the truth, and relied on the professionalism of those who released it. I have absolutely no memory of the interview with Duffy or the rubbish spoken by me on the tape. The interview was given at a time when the state of my health, both physical and, for those few short days around the time of the interview, mental, left a lot to be desired. What I said on the tape does not accord with the facts of what happened on the 27th January 1982. I rest my case.

8

ENTRAPMENT

On the Monday that I appeared on the by now famous Questions and Answers programme, a young law student out at UCD had a problem on his hands. John Menton, the Auditor of the Law Society, was looking for guests to appear in a debate he was organising about the Presidential election. He had lined up a number of guests and was hopeful that he could get the Fine Gael candidate Austin Currie to speak. He had printed the posters to advertise the event and Currie's name was on them. However, he had rung Fine Gael headquarters nearly thirty times and still could get no confirmation as to whether Currie would be coming out or not. In desperation he decided to contact Jim Duffy, the MA student, and former Chairman of the Young Fine Gael branch on the campus. Duffy readily agreed to help Menton. Both had a common interest in politics and Menton was a member of the Fianna Fáil cumann in the college. Jim Duffy left a message on the Law Society notice board telling him to come up to the MA room in the Politics Department at around quarter past four on that Monday afternoon. Duffy was trying to help in getting Currie out to UCD and Menton dutifully arrived at the MA room to meet him. Duffy had a key to Maurice Manning's office in the Department and both of them went in. Maurice Manning is a former Fine Gael TD for Dublin North-East and is currently the leader of the Fine Gael group in the Senate. Manning was elsewhere so Duffy phoned him. Duffy explained he had John Menton, the Auditor of the Law Society, with him and that Menton was anxious to get Currie out to Belfield for the debate.

Duffy passed the phone to Menton and the latter explained his frustration. He had rung Fine Gael headquarters and still could get no word on whether Currie would be coming. Manning said it would be impossible at this late stage to get the candidate out and that more or less ended the conversation. Manning promised to get him out a letter stating that Currie could not come and that this could be read to the meeting. Sitting in the office the two students began to discuss the Presidential election campaign. Menton was playing the devil's advocate saying the Presidency was a bit of a waste of time. They talked in a general way about the campaign and the three candidates for well over an hour as they sat in Maurice Manning's office. Duffy was quite knowledgeable on the whole thing given that the Presidency was his chosen field of study for his MA thesis. While they were discussing the merits of the various candidates Duffy told Menton that he had been talking to Brian Lenihan in connection with his MA thesis. What Duffy said next came as a bit of a surprise to the Law Society Auditor.

"He told me he had something which would liven up the election campaign. He said that Lenihan had admitted to him on tape that he had rung the President back in 1982. He said Brian Lenihan had told him he'd got through and the President had told him to get lost or words to that effect," says Menton. Duffy then went on to explain to Menton that if Brian Lenihan kept denying that he had made calls he would be forced to release the tape. "He then said to me that I should watch Questions and Answers that night." Menton never got to see the programme but, later that day, ran into Feargal O'Boyle, the Chairman of the Labour Party on the campus, who had been told the same thing by Duffy. "I thought it was bravado on Duffy's part. It's kind of toytown politics out at UCD and frankly I didn't believe him," says Menton.

But toytown politics it was not. Unknown to the Law Society Auditor, Jim Duffy was well on his way to leaving toytown. In a matter of days Jim Duffy was to become the best known research student in the country, better known than his lecturers and arguably the leading player in the Presidential election campaign. However, his meeting and discussion with John Menton is of some significance. After the Presidential election was over, Jim Duffy, in an interview with the Sunday Press, and later with RTE, insisted that nobody knew of the contents of his interview with me before I appeared on the by now controversial Questions and Answers programme that Monday. Yet, that very Monday there was already evidence that at least two people had been told of the contents of Duffy's taped interview with me in May of 1990. When the substance of his meeting with Menton was put to Duffy by Emily O'Reilly for her book *Candidate*, Duffy stated he was "almost certain" he hadn't mentioned the tape to the other student but added "unless it slipped out. I'd been rooting around for the tape that day and it might have been on my lips. Could I be mistaken? If I had mentioned it, it would have been accidental." However, what he told Menton does not have the appearance of a casual accident.

In an interview published in the Sunday Press last Christmas after the campaign, Duffy told the paper's political correspondent, Stephen Collins, that a number of stories being spread about him were "absolute rubbish." In particular he rejected stories that he had been paid £60,000 for the tape he had done with me. "It was also said that I was part of a Fine Gael plot and again this is absolute rubbish. No one in Fine Gael has ever heard the tape, nor would I have allowed them if they asked," said Duffy. This reply is disingenuous in the extreme. While it may be true that nobody in Fine Gael actually heard the tape, there is ample evidence to suggest that they knew exactly what it contained. On the Tuesday after the Questions and Answers programme, Fine Gael told journalists that they would produce evidence - within 24 hours - that what I had said on the programme was incorrect. In the event Fine Gael did not produce their evidence and it was left to the Irish Times to do so. It is obvious that the evidence Fine Gael hoped to produce - within 24 hours - was the same as that which the Irish Times played in conjunction with Jim Duffy.

Later in January of this year, Jim Duffy was to alter his reply somewhat from what he had told the Sunday Press. In an interview with RTE he was tackled on his assertion that nobody else knew about his interview recorded in May which he subsequently released. Joe Little on the This Week programme put it to Duffy that his interview with Brian Lenihan would have been known among his friends and fellow researchers. "They would have known I had done interviews with many people, they would not have known what the interviews contained. No one in Fine Gael, for example, ever heard the tape, nor would they have been allowed to if they had asked to," said Duffy. Here Duffy has gone further than he did with the Sunday Press and said nobody heard the tape nor knew of its contents before the Questions and Answers programme. This denial need not detain the reader too long. In the light of his conversation with John Menton set out at the beginning of this chapter, this assertion simply does not stand up.

On that Monday, before the Questions and Answers programme, Duffy was to talk to somebody of significance to events as they unfolded - his name, Brian Murphy. Murphy was a former National Chairman of Young Fine Gael and became friendly with Duffy when the latter was head of the Young Fine Gael Branch in 1987.

When Jim Duffy was first asked about his contacts with Brian Murphy before the Questions and Answers programme his memory seemed to fail him. Murphy, it will be remembered, was the young man who asked the critical question about the events of 1982 on the programme. In late December of last year, Emily O'Reilly, in the course of researching her book *Candidate*, asked Duffy about his relationship with Murphy prior to the programme. "The last time I met him in person was during the divorce referendum (in 1986) back in Meath and apart from that I'd bumped into him once or twice or spoken to him on the phone once or twice," said Duffy. However, in a follow-up interview with O'Reilly, he admitted having telephoned Murphy on the day of Questions and Answers, the next day and twice the day after that. Again, it is hard not to conclude that Duffy's original reply to O'Reilly was not deliberately vague. The number of calls passing between Duffy and Murphy is highly significant. On the Monday Murphy went on the Questions and Answers programme, on the Tuesday Fine Gael claimed they would produce evidence within 24 hours that what I'd said the previous night was untrue, and on Wednesday the Irish Times produced their article claiming they had "corroborative" evidence that I had in fact rung Áras an Uachtaráin back in 1982. On all three days, Jim Duffy was on the phone to Brian Murphy.

Murphy's role is central to events as they unfolded. Quite apart from his friendship with the MA student, Murphy had other strings to his bow. Murphy was a member of a key campaign committee that advised the Fine Gael director of elections Jim Mitchell. The committee was meant to exercise a monitoring role in relation to the whole campaign, ensuring that the director of elections' orders were being carried out. Other members of the committee included Senators Avril Doyle, Maurice Manning and a young accountant called Cormac Lucey. All members of the committee answered directly to Mitchell and nobody else.

Both Duffy and Murphy deny that they spoke about the night's Questions and Answers programme during their telephone conversation on the day it was on. Duffy denies talking about the programme as well as denying he told Murphy the contents of his interview with Brian Lenihan back in May. "We sort of discussed Questions and Answers in general, we didn't talk about the fact that he was on it because I didn't know about it. It was a surprise to me when I saw him there on Monday evening. If I'd known I wouldn't have rung him for a start," Duffy told Emily O'Reilly for her book. Murphy does not remember now if he did tell Duffy that he was going on the programme later that night. The fact that he, at least, is unsure, would seem to throw Duffy's assertion into further doubt. Frankly, in the light of both their actions and the number of calls, I find it impossible to believe that there was no discussion of Murphy's participation in the Questions and Answers programme. What could be more topical since they were discussing the Presidential campaign? It would have been natural for it to arise and an absurd omission if it were not mentioned.

Joe Kenny was General Secretary of Fine Gael during the Presidential election campaign. He was a close friend and ally of Alan Dukes. Since the election, he has moved on from his post at the party's headquarters in Mount Street. On the Monday night of the Questions and Answers programme, he was alone in the headquarters. There was nobody on the central telephone switchboard as it was too late. At about 9.30 pm. a call came through on a specially provided telephone line for the campaign on Jim Mitchell's desk. As Kenny was alone, obviously he alone can substantiate this. Kenny picked up the phone. It was Brian Murphy and he was very excited for some reason. He had just come out of the Questions and Answers show and he had something to tell. "I knew nothing about the phone calls to the Áras business until Brian Murphy informed me about it on the Monday night. He told me there was evidence that what Brian Lenihan had said on the programme was not true. He didn't tell me then about the tapes," says Kenny. It is obvious from both the excitement in Murphy's voice and the information conveyed that if he didn't already know the precise contents of the tape he had a pretty good inkling of what it contained. There is only one person who could have told him and that is Jim Duffy.

The next morning, Brian Murphy rang again, this time to the Fine Gael press office in Leinster House, Kenny took the call. At this stage, Murphy was able to tell him that the evidence he had spoken of the night before was actually on the tape in an interview Brian Lenihan had given to a research student named Jim Duffy from UCD. Kenny asked him would Duffy co-operate? Brian Murphy wasn't sure on that point. "I took the impression from my conversation with Murphy on the Tuesday that he had been in close contact with Duffy but that he was finding it increasingly difficult to maintain that contact - or at least that's the impression he gave me," says Kenny. However, as we have read earlier on in this chapter, Murphy had no difficulty maintaining contact with Duffy and spoke to him twice the next day, the Wednesday. Anyway Joe Kenny was not the contact point for Murphy with the campaign so it may be that Murphy's reticence was deliberate. It is likely that Murphy would have liaised directly with Jim Mitchell on a matter of this importance. "I surmised there was one of two reasons for this (a) that either he Murphy or Duffy was getting nervous of this thing escalating or (b), and I think it more likely, that the Irish Times were strongly advising Duffy not to speak to anybody but them," says Kenny.

By lunchtime on the Tuesday, according to Kenny, most of the top people in Fine Gael at Leinster House knew of both the tape and Duffy's identity. Later, at teatime, Kenny ran into Murphy in Leinster House. He met him near the stairs leading up to the chamber, a familiar spot where people stop and chat when in and around the house. "Murphy felt Duffy would not co-operate with Fine Gael and that Duffy was worried about questions of academic ethics."

When Jim Duffy went into the Westbury later that week to play his own selected portion of his taped conversation with me, the public knew little or nothing about the 24 year old research student. Subsequent media coverage tended to concentrate on his well documented connections with Fine Gael but stated little else. Duffy is from Durhamstown, Bohermeen, about three and a half miles from Navan in County Meath. He received his secondary education at St. Patrick's classical school in Navan town. His father is involved in local Fine Gael politics doing the national collection for the party in the area and canvassing for them at election time. While at school, Duffy tried to set up a branch of Young Fine Gael at St. Patrick's but there was little interest shown by the other students. At college the only society which Jim Duffy showed any real interest in was UCD's branch of Young Fine Gael. He became the Chairman of the branch for the academic year 1986-87. He was elected unopposed. Fine Gael were in coalition with Labour, the Government was unpopular, and the level of activity within the branch was low. With his year completed, Duffy settled down to his books and got a high two one in his degree exams which allowed him to go on and do an MA. He chose to do a one year MA which combines an exam and a thesis. He would have sat the exams in the summer of 1988 but, as we all know, has yet to complete his thesis.

Duffy's thesis on the Presidency grew out of a third year project he did on the office. It was part of a third year course on the "Houses of the Oireachtas." The course was given by Maurice Manning and Duffy's paper would have been submitted to him for assessment with the marks going towards his final BA exams. After those finals, he expanded the paper for the purposes of his MA thesis. Maurice Manning was to be his MA supervisor but had taken up a three year sabbatical posting with the college's development office. Though Manning was not his supervisor, Duffy would have consulted with him. The office of President is very much a neglected area in terms of political science research in this country. Duffy knew his research work could be rewarding. Manning was also interested in the student's field of study since he was considering writing a book on the workings of the Oireachtas. Manning has always been friendly with his students and the two had something in common as members of Fine Gael. In contrast to the other parties represented on the campus, Young Fine Gael is attached to the Dublin South-East constituency though Belfield is situated in Dublin South. Duffy played an active part in the constituency and was the branch delegate to the constituency body right up to 1989. Naturally, as a constituency activist he would have come into contact with the local TD and former Taoiseach Garret Fitzgerald. In any event, Duffy was to interview the former Taoiseach for his MA thesis. It had been suggested that Duffy would have visited the Fitzgerald home on Palmerston Road. However, there is nothing exceptional about this, if it is the case. Any number of constituency activists have been received hospitably there over the years.

Ironically, given his involvement in Fine Gael, many of Jim Duffy's friends were actually members of Fianna Fáil. One such friend was Marty Lynch whom he would have known from home. Marty's father is the former Meath TD, Michael Lynch. There were many other friends of Duffy in Fianna Fáil.

Notwithstanding this, the young research student's interest in Fine Gael did not wane after his period as Chairman of the UCD branch. He canvassed for the party in the 1989 general election in the Dublin South East constituency according to a friend who shared a flat with him at 56 Belgrave Square in Dublin's Rathmines.

In his interview with the Sunday Press, Duffy was to dismiss as "rubbish" suggestions that he had been part of a Fine Gael plot during the Presidential election campaign. Fine Gael's Director of Elections, Jim Mitchell, did the young research student no favours here. Within days of my appearance on the Questions and Answers programme, Mitchell was to boast that Fine Gael had set a trap for me that night on RTE. He declared that the party had done its research well and prepared well in advance. However, a week later, and perhaps regretting the boast, Jim Mitchell was to backtrack a bit on this assertion. Speaking in the Dáil confidence debate about the Questions and Answers programme he announced:

"In planning the questions and in briefing our representatives, we were making no more than proper and well considered preparations and we state categorically that (1) we had no prior knowledge of the existence of the Duffy taped interview and (2) we had no prior inkling that the Tánaiste would answer the question the way he did."

Whatever about the first assertion, the second is certainly not true. Mitchell only had to look at the Irish Press on the morning of the Questions and Answers programme to get an inkling of what I might say later at RTE. In an interview with the paper's political correspondent, I denied ever making any calls to Áras an Uachtaráin back in 1982 when questioned about the matter. There were other reasons why Mitchell might have known of my likely response as we shall see later and it relates to my visit to UCD on the 16th October during the campaign, just six days before Questions and Answers. There is ample evidence to suggest that both the existence and contents of the tape were well known to members of Fine Gael. We have already seen how Duffy spoke before Questions and Answers to Brian Murphy. Gail Conlon, a law student out at UCD and Secretary of the Fianna Fáil cumann there, says the existence of the tape was well known among members of Fine Gael at Belfield. Two days after Jim Duffy gave his famous press conference, she spoke with her class mate John Gannon after a lecture. Gannon is treasurer of the Fine Gael branch this year. "He told me that the tape was very much common knowledge as far back as last summer. He told me that Seamus Kennedy, the Chairman of Young Fine Gael, knew around that time too," says Gail Conlon.

That the Fine Gael Director of Elections, Jim Mitchell, had prepared well in advance is obvious. This part of his assertion is certainly true. As we have seen in chapter 6, a statement from Garret Fitzgerald went out before the Questions and Answers programme claiming that I had been one of the most persistent of the callers to Áras an Uachtaráin back in 1982. Fine Gael had briefed their members of the audience for the programme at their headquarters around 5 pm. that evening before going out to RTE. Emily O'Reilly says there was a further briefing at Garret Fitzgerald's home on Palmerston Road. "At the briefing in Fitzgerald's home it was decided to update a statement prepared by the former Taoiseach some days earlier, once again detailing the alleged events of 1982. A decision was made to attempt to raise the subject on the programme," she writes. If this is true, then it would seem to make nonsense of Garret Fitzgerald's claim that he did not know on the evening of Questions and Answers that the statement had been put out.

"On returning home late on Monday night after the Questions and Answers programme, I was interviewed by a journalist from RTE who started to ask me why I had accused Brian Lenihan of ringing that night. When I denied that I had done so on the programme, she drew my attention to the fact that the speech I had prepared several weeks earlier before Brian Lenihan made his denials had been issued by Fine Gael, of which I had until then been quite unaware. That's my involvement. No plot - no trap," Fitzgerald told the Dáil. There is a clear contradiction here. It should be cleared up.

However, there were other more compelling reasons why Fine Gael knew exactly how I would respond on the Questions programme. On October 16th my campaign brought me to UCD. In the crowd, though I did not know it at the time, was one Jim Duffy. It was a friendly meeting in a packed theatre out in Belfield. It was to be a question and answers style session with students. Also in the audience was Seamus Kennedy, then the Chairman of the Young Fine Gael branch on the campus. He like Murphy on Questions and Answers, had one question on his mind and it concerned the events of 1982.

Fianna Fáil headquarters were subsequently to conclude that it was here where Fine Gael was first to test my response on the phone calls to the Áras matter. However, before the session with the students began, Fianna Fáil's National Youth Officer Noel Whelan, was to have an intriguing conversation with Jim Duffy.

Whelan is a graduate of UCD in political science. Though Duffy was two years ahead of him at Belfield, they were on friendly terms. Back in the Autumn of 1987, Whelan shared the same flat as Duffy at 56 Belgrave Square in Rathmines. When they were together in the flat they would often talk about their mutual political interests. Whelan found Duffy interesting to talk to and their conversations often got around to Duffy's chosen field of expertise - the Presidency. Whelan accompanied me out to UCD that day. "I spoke to Duffy as we made our way into Theatre M. That's when he boasted to me that he was doing some research work for the Currie campaign. He also said he'd been approached by somebody in the Robinson campaign," says Whelan. When launching his campaign, Austin Currie had put forward the idea of involving the President in the appointment of members of the judiciary. It was contained in the policy document when Currie began his campaign. In particular, Duffy told Whelan that this idea was his own. Whelan had no reason to doubt what Duffy was saying. He knew of his area of expertise and of his involvement in Fine Gael. "A lot of the ideas that appeared on the policy side of the Currie campaign struck me as familiar, I'd heard them in my chats back in 1987 with Jimmy," says Whelan.

Meanwhile everything at the meeting at UCD went well. The questions were pretty run of the mill. Then Seamus Kennedy asked directly had I phoned Áras an Uachtaráin back in 1982. I answered it directly saying I had not. "I got the impression it was quietly planned by Young Fine Gael. Up to that the questions from students were of a very general nature," says Gail Conlon, Secretary of the Kevin Barry cumann. Jim Duffy sat in the audience unflustered by my denial. One of the reasons advanced by Duffy for the release of the tape was that my denial on the Questions and Answers programme was a blatant contradiction of all that he knew from his interview with me. "That night I arrived back in my flat just in time to hear him denying it on Questions and Answers. I thought it was amusing but the more I thought about it the more annoyed I became, because he was denying publicly information I had written about," he was to tell the Sunday Press after the Presidential election was over. His statement begs the question why was he not similarly annoyed with my previous denial just six days before at UCD and in a public lecture theatre with him present? Emily O'Reilly tackled him on this matter and he seemed vague initially. "Let's see" he told her, "I would have literally sort of said, Oh, that's Brian being Brian, and you know my articles. I know what I've written in the Irish Times and that it's true, my version is correct. But beyond that I wouldn't have said what my sources were, under no circumstances would I have done so." However Emily O'Reilly is skeptical of this assertion that he just laughed the matter off.

"But Duffy did more than laugh it off. The excited student reacted immediately, displaying once again an apparent inability to keep his mouth shut, telling several people that day that Lenihan was telling lies. He denies however that he also revealed his sources," writes O'Reilly. According to her Brian Murphy was also to hear of my denial that day at UCD. His determination to zero in on that question again on Questions and Answers seems all the stranger for that. Why should Fine Gael concentrate their attack on this matter if they knew from UCD and the Irish Press on the morning of Questions and Answers that it would not yield more than yet another denial by me? It is easy to conclude that they, or certainly Murphy at least, knew that there was evidence that suggested otherwise.

Just one day after the UCD meeting on October 17th, a letter, headed Department of Politics, UCD, arrived on my desk at the Department of Defence. The strange thing about the letter was that it was dated October 4th but was stamped by civil servants as having arrived by post in the Department on the later date. It was from Jim Duffy and he was seeking to clear some quotes he had gathered from his interview with me the previous May. This is the letter:

An Fanns Osssmb
1 7 OCT 1990

Department of Politics,
University College Dublin,
Belfield,
Dublin 4.

Brian Lenihan T.D.,
Leinster House, Kildare St.
Dublin 2.

October 4, 1990

Dear Tanaiste,

As promised, I am sending you a list of quotes from our interview of 17 May last. I would like to be able to use these, but want first of all to give you an opportunity to inspect them to ensure their accuracy. If there are any that you would wish me not to use, or else to use without giving the sources' name in the footnotes, please let me know. I am aiming (finally!) to get the thesis on the presidency completed by the beginning of November. The help which you gave me with my research will be fully acknowledged in the text.

Congratulations, by the way, on securing the Fianna Fail nomination for the presidency. I look forward to being able to observe the first presidential election in seventeen years. The date chosen for the election has caused me one problem. In the preface, should I acknowledge the help of "An Tanaiste, Brian Lenihan" or the "President-elect, Brian Lenihan" (sic)?

Yours sincerely,

Jim Duffy, B.A.

This letter clearly acknowledges my understanding of the arrangement, which covered the interview that I gave to Mr. Duffy. The interview was confidential, and its contents were only to be disclosed in Mr. Duffy's academic thesis after I had approved them. I was entitled to correct any quotations which he might submit to me.

Enclosed with the brief letter were two pages of quotes. They were all pretty innocuous giving no hint of what was actually contained in the portion of the tape that he eventually released. The following are the quotes enclosed in the letter:

BRIAN LENIHAN INTERVIEW

17 MAY 1990

On de Valera as President

Contact with Ministers:

"[He'd arrange to meet ministers] definitely every year, usually twice a year."

"He'd talk about the [the Minister's] office, what we were doing, what our objectives were, how policy was going, and so on, in a very general way. He'd add a bit of his own wisdom without trying to pressure you or anything like that. There was no question of that."

but not pol it us as well

"He never regarded himself as being above or apart from party politics. He regarded him- self . . . as part of the political office of the presidency, which is a political office written into the constitution, *and part of the political process*

"[In the 1966 election] Tom O'Higgins ran a *real* campaign."

On Erskine Childers

"[We] played down the Fianna Failism of Childers . . . and played on all [his] non Fianna Fail attributes . . . a man of culture, a cultivated man, a protestant, the minority could feel safe with him."

"[Childers] - vehemently anti-violence"

On Cearbhall O Dalaigh

"Cearbhall Ó Dalaigh was a very legalistic man, a brilliant lawyer . . . although standing several times for [Fianna Fail] he wasn't really a politician. His whole makeup and tem- perment was different. He hadn't got the flexibility that is normal of a person with politi- cal training, someone who regularly contests political office, served in parliament, and so on. You develop a give and take, an attitude of mind that's flexible. A person with that attitudes and approach, temperment, obviously wouldn't embarrass a government. He'd temper what he'd say with what the Government's view was. Along with that, Ó Dalaigh had a very strong integrity. If he felt a certain way, he'd push for his rights under the law and the constitution to say it, right up to a conflict point. To that extent he wasn't suited."

"He was an argument for being very watchful about who you appoint president."

On Patrick Hillery

Events of January 1982:

"Looking back on it, it was a mistake."

"A very cautious man . . . wouldn't break new ground."

- 1 -

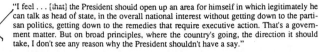

"I remember saying to that group of us, 'Look Here! Paddy's not going to have anything to do with this.'"

"[Hillery] has got much warmer with Haughey since the 1987 election."

"[Hillery] went too much into retreat in regard to his personal involvement"

On the Presidency in general

"I feel . . . [that] the President should open up an area for himself in which legitimately he can talk as head of state, in the overall national interest without getting down to the partisan politics, getting down to the remedies that require executive action. That's a government matter. But on broad principles, where the country's going, the direction it should take, I don't see any reason why the President shouldn't have a say."

"Childers was the man who had the best approach to it. A fellow like Ó Dálaigh is dangerous. With all due respect to academics and lawyers there's a danger there because it is a highly sensitive political job his [Ó Dalaigh's] antennae were not geared in that direction at all."

I was at a distinct disadvantage reading through the quotes. I had no memory of having done the interview in the first place. That I had no particular memory of the interview is perfectly compatible with my medical condition at the time of the interview back on the 17th May. However, my own common sense told me that some of his quotes were either inaccurate or wrong. There were fifteen separate quotes in all. Reading through them, I rejected over half of them, drawing a line across those that I did not approve. In all I rejected eight of his quotes, approved six and amended just one. I drew an X beside those that I considered worthy of inclusion in his thesis. Having completed this, I left it there with the file in the office. I did not consider it a matter of urgency to reply quickly to the young man's request.

Among the quotes submitted to me by Mr. Duffy for approval, two were taken from the section of the tape which he disclosed at the press conference. By submitting these quotes to me with his covering letter, there was a clear understanding that they would not be disclosed until approved by me. Furthermore, all the quotes were taken from almost every section of the interview, coming from ten of the thirty-eight pages comprising the complete transcript. Mr. Duffy's letter, in the light of his enclosed quotes, shows that he accepted the entire interview to be confidential.

In retrospect, it was a strange letter to receive. It arrived in the middle of the Presidential election campaign and with less than a week to go to the Question and Answers programme. None of the quotes gave any hint of the contents of the tape as eventually played by Duffy. The interview itself had happened on the 17th May. It had taken Duffy all of five months to submit just fifteen quotes from a lengthy interview. When the questions did arrive all that they amounted to were a pretty general set of observations about various different Presidents and the Presidency itself.

In January of this year, Joe Little of RTE's This Week programme questioned the research student on why he had not checked back with me before going ahead and playing the portion of the tape. "Well, I had given him a list of quotes quite a while before that and he hadn't replied and it had been clear in my letter that I was waiting for his right to deny them if he wished to deny and he never issued a denial, so," replied Duffy. The use of the phrase "right to deny" is more the language of an investigative journalist than an academic research student. The quotes he sent to me for approval were for inclusion in an MA thesis, not a press conference given by the Irish Times. It was incorrect also to state that he had sent me the quotes a long time before that as the letter was only received by my office on October 17th. The extent to which Duffy has confused his role as occasional writer for the Irish Times and academic researcher is disturbing. His interview in December of last year with the Sunday Press is testament to his continued confusion on this point. In his articles for the Irish Times, which were published at the end of September, Mr. Duffy, on the basis of his taped interview, referred to phone calls to President Hillery on the night of January 27, 1982, by Charles Haughey, Brian Lenihan and Sylvester Barrett. He told the Sunday Press that "there was no reaction about the allegations of '82 and I wasn't particularly surprised as there was a general acknowledgement that it had happened." The problem for Duffy is that when I consented to be interviewed by him, it was not on the basis that our discussion was to form the background for his series of articles in the Irish Times. It was he, himself, who manoeuvred himself into a situation where there was a clear conflict of interests. His admission that he used material gathered for his thesis in the Irish Times is a breach of academic ethics. His duty as an academic researcher was to check back with me, he did not do this. Furthermore, in his interviews with Emily O'Reilly, he stated that the excerpted quotes sent to me with his letter of the 17th October contained an admission by me that I had made calls to Áras an Uachtaráin back in 1982. This is simply not the case. A cursory glance at the quotes forwarded by him makes this clear. The dots are his not mine, as is clear from the actual copy of the letter:

"Looking back on it, it was a mistake."

"A very cautious man ... wouldn't break new ground."

"I remember saying to that group of us. Look here! Paddy's not going to have anything to do with this."

These quotes do not come near to me admitting that I rang Áras an Uachtaráin back in January 1982. Far from it, they actually back up my version of events set out in detail in Chapter 7 of this book. The quotes merely show that I opposed ringing the Áras at the front bench meeting then, and there are plenty of people around still who testify to that fact.

To recap then on the campaign. On the Tuesday after the Questions and Answers programme I had plenty to do. There was a party political broadcast to record for television and Today Tonight wanted to interview me again. Olivia O'Leary had inter- viewed me at my office in Defence but, in the light of Garret's allegations on Questions and Answers, she wanted to do it again. Just after lunch I made my way out to RTE and re-recorded the interview. She put Garret's question to me and I replied "Other people may have phoned the Áras about what was going to happen, but I had nothing to do with it, good, bad or indifferent." I was glad to be able to do the interview again and felt I had done better the second time round. The interview, along with a profile, went out later that evening on RTE. I hopped on the campaign bus and went straight to Bray where I was to begin my tour of County Wicklow. We would be in the county all day, finishing up that night with a rally in Aughrim. I would stay overnight and come back to Dublin in the morning. Unknown to me on that Tuesday, events were pushing inexorably to a crisis. Jim Duffy was to pick up the phone and ring through to Dick Walsh, the Political Editor of the Irish Times. His ostensible reason for ringing was to discuss two further articles he was to write for the paper. Their discussion quickly centred on what Garret Fitzgerald had alleged. Duffy claimed to the Irish Times Political Editor that he had evidence that contradicted my version of events on Questions and Answers. I am indebted to Emily O'Reilly for taking up the story at this point:

"According to Duffy, Walsh then told him that the conversation with Lenihan should be made public knowledge, that the proof that Brian Lenihan had lied should be published, Duffy refused. Walsh said he understood his position but suggested that perhaps the paper might interview him instead, give Duffy an opportunity to say what he knew on the basis of his research that Lenihan had lied. Duffy rang off saying that he would consider it."

At this point, Duffy began to consult with his academic tutors and lecturers at UCD, as to what he should do. Brian Farrell told him in no circumstances to reveal the tape. The interview had been gathered for academic purposes only and he should not reveal his sources. Dr. Tom Garvin, now head of the Department of Politics at UCD, also counselled against. In an interview with RTE since the election, Garvin stated: "Unfortunately, however, he (Duffy) is applying the ethics of journalism rather than the ethics of academic research to his use of the tape recording." In the interview Dr. Garvin seemed to be labouring under the illusion that Jim Duffy's interview had not been done with me in confidence. That this is not the case shall be demonstrated later in this chapter. However despite that slight misunderstanding, Garvin was adamant that Duffy had breached academic ethics.

Garvin said that the primary rule in academic research is that you do not use any material whether it is confidential or not, in any way that might damage that source ... "And in effect, what Jim has done is perpetrated a breach of this number one rule. Now, of course, Jim hadn't been apprised of this rule. We have always tacitly assumed that this rule was understood. If you like, there has been a traditional gentleman's understanding, if you like. And I'm afraid he has broken the rule. Now, he has excuses - he was pushed in many ways. He was challenged to produce the tape, he was provoked in many ways and I have a lot of sympathy with him. But I'm afraid he has done his colleagues and his other students who might want to do research of this kind a lot of damage."

Since the election, Professor Garvin has written to me personally to express his regrets on the matter. "Jim Duffy was advised by us, sometimes in very strong terms, not to go public with that tape. By doing so, he violated the primary unwritten rule of academic research, which is that you do not use information in such a way as to damage the informant."

Still casting around for academic approval, Duffy consulted both Maurice Manning and the historian Michael Laffan. It is incredible to read in Emily O'Reilly's book that Maurice Manning, when approached by Duffy for advice, told him to go and see somebody else. Laffan advised against publication. Later, he was to explain to the Irish Times his reasoning: "Academics should take the long view, not jump in, especially in the middle of an election campaign". Laffan is critical of Duffy's decision to release the tape and hopes that it will not lead to what he describes as a "bonfire of archives." While it may not lead to a bonfire, it does seem unlikely that politicians will now trust academic researchers because of the controversy.

In his interviews with Emily O'Reilly, Duffy maintained that because of these consultations with the academics on Tuesday afternoon he was veering against disclosure: "Duffy claims that the net effect of his conversations with the academics was to reinforce his determination not to reveal the information. He rang Dick Walsh of the Irish Times again and told him so." However, this version from Duffy would seem to be contradicted by one eye witness account from UCD that Tuesday.

Michael Fealy is a final year law student at Belfield. He, like John Menton mentioned at the beginning of the chapter, is involved in both the Law Society and the Fianna Fáil cumann on the campus. Fealy knew Duffy well and was also involved in organising the Presidential debate for the Law Society. The motion for debate was "Lark in the Park" with the intention behind the whole thing to examine the actual relevance of the office as opposed to the candidates contesting for the office.

Because of the articles Duffy had written in the Irish Times, Fealy had asked him to participate in the debate. Fealy ran into Duffy outside the campus restaurant at around half past one that Tuesday. At this stage, Duffy had spoken to Walsh in the Irish Times and presumably had consulted with some of the academics.

The two chatted about Duffy's possible participation in the debate. The conversation soon wound its way around to the Presidential election. Duffy would have known Fealy's political involvement as he had attended the Fianna Fáil cumann's annual general meeting when Fealy was elected treasurer. It is not considered unusual for activists of different persuasions to attend rival AGMs out at UCD. In fact, the particular AGM was the first time both of them had met. Fealy cocked up his ears at what Duffy said next. Duffy told him that he had done an interview with Brian Lenihan back in May and that the Tánaiste had admitted making calls to Áras an Uachtaráin back in 1982. He also went on to say that this would probably be appearing in the Irish Times the next day. "The Irish Times", he told me, "were discussing the legal implications of publishing it with their solicitors," says Fealy. The importance of what Duffy told the law student is that it clearly contradicts his assertion to Emily O'Reilly that he had doubts, given the advice given to him by his academic mentors. This would seem to indicate that Duffy was far less plagued by concern about academic ethics than he has tried to maintain since the Presidential election.

On the Tuesday morning, Duffy also rang his old friend Brian Murphy. According to Emily O'Reilly's account: "He told him that the Questions and Answers programme had caused difficulties for the Irish Times as they had run a story stating that Lenihan had made the calls. He told him he had solid evidence that this was the case. Murphy passed on the information to Fine Gael's Director of Elections, Jim Mitchell." The pressure to publish the tape, it would appear from this account, was coming not from Fianna Fáil but rather the Irish Times, and this is borne out by the run of events. Later that evening, Duffy played the tape to the Editor of the Irish Times, Conor Brady, and to Dick Walshe and Denis Coughlan of his political staff. "Duffy then agreed that the Irish

Times could run a low-key story stating that they had corroborative evidence that Lenihan, Sylvester Barrett and Charles Haughey
had made phone calls to Áras an Uachtaráin, but not giving any
hint as to what this evidence was," according to O'Reilly.

However, Wednesday's Irish Times was anything but low-key.
Right across the front page was their lead story claiming they had
"corroborative" and "independently available" evidence that what
I had said on Questions and Answers was wrong. In Aughrim, I
surfaced early from my bed and studied the morning newspapers.
I was quite apprehensive about the contents of the Irish Times
story. I put through a call to the Government Press Secretary, P.J.
Mara. It was only at this stage that people began to piece together
who the source behind the Irish Times story was. P.J. and Fianna
Fáil headquarters had learnt of the Duffy tape independent of me.
I was able to tell P.J. on the spot about the interview with Duffy as
I had been reading and correcting the letter he had sent me the
week before. However, for reasons well set out earlier in the book
I was unable to tell him of the details of my interview with Duffy.
I was sure of two things: one – that I had not called the Áras or
spoken to the President on the night in question, and secondly
that the interview with Duffy had been conducted on the basis of
confidentiality.

That morning, I flew by helicopter to Blessington. It was a
lovely clear morning as we flew over Turlough Hill and down by
the lake to Blessington. It was an unscheduled stop in the tour and
there was a small number of activists from the local party there to
greet us. We landed in the back garden of The Downshire Arms
hotel. From there, it was back to Dublin and my office at the
Department of Defence. In the meantime, P.J. Mara had put
through a phone call to the Editor of the Irish Times, Conor
Brady, reminding him that the source for their story was a student
engaged in academic research and that Jim Duffy was also a
member of Fine Gael. Back at the office, I pulled out the file that
contained the letters Duffy had sent me in relation to our interview. This was later passed to the Director of Elections Bertie
Ahern. To my mind, reading back over the letter Duffy had sent
me, there seemed to be little to the interview. As illustrated earlier

there was nothing in the excerpts that I viewed as damaging in any particular way. I had presumed, wrongly as things turned out, that the excerpts were broadly reflective of what I had said in the interview. There was no hint of what was to come out later the next day in those excerpts.

I was determined to get to the truth of the matter and put through a call to Sylvester Barrett to confirm my memory of events back in 1982. I caught him at his home in Clare. He confirmed my version of events that night as set out in Questions and Answers. He told me that he alone had rung, and was definite that I had not, and in a later telephone call agreed to go on television stating that the following day. Nicholas Coffey from Today Tonight was dispatched down to Clare to do the interview. Unfortunately this interview was to be buried in the maelstrom of events and coverage that followed Jim Duffy's premature release of a portion of his interview with me. I was so certain of my position following my conversation with Sylvie Barrett that I consulted with lawyers about a possible legal action for libel against the Irish Times. It was with relative peace of mind that I left to campaign in counties Monaghan and Cavan that afternoon. Again it was another overnight stay and the reception was very warm.

However, pressure had been building throughout that morning. Gay Byrne, on his popular morning programme, had called on the Irish Times to make their "corroborative" evidence available if indeed they had it. In the Dáil that morning, opposition deputies tried to raise the Irish Times story on the order of business. All eyes were on Fine Gael who had told the newspapers the previous night that they would produce evidence that my version of events on Questions and Answers was untrue. They had said they would produce it within 24 hours and time was running out. Alan Dukes' attempt to raise the matter was ruled out of order by the Ceann Comhairle. Dukes told the House: "Sir, you leave me with no option but to give you notice that my party will put down a motion of no confidence in the Tánaiste." The following day's newspapers claimed that it was Dukes who first mentioned the existence of a tape. However, it was John Bruton, then deputy leader of the party, who told the Dáil in very explicit terms what was contained in the Duffy tape. "A Cheann Comhairle, is it not the case that the Tánaiste admitted on a tape that he had made such representations." It was the first explicit and public mention by anyone that pointed to the possible contents of the tape. It is not clear what role the current leader of Fine Gael played in events. In the Dáil confidence debate the next week, John Bruton was to be one of the few deputies who would rush to defend Jim Duffy and what he had done. It may be that his defence of Duffy owed more to the fact that the research student was a Meath man, a member of Fine Gael and his father an activist in his own organisation.

On the News at One programme on RTE, Bertie Ahern confirmed that I had done an interview with a research student and that this appeared to be the source of the Irish Times story. Subsequent to the election, Jim Duffy has indicated that it was Fianna Fáil's disclosure that he had conducted an interview with me that forced him to publish the tape. He said his reluctance went right up to the Thursday. Duffy said that he was angered by the Fianna Fáil denials he read on Thursday's newspapers. "They (Fianna Fáil) were using my silence as a form of alibi for Brian Lenihan. My reluctance to reveal my information was being claimed by them as evidence that there was no information. I did not want to damage Brian Lenihan but I was unwilling to let my silence be used to get him off the hook," he told the Sunday Press. There is plenty of evidence that, over the Wednesday, Duffy was again confusing his role as academic researcher and a more ill defined journalistic role. His use of emotive words like letting people "off the hook" owes more to Woodward and Bernstein than the quiet more subdued language of academia. The pressure on him from all sides was beginning to tell. He wrongly assumed it was Fianna Fáil that was putting him under pressure. There was considerable pressure from Fine Gael, a personal friend and, of course, the Irish Times.

On the Wednesday, he spoke to Brian Murphy on two occasions. Emily O'Reilly captures the mood of one of these:

"Meanwhile, Jim Duffy had arrived on campus. He had heard his name mentioned on the Pat Kenny Show and had again contacted Brian Murphy, who, under pressure from Fine Gael to get Duffy to give them the tape, told the student that the only option now was to publish it. According to Murphy, Duffy seemed naively unaware of the political storm he had caused."

What is odd about this is that Jim Duffy seemed to have remained quite calm when listening to his name being mentioned on the Pat Kenny Show but became infuriated when his name was put to Denis Coughlan on the News at One by Shane Kenny. If he was naively unaware up to this of the political storm he had created he was soon brought down to earth. There were journalists from RTE, the newspapers and apparently people from Fianna Fáil headquarters tearing around the campus looking for Jim Duffy. In a nervous state, he apparently took refuge in the college chaplaincy. It was from here that he rung the Irish Times yet again. The Editor of the Irish Times, Conor Brady, argued he should see a lawyer. "A company car containing a driver and The Irish Times duty editor Meave Ann Wren, duly arrived at the Chaplaincy and Duffy was whisked off to Hayes and Sons on Stephens Green who handle part of the Irish Times business," says O'Reilly.

The result of all the pressure seems to have been to throw Duffy back into the comforting arms of the Irish Times and their solicitors who advised him it would not be illegal to publish the tape. However, that night he spoke for the second time that day to Brian Murphy who was on the Currie campaign and who urged him to release the tape.

The choices confronting the young man of 24 were now pretty stark. Would he follow the advice of his academic mentors, or would he go along with Fine Gael? Or would The Irish Times - who were also urging him to release the tape - be his final choice? At this stage Jim Duffy is in an ethical minefield where he has confused three different and quite distinct parts of his life. There is Jim Duffy the young man doing an MA thesis. There is Jim Duffy the Fine Gael activist who has been telling people he has been contributing on the policy side of the Currie campaign. Finally there is Jim Duffy the putative journalist and occasional writer on the Presidency for the Irish Times. All three of these personae were to blame in bringing him to this point. It was the decision to blur the lines between the three. He decided to ignore the academic advice in relation to the tape, he decided to maintain contact with Brian Murphy a leading member of the Currie campaign, he chose to tell people he was contributing to that campaign himself, and finally, as we shall see shortly, it was he who decided to break his confidence with me. Jim Duffy made the decisions, not Fianna Fáil. The Irish Times chose to facilitate that choice.

It was a curious press conference on the Thursday at the Westbury Hotel. The young post-graduate research student was accompanied to the press conference by two executives from the the Irish Times, Eoin McVey Managing Editor and Ken Gray, the Deputy Editor. Jim Duffy then played the tape. It was not a press conference in the normal sense of that word. Neither The Irish Times Executives nor the young man at the centre of the whole controversy, Jim Duffy, could be questioned by the journalists present. A statement from Jim Duffy was handed around to journalists:

"In view of the recent controversy concerning my recording of an interview with an Tánaiste, I wish to make the following statement. The interview in question was recorded by me with the full knowledge and consent of an Tánaiste on May 17th last. It covered a wide range of topics relating to the Presidency. In it, an Tánaiste outlined in some detail his knowledge of events of January, 1982. Some of the information disclosed to me at this interview confirmed various facts told to me by other sources. These formed the basis for an article on the Presidency written by me and published in the Irish Times on September 27th last. To date, I have received no denial concerning the information published in that article and I stand over the accuracy of its content.

"I have decided to make available to a limited number of people a short extract from the recording by the Tánaiste in which he describes the events. At the time, the Tánaiste asked that portion of the 40-minute interview be treated as strictly confidential and I am honouring that request.

"I wish to make it clear that the decision to make available the text of a portion of the interview was taken with great reluctance. I was left with no option in view of the political pressure I was subjected to when it was made known that I had done a recorded interview with the Tánaiste.

"I wish to say that I have no ill-feelings whatever towards the Tánaiste whom I respect and who was of enormous assistance to me in my research. The recording of the interview has been placed in safe custody."

This statement simply defies comprehension.

First of all, the statement shows that Duffy has breached an academic ethic by using material gathered for his MA research in a newspaper article for which he has been paid.

He approached me on the basis that he was an academic not a writer with the Irish Times who was going to write about the interview for the paper or release it to the public in any way.

Moreover, he justifies his release of the portion of the tape not for the sake of his academic research, but rather to defend what he wrote in the Irish Times on the 27th September 1990.

If he had wanted to defend his material written then he should have relied on his other sources and not me. He has claimed that I was just one of a number of sources that formed the basis of this article.

The statement is entirely wrong in asserting that the interview on May 17th 1990 was anything other than in confidence.

Duffy's statement about "making available to a limited number of people a short extract from the recording by the Tánaiste" when those people were active journalists working for the Irish national newspapers, radio and television, must rank as one of the understatements of the century. He was aiming, not at "a limited number of people", but at millions throughout Ireland and many parts of the world. The most sinister aspect to Duffy's release of the tape is the fact that he knowingly released information which he himself believed to be untrue. He, therefore, gave wider currency to an allegation which up to that point nobody regarded as fact. In his interview with RTE on January 13th of this year he was challenged on this very point. Here is the exchange on the subject between Joe Little and Duffy on the This Week programme:

Little: At that time ... you didn't claim that the phone calls had got through to the President, isn't that the case?

Duffy: That's true, I didn't believe they got through.

Little: If you didn't believe they got through, why did you decide to reveal the research interview with Brian Lenihan where he claimed that he got through?

Duffy: Well, it's his claim, I don't accept it.

Little: But it does seem a strange decision to take to publish information which you yourself suspect might be untrue?

Duffy: Well, I was publishing information that was simply setting the record straight about phone calls having been made and the accuracy of my sources. The fact that one source exaggerated his role was not my fault.

However, it was up to him to check back with me on a matter that he felt to be untrue. His duty to his chosen academic research was to get the facts right. He never gave me the opportunity to correct this either in the quotes submitted to me or subsequently.

In my interview with him, I clearly stated that all our discussion of the events of 1982 was confidential. At the press conference in the Westbury, Mr. Duffy and the Irish Times chose not to disclose the full extract from the tape of our conversation about the events of 1982. The full extract clearly demonstrates that the conversation was confidential. Now, for the first time, I am revealing the relevant extract, which is enclosed as an appendix to this chapter. At the press conference, Mr. Duffy and the Irish Times stopped the tape at a crucial point, failing to disclose the following exchange of words between me and Duffy.

Brian Lenihan: ... No actually the whole motivation now was strictly political. You mentioned first yourself there, would be, to get into, as you say, be the government, from that launching pad to go to the country, you know.

Well between ourselves, I mean you're not going public with this.

Jim Duffy: No, no, no.

Brian Lenihan: It was mainly Haughey's idea actually you know and o.k. he asked me to get Barrett, he asked

Barrett and I to go along because we were the
most friendly with Hillery ...

I shall end this saga with one quotation from the controversial
tape. A few minutes after the recording began the confidential
nature of the interview emerges. I put the following question to
Mr. Duffy:

You are not going to print ... starting any
campaign or that?

I was making it clear that the purpose of the interview was
limited to its use as a source for one purpose and one purpose
only, a research thesis for an MA degree as specified in Mr. Duffy's
arrangements with my secretary.

The interview was not for publication.

Extract

THE CONFIDENTIALITY OF MY INTERVIEW WITH DUFFY

Duffy: I see ... Eh ... In 1982 the ... Em ... attempt to get Hillery to refuse dissolution. Where (did) the idea first spring from?

Brian: Well it sprung from a meeting of a group of us after the vote down below, by down below I mean now the chamber room over there. At that time - well we still have - the parliamentary party offices. We were in opposition then of course. Our general opposition offices were upstairs, over the group of restaurants, so we all just adjourned upstairs, and have discussions, discussed it around about amongst the number of us.

Duffy: I believe there were eight phone calls made.

Brian: Well there weren't eight. there were two or three, there were two or three certainly.

Duffy: But you made a phone call?

Brian: Oh, I did yeah.

Duffy: Yes, Sylvester Barrett?

Brian: Sylvie, that's correct.

Duffy: And Mr. Haughey?

Brian: Yes, that's right.

Duffy: And did any of the phone calls get through to the President straight?

Brian: Oh, yeah, I mean I got through to him. I remember talking to him and he wanted it ... he wanted to lay off it altogether. I mean there was no doubt about his mind about it. He didn't want ... In fact looking back on it, it was a mistake on our part to, to ... because Paddy Hillery would know, he wouldn't want to start breaking new ... He was not the sort of man, a very cautious man, you know and the sort of fellow that wouldn't - didn't - wouldn't break new ground, well of course Charlie was gungho and there is an argument

as you know under that. We will have to improve the
phraseology of that.

Duffy: Definitely.

Brian: No question about that.

Duffy: It's ridiculous as it stands.

Brian: It's hopeless, now I'm not going to talk about it, that's
... no doubt about that and you see it's ridiculous
when it puts everybody in a predicament that I mean
... when it's open to that sort of interpretation that
existed that particular night we are talking about.
that's wrong. But Hillery had, there's no doubt about
Hillery but taking a cautious interpretation.

Duffy: I believe that MR ...

Brian: He wouldn't countenance ... the fact ... He was very
annoyed about that I'm a very good friend of his, I
know he was annoyed with the whole bloody lot of us.

Duffy: I've heard that from a few people.

Brian: That's true.

Duffy: I understand from a civil servant that Mr Haughey
went to the Áras himself - is that the case?

Brian: No, I only know about the phone call, I remember
distinctly - and I've described to you the phone call - I
don't know whether Haughey went up himself
personally after that.

Duffy: I was told he went to the Áras and was refused
admission and told to leave.

Brian: Was that subsequent to this?

Duffy: It was on that night, yes, Ah ... sometime on that night.

Brian: I honestly don't know that now. I cut it. Once I saw
Hillery's reaction I remember distinctly saying to that
group of us ... I ... remember distinctly saying look it
here Paddy's not going to have anything to do with
this. That's quite plain. That was my view.

Duffy: I see.

Brian: I wrote it off as an idea after that to tell you the truth.

Duffy: When ... What was the idea behind it, was it just to get
into power or to get into power and then call an

election with the trappings of power?

Brian: That was ... that was the idea that - O.K. - if the President could interpret that this way then it was open to him, that was it ... it would help the electoral prospects ... that is the only rationale I could see of it at the time, I remember that distinctly.

Duffy: There was no intention of staying on for a long time?

Brian: Ah, no, no, no ...

Duffy: There is actually one problem that does arise from the Constitution. If Haughey had formed a new Government he couldn't have changed Fitzgerald's eleven Senator nominees, as a result the new Government would be a minority in the Senate.

Brian: That's interesting.

Duffy: And what's more there is another very important Presidential power which allows the Senate to petition the President to refer bills to the people in referenda and that would come into play if the old Government controlled the Senate ... so his use of that power could have brought in three other powers that would be functioning then that haven't worked before.

Brian: That's a very valid point, that is true.

Duffy: So that's something wasn't actually realised at the time.

Brian: Yes, that wasn't realised the consequence of it ... no actually the whole motivation now was strictly political. You mentioned first yourself there, would be to get in, as you say, be the Government, from that launching pad to go to the country, you ... Well between ourselves, I mean you're not going public with this?

Duffy: Oh, No, No.

Brian: It was mainly Haughey's idea actually you know and O.K. he asked me to get Barrett, he asked Barrett and I to go along because we were the most friendly with Hillery and to ring Hillery as ... he asked me to ring Hillery, he knew ... well I was particularly friendly Hillery in the Government prior to that as I told you. I got him to go for the President, I think, but eh I was

one of the people and that Barrett was also very
friendly with Hillery being a Clareman and so on. So
he got Hillery and Barrett and I to do it. But I rang
Hillery in front of them. I spoke to him in front of
them. I remember distinctly putting down the phone
telling Haughey and the whole lot there, look it here
boys this is not on. That man is going to interpret the
Constitution and he is cautious and conservative
manner ... that's his interpretation and he is the sort
of guy I said, he's going to stick with that, that's that,
forget about it. I remember saying that, forget about
it. Anyway he may have gone up, I don't know.

Duffy: I see, was it ... was it that ... did Haughey feel his
leadership was under threat at this stage?

Brian: Yeah. Well he was going kind of gungho for the, this
would be ... well there was all that of course ... that's
another factor ... sure that was all part of the
surrounds of that time within the party, you had this,
the Colley thing, and then the O'Malley thing ... and
so on and all of that was in the party at the time. It was
the worst time ever that the party went through that
general period in '81, '82, '83 you know yourself the
whole history and yeah ... that would have been a
factor in it too.

Duffy: I see, let's see what's next for me to touch on ...

9

PD PERCEPTIONS

That Thursday was quite different to anything I have experienced before or since. Jim Duffy's press conference was exercising all our minds. As the campaign bus made its way out the coast road past Clontarf and the Bull Wall, we all speculated about the possible reason why the young MA student was calling his conference at this particular time. I was so confident of my own memory of the events back in 1982 that I felt that perhaps Duffy was calling the conference to scotch the rumours about the contents of his interview with me once and for all. Since the Tuesday after the Questions and Answers programme, Leinster House had been alive with rumours but I had been getting on with my campaign. I had already assured Bertie Ahern and other colleagues that I did not think there was anything in the interview that would prejudice my version of events. I was absolutely certain of my recollection of the events of 1982. I did not think that there could be anything damaging in the interview, as I assumed that the quotes Duffy had sent me by letter were a reasonable representation of the type of exchanges between us in our interview. I had no memory of anything else, and nothing else to go on. I even thought that Duffy, having become embroiled in the campaign, was now going to disentangle himself by ending all the rumour. Since the interview had been conducted for academic purposes only, I presumed that perhaps Duffy would explain to journalists that he was under an obligation not to reveal the contents.

After a brief stop at Sutton Cross it was off to Donaghmede Shopping Centre on the northside of Dublin. We were aiming to do all of the big shopping centres on the northside that day. It was while on our way there that the news of the Duffy press conference came through. The Fianna Fáil press officer Niamh O'Connor had arranged with someone in the Westbury to relay on any news as soon as it was all over. When the news came through, it was a political depth charge to all inside the bus. The revelations were a shock. Michael Woods and I, the campaign manager Michael Dawson, and Niamh O'Connor all retreated to the small back room on the bus. The others on the bus, including Gene Kerrigan of the Sunday Tribune, still didn't know what was going on and must have wondered what was up when we all retired to the back. It was time to talk and straighten things out.

I knew I hadn't spoken to or rung President Hillery on the night in question. It was clear to me that what I'd said on the tape was wrong but I couldn't explain it because I had no recollection of saying it to Duffy. I knew only of the quotes Duffy had sent me the previous week but none of these had contained anything about me ringing Áras an Uachtaráin or speaking to the President back in 1982. So apart from these quotes received by letter I could not remember anything of the interview I'd had with the UCD student back in May. I rang the Taoiseach Mr. Haughey to explain the position. He confirmed my version of events and suggested that I should seek to clarify the matter with the President and say publicly that I was doing so. Frankly this idea appealed to me. It struck me immediately that he was the only person who could straighten things out and clarify my version of events. A call was put through to Áras an Uachtaráin later but the President was not in and a message was left to the effect that I wanted to talk to him.

There were hurried consultations going on in the room on the bus and a number of mobile phones were going at once. Some journalists had put in requests for interviews including Seán Duignan of Six One News. To put it mildly I was in a difficult situation. I had not seen exactly what was on the tape nor even a transcript of what was on it. Yet despite all this there were people on the bus urging me to admit that I had made contact with the Áras back in 1982 on the basis that I could explain away my denials on the Questions and Answers programme during the remainder of the campaign. But to me this was unacceptable. I was determined on one thing - to tell the truth and nothing but the truth - that I did not ring or speak to Dr. Hillery and that what I had said on the tape was a mistake and therefore untrue. I had to be honest with myself if I was to be honest with people.

Outside, the activists waiting to welcome us must have known something was up. The bus was parked across the entrance to Donaghmede Shopping Centre and nobody was getting out. There was an RTE camera crew and interviewer waiting with them. I went out to press the flesh but was followed at every footstep by Brendan O'Brien from RTE and a camera crew. He had been at the press conference given by Duffy and the Irish Times in the Westbury and was repeatedly putting questions to me about the contents of the tape. I ignored him and kept on with meeting the voters. He had the advantage of a copy of the transcript in his hands whereas I had seen nothing yet.

I decided there and then to go directly to RTE and clear the air on the whole matter. I felt that if I was going to counter this thing it would be better to do so quickly. The tour around Donaghmede was called off and I got in a car and set out for RTE. I put through a call to P.J. Mara on the way and asked him for his advice on how to approach the interview. It was going to be one of the most difficult interviews of my whole career. I was travelling to Montrose in the full knowledge that by telling the truth I would possibly be doing irreparable damage to my campaign for the Presidency. The truth as I saw it would seem incredible to anyone who was viewing. But what was I to do? I could have followed the false gods of perception and credibility into a labyrinth of real lies and fudges. It had been suggested to me that it would be wise to admit ringing and speaking to Dr. Hillery and that people would perceive that to be more credible given the contents of the tape. It was this sort of ethical dishonesty subsequently that caused opposition spokesmen, the PDs and many in the media to demand that I be punished in the interests of government credibility, irrespective of whether I was telling the truth or not. I decided to stick with the truth and trust the people. I put my own reputation for being an honest politician up front with them. P.J. Mara advised me to look straight into the camera and I agreed with this honest approach although it was to cause much comment later.

After I'd finished in Donaghmede, my son Niall was to continue with the planned tour of the other two shopping centres that I would not be getting to. At Northside Shopping Centre Niall met up with the local TD Ivor Callely and the Taoiseach's son Sean Haughey. He explained what had happened and was shown around the shopping centre. He then went to Artane Castle where he met the Taoiseach Mr. Haughey.

Niall, for the first time in his life, enjoyed the odd experience of being shown around a shopping centre being introduced to voters by the Taoiseach as if he were the candidate! There were odder moments to come in a campaign which had more than its fair share of them.

Out at RTE, I met Bertie Ahern. We were both shown into a private room by the station's Head of News Programming, Joe Mulholland. I had heard snatches of what was on the tape but nothing more. I told Bertie that I would speak the truth as I understood it, but we both saw the enormity of the problem in that I was shortly to go on prime time television and give my version of events which was in direct contradiction to what was on the tape.

The Six One News interview began with the Duffy tape excerpt being played. It was my first time to hear it in full and there were about 600,000 people watching. The comparable RTE TAM rating for the same programme a month before that was 200,000 less than that figure. Seán Duignan turned to me and began to question me about the contents of the tape. The essence of my position is best summarised in my reply to his question: "I did not ring President Hillery on that night, I did not speak to him on that night or on any other night in connection with the constitutional matter referred to or any other matters". Facing the cameras instead of the interviewer I pressed home these points, and also stated that I was seeking a meeting with President Hillery to clarify my version of events. When pressed further by Seán Duignan about the contents of the tape I said that I must have been mistaken in what I had told Duffy. It was I said "a casual discussion to which my mind was not attuned". I finished the interview by saying that "I have a long reputation of being honest in public life. People out there know that ... What I want the people to judge is that what I am saying is right."

I knew the interview was going to be difficult and that many people would find it hard to accept the truth of what I was saying.

What effect the interview had with the public is not easy to discern, but media commentators and opposition spokesmen at Leinster House reacted with amazement. Later there was to be much comment on my "face to camera" technique in the interview with one TV critic remarking that even my enemies must have cringed.

However, to me it was the only way of conveying the truthfulness of what I was saying. I could have spent the whole interview debating in a combative way the details of what was contained in the tape. This would have led nowhere. I wanted to make a public appeal to all of those people watching without interference. The phrase "mature recollection" was criticised, but in the light of what I'd apparently said on the tape, how else could I explain my current position? I couldn't explain a taped conversation that I did not remember, and the horrific details of my medical condition, when I gave the Duffy interview, were only pieced together much later.

After Six One, I went to do an interview with Seán O'Rourke for the 6.30 radio news. It was very much the same thing as on the television. I criticised Jim Duffy for going outside the bounds of all ethics in revealing the contents of the tape. "The realities involved are a discussion with a student in UCD that I was befriending and trying to help out, and he has turned against all academic ethics and published a tape, without recourse to me, which he committed himself to do in the course of correspondence to me in which I was already checking out some of his quotes and rejecting them," I told O'Rourke.

It was because of what I had mistakenly said on the tape that made the Six One interview so hard to accept and not the manner in which I said it. I knew before the interview that this would be the case. There were two incompatible versions of what I did back in 1982 and both of them uttered by myself. The truth, therefore, had become so incredible that the more I repeated it, the more obscene it would become to those who did not believe me. The extent to which this is true is brought out vividly in the reaction to my appearence on Six One News by Tony Ward, the former Irish rugby international. Ward, along with other celebrities, was asked by the Irish Independent for his reaction to my interview on the television. Ward clearly did not believe me on Six One. "The whole thing made me cringe. It was pathetic to see someone continuing with a lie when the truth was there for everyone to hear. I just wanted to say, stop! stop! Get off the television!"

From RTE I went to the Incorporated Law Society in Blackhall Place where I was scheduled to appear before a Lawyers For Lenihan reception. Before going into the reception, I held an impromptu press conference with journalists, mostly from the written media, on the day's events. I explained my position in relation to the President and that I did not wish to embroil Dr. Hillery in any controversy. It was for my own peace of mind and to establish the truth that I was seeking to meet him. "I will not ask the President to make a public statement - that is his business, but I will tell you what he said," I told them. I was determined that whatever the President told me should be passed on, even if he had told me I had spoken to him back in 1982. There were many of my old colleagues from the law library at the reception and they were all very supportive. Among them was the barrister Adrian Hardiman who made a speech supporting my candidacy for the Presidency. It was a courageous speech for him to make and one for which I was very grateful. He is one of the few prominent members of the PDs who acquitted himself with honour during the Presidential campaign. I would like to mention Peadar Clohessy TD of East Limerick in this category also.

After that, it was straight back out to RTE for an interview with Today Tonight. Montrose was packed with politicians of every sort, so much so, that it had all the appearance of a general election night as the results are pouring in. Before the programme Alan Dukes, Dick Spring and the opposition were in one room and we were in another. It was the same old questions all over again. However, at one point, Olivia O'Leary, getting closer to the truth than either of us knew at that stage, asked was I drugged when I gave the interview to Duffy. I replied in the negative. She was the only journalist to ask that question.

When the election was over, I was to discover how close she had come to the truth after I had asked my doctors to check back on the dates and details of my medical records. Perhaps it was just as well that it worked out like that because a medical controversy would have been used as yet another brickbat to cast at me in the closing days of the campaign.

The political reaction to the release of the tape and the subsequent interviews was predictably bad. Mary Robinson said that I had apparently lied, adding that "not even Brian Lenihan could wriggle out of this one". She also defended Jim Duffy's actions saying that she would understand the pressure he was under. Fine Gael followed up by tabling a motion of no confidence in the government. Jim Mitchell shouted out in the Dáil chamber that "Brian Lenihan should be hauled in here and hung, drawn and quartered". The PD leader and Minister for Industry and Commerce, Des O'Malley, told the media before leaving for GATT talks in Strasbourg that the "present situation is very disturbing".

This gave rise to speculation that the PDs would not support the government in the no confidence motion. Meanwhile, the PD Chairman, Michael McDowell, had his own reaction to pitch into the debate. "It undoubtedly has clear implications for Mr. Lenihan. It produces problems for the people, for the government and for the PDs," he said. Not for the first time, McDowell would be attempting to influence the course of government from outside. The really disturbing thing about the PDs at this moment is the extent to which they appear to have two reactions to every event that takes place. It makes government very difficult if one of the partners to a coalition has one view for their colleagues and another for public consumption in the media. At least two members of the current government, Albert Reynolds and Michael O'Kennedy, have expressed their concern about this dual approach deployed by the PDs.

Earlier that day I had instructed my private secretary, Brian Spain, to contact the President's office in Áras an Uachtaráin to set up a meeting. He was unable to do this because the President was away and would only be back that night. The next morning Ann and I were flying to Cork where we were to continue the campaign. Overnight there had been strong resistance to the idea of visiting the President to clarify my version of events. The charge had been led by opposition spokesmen the night before and had been taken up by the morning newspapers. The Irish Independent expressed its concern in a front-page editorial counselling against embroiling the President in the heat of the campaign. For these reasons I decided to withdraw my request to meet with the President on the matter.

Down in Cork we were mobbed by supporters at the Airport, with a jazz band there to welcome us at Arrivals. At a press conference I apologised publicly for the mistakes I had made in the Duffy interview. We had all gone to Cork expecting a hostile reception in the wake of the Duffy tape controversy. Instead, we were treated to the warmest welcome we had got on the campaign so far. On the streets of Cork, jammed because of the Jazz Festival, I was mobbed by well-wishers. It was almost as if the tape business had galvanised Fianna Fáil supporters and friends in a very real way. It was then that I began to realise that the Fianna Fáil organisation had been quite complacent up to this but now the sleeping giant was awake when one of their own was clearly in danger.

The revivalist atmosphere that caught the campaign at this stage is well captured by Justine McCarthy of the Irish Independent who wrote of that day in Cork City: "At Wilton Shopping Centre a crowd as big as any ever seen on a general election campaign cheered and clapped as the People's President coach pulled into the car park ... It could have been a rock star who had descended in their midst. Children jostled for autographs, middle-aged men and women - with elbows of iron - fought their way into his presence, veterans of the Party were brought forward to shake his hand. Though Mr. Lenihan was limping, the expression on his face told of a very happy man. "I have never seen the like of it in my life", he announced in the shopping centre. "This indeed is rebel Cork. You do the heart good".

It was then all over the county where there were extraordinary scenes wherever we went. In Mallow the following day, we were escorted through the town by a piped band. On we went through North Cork and into County Limerick: Buttevant, Charleville, Kilmallock, Bruff, Hospital and Caharconlish. It was freezing weather and we were always hours behind time, yet people waited patiently at every stage. Everywhere we went that week-end it was the same, huge crowds and long delays.

Meanwhile, in Dublin, things were taking on a life of their own. Fine Gael's director of elections, Jim Mitchell, confirmed that the party had laid a trap for me when I was questioned about calls to Áras an Uachtaráin on the Questions and Answers programme. He confirmed that Brian Murphy, the man who had asked the crucial question, was a former national Chairman of Young Fine Gael. "Obviously we had done our research and we planned it very well. In that sense it is true to say we had set a trap," declared Mitchell. He denied that Fine Gael knew that this would be followed by the release of the tape. The latter denial is all the stranger given that just one day after the Questions and Answers programme, Fine Gael were boasting to the media that they would produce evidence within 24 hours that I had been involved in attempts to ring Áras an Uachtaráin back in 1982.

On the Friday, Bobby Molloy flew into Ireland and issued a statement which emphasised the PDs role in providing stable government, which seemed to carry the suggestion that they did not want the whole affair to threaten the survival of the government. However, there were again two sides to the PDs. Mary Harney, the Junior Minister at the Environment, told the media that "there must be a strong possibility that the crisis could bring down the government". Later, on the Friday night, the party's leader Des O'Malley flew into Dublin. He had hoped to make his way straight to Kinsealy to see the Taoiseach but judged it too late. In the end, he met with party colleagues apparently at the home of PD Chairman Michael McDowell, who lives in Rathgar. Present at the meeting were the party's three ministers, Pat Cox a member of the European parliament and some of the party's press officers.

Emily O'Reilly catches the mood of this meeting quite well in her book *Candidate*. "He (O'Malley) would speak to Haughey in the morning, he told the gathering, and tell them that the PDs would resign from the Government if he did not sort the matter out. It was a problem of Fianna Fáil's making, not theirs. A view also voiced at the meeting was that the idea that Lenihan would resign could be sold to him (presumably by Haughey) on the basis that he would get a sympathy vote if he did. The meeting decided that Lenihan's resignation would be demanded, but that this would never be explicitly stated in the media".

I emphasise those last two sentences for a reason. Firstly, the idea that resignation would help get me a sympathy vote was precisely the reason eventually used by Mr. Haughey when he tried to sell the idea to me. So, clearly from the outset the PD tail is wagging the Fianna Fáil dog and Mr. Haughey is playing along with it. The last sentence is significant in that it shows the extent to which the PDs knew they were pursuing a dishonest hidden agenda from the beginning and were anxious to hide the fact that they were demanding my resignation. To the public they were just trying to restore credibility in government, but behind the scenes they were looking for my head on a plate.

On the Saturday, Des O'Malley went to see the Taoiseach at his house in Kinsealy. The meeting did not seem to resolve the issue to the PDs satisfaction and they met again, this time at O'Malley's Dublin home. On RTE radio that day, the PDs hardened their line with their MEP Pat Cox stating "We would like to see the government continue, but not at any price. If needs be, there may be an election - because trust and credibility in small things is indivisible from trust and credibility in big things in government." Again the PDs are not spelling out exactly what they want done but Mr. Haughey has been told in no uncertain terms what their price is for continued participation in coalition. Mrs. Robinson, the same day, states "the controversy should not be allowed to detract from the decency of Brian Lenihan's record of public service or be allowed plunge the country into a general election." Fine Gael are becoming worried that it is Mrs. Robinson and not Austin Currie who is benefiting from the tape affair.

On the Sunday, I begin my campaign in the South East. There was a huge crowd of about five thousand people out in Wexford town and earlier there had been massive numbers in Gorey, Enniscorthy and New Ross. For a moment, one could have been forgiven for thinking it was Kelly the Boy from Killane and not Brian Lenihan the Presidential candidate in 1990. On Monday, it would be on to Waterford and Kilkenny. Again there are huge crowds everywhere we go and a vibrant atmosphere to the campaign. However, an Irish Marketing Survey opinion poll printed in the Sunday Independent dampens down any over enthusiasm that might have been generated from the huge crowds and ecstatic reception. Taken in the Dublin area only, the poll shows that my support has plummeted to just 32% with Mrs. Robinson leaping ahead with 51% and Currie trailing on 17%. This reversal is the first indication of how the Duffy tape business is affecting the campaign.

On RTE's This Week programme, Dessie O'Malley is tackled for the first time on his own recollection of events back in 1982. He, too, was on the Fianna Fáil front bench at the time. "To the best of my knowledge a number of people rang Áras an Uachtaráin that night," he told the interviewer, adding that the number could include Brian Lenihan. "I wasn't present when the actual calls were made - I couldn't put my hand on a bible and say," he later told the interviewer. He pointed out that it was his understanding that there was more than one call. How many more he did not specify. In March of this year he was to become less circumspect in an interview with the Irish Times. The paper's political correspondent asked him whether I had made a telephone call to President Hillery in 1982. Mr. O'Malley responded as follows:

"I think what happened in 1982 is largely irrelevant now. What I was concerned with was what happened in 1990 and it is not anyone's opinions, or anyone's versions of the matters that are involved. Mr. Lenihan has given two diametrically opposed accounts of what happened and they can't both be true ... I have always thought it was what happened in 1990 that was relevant."

Later, in the same interview with the Irish Times, he confesses he was not in the room when the alleged phone calls were made back in 1982. However, he then goes on to repeat the claim that "he understands" other calls were made apart from Sylvester Barrett's. Pressed on the point, he goes further than he did at the time of the election and says that "he understands" that I was one of those who made a call. He has now gone a lot further than at the time of the election. If he now "understands" that I was one of a number who made calls, who are the others? Despite not being in the room, he seems to have a very detailed knowledge of who called Áras an Uachtaráin that night. He must surely know that whenever my name is linked to the allegation of having phoned the Áras, so too has the name of the Taoiseach Mr. Haughey been mentioned. If "he understands" that Mr. Haughey was among a number of people who called, why doesn't he tell us? After all, it was his party that was worried last year about the credibility and integrity of the government. One could be tempted to paraphrase Pat Cox in relation to his own leader - credibility in government begins with small things and goes on to bigger items.

Mr. O'Malley's claim that what happened in 1990 was more important than what happened in 1982 is disingenuous in the extreme. It is a convenient formula for him to get around answering the difficult questions thrown up by his own attendance at the Fianna Fáil front bench meeting back in 1982. At that meeting, the decision was taken to ring Áras an Uachtaráin to explain the reasons for our party statement. It is quite dishonest of him to suggest now that I was among those whom "he understands" made phone calls if he is not going to be frank about who else he believes called. After my dismissal, the PDs said the whole controversy could have been avoided if people had admitted to their mistakes. Does Mr. O'Malley believe that it was a "mistake" for the Taoiseach Mr. Haughey to deny he ever threatened an army officer on the phone to the Áras? We should be told. Has he ever tried to confirm "his understanding" with Sylvester Barrett? Mr. Barrett has stated that he rang the Áras on two or three occasions on that evening at the request of Mr. Haughey and the front bench. Mr. Barrett also confirms that I did not ring.

On the Monday after the tape release, we stayed at the Ferrycarrig hotel in Wexford. That morning I get up to do an interview with Kevin Myers of the Irish Times over breakfast. From there, it was on to Waterford. Around lunchtime I met Bertie Ahern in Jury's Hotel, Waterford. The hotel is situated on a hill and has a commanding view of the city. Bertie lands by helicopter.

The main subject of discussion between me and my director of elections is whether I should resign. When Mr. Haughey sent him down to Waterford, it was with instructions to get me straight back to Dublin to meet the Taoiseach at Kinsealy.

However, Bertie did not think that necessary and urged me to continue with my campaign. Bertie said the PDs were raising difficulties over the whole controversy but in particular about the motion of confidence vote in the Dáil. After a general discussion we got down to talking about resignation. I said to Bertie that resignation would wreck my campaign. Bertie agreed with this. I then put it to Bertie that I would resign from government if I lost the Presidential election and that I wished this to be conveyed to the Taoiseach and to Mr. O'Malley. Bertie said that was very reasonable. Our discussion completed, Bertie took the chopper back to Dublin and conveyed the message on to the Taoiseach.

The tour of Waterford continued, while up in Dublin Mr. Haughey called an impromptu gathering of ministers to his home at Kinsealy. I, and my sister Mary, were the only ministers, apart from the PDs, who were not invited to this meeting. My resignation is discussed and is seen by many as the only way out of the current impasse. Mr. Haughey told his colleagues that there was no alternative as the PDs were putting the boot in. The meeting was given the very strong impression that Mr. Haughey put a much higher priority on avoiding a general election than winning the Presidential election.

That evening, my campaign moved from Waterford into Kilkenny. There was a rally in the Newpark Hotel that night. That evening, as I rested before the rally, a call came through from Dublin. It was my son Brian and he was very concerned. He had got wind of what was up. He told me that journalists with the national newspapers were being briefed that evening to expect my resignation in the morning. I had thought that the meeting with the Taoiseach in his home would just be to keep up with events as they had developed between him and the PDs. It now appeared that a public execution was being planned for the morning and the plot was already written in Kinsealy. Later in the evening Michael Dawson received a number of calls from national newspapers asking was it true that I was going to be asked to resign in the morning. Media contacts told us that the story was being put out by sources close to government.

In Dublin, Brian junior and Esmonde Smith moved quickly to dispel the rumours circulating. They feared that an attempt was being made to orchestrate a resignation by making it virtually a fait accompli in the morning's newspapers. They set about telling their own contacts in the various newspaper offices to ignore all suggestions from highly placed government sources, no matter who, that Brian Lenihan was resigning. They warned off individual journalists, alerting them to the fact that the Tánaiste was not resigning. It was a frightening evening in many ways. Here I was after over thirty years in politics and I was being deliberately isolated with just a very few friends that I could depend on. There were no phone calls from political colleagues warning me of what was afoot, just a deafening silence.

That night, something quite surreal happened in the ballroom of the Newpark Hotel. About a thousand activists cheered and sang while I and my family stood on the stage. The music started up and everyone in the audience began to sing "We'll rise and follow Charlie". It was odd to have to put on a brave face and sing along when I alone knew what was going to be suggested the following morning.

Before going to sleep that night, Brian junior rang through with the contents of the next morning's newspapers. He had made the trip into Dublin to get the first editions. They were not as bad as we thought they might be. Tomorrow would be another day. I was certain of one thing. I would not be resigning.

10

DISMISSAL

The helicopter journey to Kinsealy was pleasant. It was a clear morning, if a little crisp. There was a slight chill in the air. Niall and Conor took in the landscape. Michael Dawson, the Campaign Manager, was apprehensive of what was to come. Viewed from the air the countryside looks peaceful. The journey from Kilkenny passed over some of the best farmlands in the country, leaving the Curragh racecourse to our left. The Haughey mansion at Kinsealy is even more impressive from the air with its woodland and adjacent lake. As the helicopter circled, we spotted through the trees at the bottom of the avenue a large gathering of journalists clustered around the entrance. News of the meeting with Mr. Haughey is plastered over the morning papers. We are greeted at the helicopter pad by Ciarán Haughey. Bertie Ahern is standing nearby. Bertie and I go into an adjoining prefabricated hut. The lads stand around chatting in the hangar. Bertie puts me in the picture and tells me that the Taoiseach would be asking me to resign from the Government. It came as no surprise given the turn of events the night before. After a short spell our preliminary chat is over and we make our way up a path and into the house. Bertie tails off to make a few phone calls. The lads are shown downstairs to the kitchen where Maureen Haughey treats them to a cup of coffee.

I met Charlie alone in his private study. The Taoiseach stated that O'Malley and the PDs were being very difficult. He had met O'Malley on the Saturday previous to our meeting and the PD leader had said that his party's support for the Government in the Dáil confidence debate could not be guaranteed unless I was dealt with. The Taoiseach said he had met O'Malley again on Monday and that O'Malley's bottom line was my resignation, or else the support of the PDs would be withdrawn the next day, which would, of course, mean a general election.

The Taoiseach advocated that the best option open to me was my resignation. He said my resignation would help rather than damage my campaign for the Presidency. He said most people would respect me for standing down in the national interest, in order to avoid a general election. Pressing his point further Mr. Haughey said that if I resigned, Dessie O'Malley would issue a statement congratulating me on my decision. The Taoiseach also promised that if I resigned, he would keep the Defence portfolio and the position of Tánaiste vacant, so that if I lost the election I would be immediately re-instated. Mr. Haughey also intimated that Dessie O'Malley's statement on my resignation would include an endorsement of my candidature for the Presidency, thereby improving my chances of victory.

I listened to all of this patiently. I then countered that my resignation would be tantamount to an admission that I had done something wrong as Tánaiste and Minister for Defence which rendered me unfit to serve as a member of the cabinet. It was public knowledge that I had performed well as Minister for Defence and at no stage had anyone suggested otherwise. If I regarded myself as unfit to be Tánaiste and Minister for Defence, then I was unfit to be President. If I resigned, I argued, my campaign would become unsustainable and I would be laughed out of court. The only thing against me was that I was telling the truth in regard to the telephone calls made over eight years ago. I put it to the Taoiseach that he and Mr. O'Malley knew that I was telling the truth because both of them were on the Fianna Fáil front bench on the night the phone calls were made.

I said to the Taoiseach that the people should be allowed to decide the issue in the Presidential election and I guaranteed that if I was defeated in that contest I would resign from the government. I felt this proposal of mine was eminently fair as it would allow the election to proceed on its own merits and it would also avoid the need for a general election. I thought that from Mr. O'Malley's point of view this alternative should be perfectly acceptable. The Taoiseach told me that O'Malley would not agree to it, that all options had been discussed and the only acceptable solution was my resignation. I asked for time to consider the matter and it was agreed that I would go into Leinster House to discuss things with any of my ministerial colleagues who happened to be about.

The meeting had lasted 20 minutes. Queen Beatrix of the Netherlands was arriving at Dublin Airport in a few minutes time, on the opening day of her formal state visit to Ireland. Mr. Haughey, as Taoiseach, would have to be there to welcome her. Time was short so he and Mrs. Haughey, along with the Aide de Camp, Commander Lawn, rushed off to the airport.

Bertie, the lads and I gathered in a room that looks out onto the lawn at the rear of the building. I told all of them that the Taoiseach had asked me to consider resigning and that he had said this would help my campaign. I told the lads their opinion was as good as anyone else's. We chatted for a while and canvassed the different options. Michael Dawson, as Campaign Manager, was determined that resignation would damage the campaign. Conor and Niall agreed with him. It was suggested that if I was to resign I should only do so at the eleventh hour, when it was absolutely certain that there was no other way of avoiding a general election. In other words, that the pressure should be maintained on the PDs to be the ones to bring down the government. At this stage Bertie Ahern intervened to say that things were getting pretty desperate. The PDs, he said, were going to resign from the government at five o'clock that afternoon, if Brian Lenihan hadn't resigned by then.

There were still hordes of journalists and photographers at the gates of Abbeyville. Someone mentioned that it might not look good if we were photographed leaving Kinsealy by car as it would lend an image and atmosphere of crisis to events. Ciarán Haughey volunteered to spin us to the Department of Defence by helicopter. Bertie Ahern left in his own state car. We were met at the department by my private secretary, Brian Spain. As we piled into his small family car, Brian Spain brought me down to earth with the words: "Tánaiste, it's time to start looking after yourself."

When we got to the Dáil, I went straight to my office where I was joined by Ministers Ray Burke, Padraig Flynn, Vincent Brady and of course Bertie Ahern. Ray Burke and Vincent Brady said I had no choice but to resign. Brady was particularly emphatic. Padraig Flynn left the matter to myself. Later on in the discussion Albert Reynolds joined us. He had been abroad and came in at the tail end of the discussion. He didn't see what all the fuss was about. Albert Reynolds saw no reason for resignation, and no reason for haste, the debate on the Dáil motion not being due to take place until the following day ending at seven o'clock. He did not believe, as Brady seemed to think, that I had no choice in the matter. The discussion broke up and I went downstairs to the restaurant to join Conor, Niall and Michael Dawson for something to eat. Albert Reynolds left straight away for Granard where we would meet up again in the afternoon. The campaign tour was in Longford-Westmeath and would finish up that night with a rally in Athlone.

While this discussion was going on at Leinster House, the Taoiseach Mr. Haughey was out at Dublin Airport welcoming Queen Beatrix of the Netherlands. There was only one thing on the journalists' minds. "I will not be asking for the Tánaiste's resignation from cabinet. I will not be putting him under any pressure to resign, nor will his cabinet colleagues. It is entirely a matter for my old friend of thirty years," Mr. Haughey told the press at the airport.

After lunch, I paid another visit to Mr. Haughey, this time at his office in Leinster House. Bertie Ahern accompanied me this time. Mr. Haughey again repeated his promise made earlier in his private study at Kinsealy that morning. If I resigned and lost the election I would be re-instated as Tánaiste and Minister for Defence. This time Mr. Haughey was pushing resignation harder than before. He handed me a three page prepared resignation statement. I said I wanted time to consider the matter. Mr. Haughey said that there was a certain time-pressure as the PDs were meeting at 5 pm that day. I couldn't understand what this pressure might be, but I said I would definitely get word to him on my final decision before five o'clock.

We went to the heli-pad in Stillorgan where I met Frank Dunlop. Frank, a former Government Press Secretary, was handling public relations. I told him of the position, explaining that I had given no commitment to resign, and would be thinking things

over until five o' clock. In the helicopter I got to read my resignation statement, readied up for me earlier by somebody on Mr.
Haughey's staff. It was a bland document which talked of the need
to avoid a general election, so that the good work of the government could continue. It was going to be a long, long day. It was a
difficult decision to have to make. If I resigned, my credibility and
reputation would be destroyed. On the other hand, if I refused to
resign I ran the risk of causing a general election which nobody
wanted but for which I would be forced to share the blame. It was
a silent trip to Granard in County Longford with just the occasional word passing between Conor, Niall and myself as we
contemplated the enormity of what was to come.

The helicopter touched down near the town. Albert Reynolds
was there to meet us. An ITN camera crew was there to record our
arrival as well as photographers from the national press. We were
already behind schedule and the trip was to take us by Granard,
Edgeworthstown, Ballymahon, Lanesboro, Mullingar, Tyrellspass,
Kilbeggan, Moate and finally the rally in Athlone. All place names
to conjure with, each one sparking a fresh memory from my past.
Along the way, I met old friends dating back to my first election in
the Longford-Westmeath constituency when I was a very young
man. I sat up at the front of the bus with Dave Watson the driver,
a cheerful Irish-Scot. We bowled along the Edgeworthstown-
Longford road and I mused on whether I should resign. The
clouds had burst into rain and the darkness of evening was
drawing on. It was just me and my decision alone.

For a while Albert chatted with me at the front of the bus. He
advised me not to resign. My own instinct was to stand and fight
for the truth or else lose all respect by resigning without reason
under PD blackmail. I had to be true to myself if I expected people
to support and vote for me, and there was just one week to go. But
I had a dilemma - the Taoiseach wanted my resignation and time
was running out. The decision was mine and it was a lonely one to
have to make. In deciding not to resign I knew I would be drawing
down a barrier between myself and most of my ministerial colleagues and all those urging me along a different path. I stood up
from my perch at the front and walked down to the end of the bus

where there was a small partitioned-off room. My wife Ann was sitting there on her own. I told her I was not going to resign. Her eyes filled with tears. I held Mr. Haughey's resignation letter in my hand and suddenly, becoming conscious of it, I held it up to her and joked, "I don't suppose I'll be needing this." She looked at it for the first time and threw it aside.

At Longford town I instructed Michael Dawson to ring the Taoiseach and tell him that I would not be resigning. It was important he should know before five o'clock as he had told me that was the PD deadline. There was an impromptu rally in the ballroom of the Longford Arms Hotel as it was raining outside. After my speech, Gerry Reynolds, the Midlands Correspondent for RTE, requested an interview. The camera crew were set up and the arc lights turned on. I was a bit apprehensive as Dawson had not come back to me yet to confirm that he had told the Taoiseach I was not resigning. So rather than have the Taoiseach learn of my decision via RTE I fudged a bit on the resignation question.

The campaign went on and the bus rolled off towards Lanesboro. Many miles away and down the Shannon the fierce pressure of events was taking on a life of its own. Gerry Slevin, Editor of the Nenagh Guardian, was also under pressure with a newspaper to get out. Tuesday was always a busy day in the life of this provincial newspaper. The paper goes to press on a Wednesday and a lot of the material comes in on the previous day. A long three page fax came through in one piece at twelve minutes past four in the afternoon. It was brought into him but he had other things on his mind and set it to one side, after splitting it into three pages and stapling it. The statement was from the Minister for Science and Technology, Michael Smith,one of the local Fianna Fáil TDs. "I pieced it together and took it to be an ordinary message boosting Brian Lenihan in the Presidential campaign." But when he got around to reading it he was taken by surprise. The first two pages were innocuous enough. However, on the last of the three pages the final two paragraphs of the statement read as follows:

"Brian Lenihan has decided once again to put Ireland and the Irish people first. His resignation from Government was a very difficult and personal decision but one he took to ensure continuing strong government and avoid an inevitable general election, an election which the Irish people don't need or want.

"Despite the recent media storm about events 8 years ago, Brian Lenihan has been and remains a decent honourable and most likeable person. He has served the country well in good days and in bad. He has made a remarkable recovery in his health and with your help on November 7th he will be elected to be a great President over the years ahead."

Gerry Slevin had not been taking much notice of the developments in the Presidential election campaign that day, things were so busy. However, he still thought he would have heard it if Brian Lenihan had resigned.

"My initial reaction to the statement was that it must have happened, Brian Lenihan has resigned. I asked others in the office had it happened and they all said no. For a second I thought Michael Smith was trying to get in first because of the intense rivalry between him and Michael O'Kennedy in this constituency," he says.

He decided to get to the bottom of the thing and rang through to RTE and asked to be put through to the newsroom.

He introduced himself and asked had there been any developments in the Brian Lenihan business. He was told "No." He told the journalist in the newsroom that he had a statement from Michael Smith saying that Brian Lenihan had resigned. There was a momentary silence at the other end as the full consequence of what he was saying sank in. RTE asked him to fax them the statement.

At around twenty past four Michael Smith rang the Nenagh Guardian and Slevin identified the voice immediately. Smith spent no time beating around the bush. He mentioned the statement, a note of urgency entering his voice, and added, "If you go down towards the end of it there's something that shouldn't be there."

"I think I realise that," said Slevin. Smith pointed out that what he had in the paragraph was not true and asked Slevin to keep it out of the paper. In normal circumstances a local newspaper might be expected to agree to such a request from a local politician. However, at this stage Gerry Slevin told the Minister that it was out of his hands as RTE had a copy of the statement. Smith said "Oh God" and put down the phone. He rang back again at about ten to five and asked him had he given the statement to anybody else, to which Gerry Slevin replied "No."

Back in Longford on the bus everyone listened to the RTE news bulletin at five o'clock in stunned silence. Whatever lingering doubts I had about my decision not to resign they had now disappeared. My first impression on hearing that news was that it had been a planned thing. It struck me immediately that the statement was issued by Smith in all sincerity on his part believing I had resigned. I surmised, perhaps wrongly, from my years of political experience, that Smith had also been offered the Defence portfolio by the Taoiseach. I then fully comprehended that the assurances given to me by the Taoiseach at lunchtime about my re-instatement as Minister for Defence were just part of a process of getting me out of the way.

In Lanesboro, there was a short meeting in the town hall. The town straddles the Shannon, Longford on one side, Roscommon on the other. Here the mood is determinedly against resignation, though I tell nobody that I meet, that my mind is made up and I'm not resigning. The schedule is well over time. We make our way back to Athlone stopping off in Mullingar. In the meantime Dawson has told me he has been in contact with the Taoiseach and given him my message. It is then, in Mullingar's Greville Arms that I publicly confirm for the first time that day that I am not resigning. There are two cameras there to record it but both of them are British television crews. On the bus Niamh O'Connor has conveyed the news to RTE. Brendan O'Brien and a crew from *Today Tonight* are on their way down at breakneck speed from Dublin. The RTE newsroom has also sent Gerry Reynolds chasing after the bus because his earlier interview is now of little worth. Both the camera crews meet up with me at the town of Moate. In the middle of its wide street I do the interview for the news bulletin that night. Back on the bus, a short distance outside the town, Brendan O'Brien does his piece.

Then, it is on into Athlone with the rest of the cavalcade

travelling ahead. Ann and I go first to our old friends, the O'Callaghans, where we are staying that night. At 7 pm that evening the Progressive Democrats have been meeting in Dublin. After meeting for about two hours at their Molesworth Street headquarters in Dublin, Dessie O'Malley emerges to tell waiting reporters: "Since no final response has been received from Mr. Haughey to the point raised by me at our meetings, our parliamentary party has agreed to meet tomorrow to consider such a final response from Fianna Fáil, if it is received." Following that meeting the PDs apparently threatened to pull out of the government the following morning unless my resignation had been secured.

At the Prince of Wales Hotel in Athlone things are chaotic. There are between two and three thousand people crammed into the hotel for the rally. The venue for the rally is far too small and the supporters are spilling out onto the street disrupting the traffic flow through the town, something of a bottleneck at the best of times. My son Brian, a barrister friend of his Esmonde Smith, and Frank Dunlop are down in Athlone ahead of a posse of ministers. Smith, a former adviser to Jack Lynch, has been helping the campaign writing speeches. Bertie Ahern has been sent down by the Taoiseach who is clearly still dissatisfied with my earlier message that I would not be resigning. Padraig Flynn is also down on the same mission. Two rooms upstairs in the hotel have been set aside for them and they are wondering if they will be able to change my mind. The two ministers are joined by Albert Reynolds. The atmosphere in the Prince of Wales was frenetic. At one point, there were bad tempered exchanges as my sister Mary O'Rourke upbraided the ministers for their attempts to get me to resign. "You come in guile Padraig Flynn, not in friendship," she reportedly told her colleague. Downstairs the mood was becoming hostile. The activists, supporters and friends had been waiting a long time for my arrival. In the delay, word had got around that there were ministers upstairs in the hotel who had come down from Dublin to get me to resign. Feelings were running high and the ministers would not go down to the lobby for fear of what might happen. When I did arrive at the hotel I was mobbed by people. Members of the local organisation formed a tight ring around me to keep the well-wishers at bay.

As we pushed down the hotel's narrow corridor and into the conference hall the audience were chanting "No resignation, no resignation". The sound carried upstairs where both Bertie Ahern and Padraig Flynn waited, unable to join me on the platform because they were afraid of what they thought was a hostile mob. Albert Reynolds and my sister made defiant speeches and I told a delighted audience that I would not be resigning.

Back in Dublin there has been a picket outside Fianna Fáil's headquarters in Mount Street demanding that I not be asked to resign. According to my son Paul the phone in our home in Castleknock has barely stopped ringing all night with callers urging me not to resign. Members of the Fianna Fáil organisation from all over the country are leaving messages at party headquarters, my home, and finally in the Prince of Wales Hotel itself urging me not to resign. It is almost as if the more I confirm that I am not doing so, the more the messages come through. My constituency Chairman, Eamon Nolan, has also left his message from Dublin West at the Hotel.

After the rally I made my way out of the hotel. The crush was frightening. We spent the night with the O'Callaghans who live a few minutes from the centre of the town. In the confusion I had failed to meet up with Bertie Ahern. However, he had spoken to Conor that night and assured him that I was not needed the next morning in the Dáil. Later that night before going to bed, I put through a call to Bertie on his car phone. It was twenty past midnight and he was on his way back to Dublin. I confirmed that I would not be resigning and asked him to pass it on to the Taoiseach, which he dutifully did. It was agreed that I need not be up for the Order of Business in the Dáil the next morning. There was no need to be there as the Dáil would go straight into debate on the confidence motion with the vote already arranged for 7 pm. I got some sleep and Conor rang through to the Prince of Wales to tell Michael Dawson, the campaign manager, that the helicopter ordered for the morning was no longer necessary. I had decided to make my own way up and at my own leisure.

Before I'd woken the next morning, and unknown to me, the Kildare deputy Charlie McCreevey put through a call to the Junior Minister at the Department of the Environment. It was around 7 am and he was appealing to Mary Harney to hold off pulling the plug on the Government. They were threatening to withdraw from the Government before the debate got underway. McCreevey had been on friendly terms with Harney since their joint participation in the heaves against Mr. Haughey back in the early eighties. The Kildare deputy did not join the PDs but maintained his earlier friendship with them. He was an influential link in setting up the negotiations before the formation of the current coalition. McCreevey told Harney that they should put off their meeting until after the Fianna Fáil parliamentary party met. He assured her that Mr. Haughey would get a mandate to do whatever he liked from the TDs.

That morning at the O'Callaghans' home, there were to be some pretty extraordinary scenes. Despite being told the previous night to cancel the helicopter, Michael Dawson had pressed ahead. Both he and the press officer, Niamh O'Connor, were clearly under great pressure to get me up to Dublin. They both arrived at O'Callaghans' door asking to see me. Maureen O'Callaghan told them that I was resting and that as far as she understood, I was not travelling to Dublin by helicopter. Dawson would not accept this and insisted on hearing that from me. Maureen had no intention of waking me up and told him so. When he persisted she told him politely that she was going for her breakfast. While she made the tea, Dawson and Niamh O'Connor stayed outside communicating with Dublin by mobile phone. There were streams of calls coming through.

Sometime later the helicopter piloted by Ciarán Haughey came by overhead. As I lay in bed I was woken by this thunderous noise over the house. The clatter of helicopter blades and the noise of the engine so nearby seemed a little unnecessary. Still dozing I sat up in the bed. My son Niall came up to the bedroom. He looked out the upstairs bedroom window and saw, less than ten feet away, the undercarriage of the helicopter. My first comment to him sitting up in the bed was to joke that it was getting like

Vietnam around here! It was 9 am and I was still tired from the night before. It was my intention to get more sleep so I told Niall to instruct those outside that I would not be travelling to Dublin till later. He went out and relayed on the message.

Then a series of calls came through. One of them was from my private secretary Brian Spain who was in a bit of a panic. The Whip's office had been on to him telling him I was needed up in Dublin for the Order of Business. He told Conor that Vincent Brady was quite adamant that I was needed in case there was a vote on the Order of Business. I knew from the night before, from both Mary O'Rourke and Bertie Ahern, that this was not the case. In fact, a few minutes later, Bertie rang and spoke again to Conor. He said there was absolutely no need for me to be in the Dáil that day as the vote was not until 7 pm. Bertie seemed to be calmer and more relaxed than everybody else up in Dublin that day. Yet the calls kept coming through. It was clear an atmosphere of panic and paranoia was being created up in Dublin. An official from the Department of Defence rang through to my driver in his car suggesting that I was being held hostage by my family and that if I didn't come up soon, they would ask the Gardai in Athlone to get a search warrant. The driver told the caller they must be off their head. The allegation that I was in some way a hostage of my family was ludicrous. My host Brendan O'Callaghan was a former Chief Superintendent of the Gardai – hardly the kind of man to preside over the kidnapping of a Tánaiste and Minister for Defence. It was clear to me that pressure for my early return was being applied at a very high level.

With these antics over I came down for breakfast and sat listening to the radio as it broadcast the opening exchanges in the Dáil confidence debate. I listened to Mr. Haughey denying opposition charges that he had telephoned Áras an Uachtaráin back in 1982 and threatened an Army officer.

As I sat over breakfast I considered the various options open to the Taoiseach. The country was facing a general election unless something could be done. My own role, I felt at this stage, was pretty marginal. It was up to both the Taoiseach and Mr. O'Malley to sort things out. I had already well indicated that I would not be resigning. My presence at Leinster House would just see me subjected to further and unnecessary pressure to resign. I had done nothing wrong and there was simply nothing to resign about. My belief that the Presidential Election should be decided by the people and nobody else was echoed by Mr. Haughey in the Dáil debate:

"The Presidential election campaign is not a government matter; it is a matter for the people. To attempt to take the election away from the people in this way and to try and have it decided here by a vote in the Dáil is not democratic, it is an infringement of the people's right to decide who should be President."

Not only was the election a matter for the people but the telephone calls to the Park had happened nearly nine years previously and had not caused any controversy in the intervening period. I felt that if the PDs brought down the government on this issue, then they would be blamed by the people for the ensuing general election. My own instinct was that when it came to the crunch they would back off. All that was required was to face them down. After all, with only 3% support in the most recent opinion poll, the PDs could face annihilation in the election, an event which, in my humble opinion, would have been in the national interest.

Up in Dublin the parliamentary party was having its first and inconclusive meeting. It began around 11.30 am but was soon adjourned, as the Taoiseach had to attend a luncheon appointment for Queen Beatrix. "Of all the days, why do we have a queen visiting?" Mr. Haughey asked the deputies. In his opening remarks, Mr. Haughey spoke of the very difficult situation facing the government and how he hadn't the opportunity to discuss the matter with the Tánaiste and that "it was a matter of grave concern that he could not contact him". He went on to state that it was a very serious situation from a constitutional point of view if he could not make contact with me. That this was not the case was quickly established. At this point in the Taoiseach's speech, Senator Edward Bohan interrupted him saying, "It's not that difficult to contact him. He was in Athlone last night and I was talking to him myself this morning on the phone."

Mr. Haughey began to lose his temper at this point and gruffly told Senator Bohan that, if he was in contact with him, to tell Brian Lenihan that the Taoiseach wanted to talk to him. The meeting then adjourned until the afternoon. After the meeting my constituency colleague, Liam Lawlor, and Senator Bohan stood around chatting in the corridor just outside the Whip's office. While they were there Mr. Haughey came along, still, it seems, in a bit of a temper. He told Eddie Bohan in front of Liam Lawlor, "If I cannot contact my Tánaiste and Minister for Defence I'll have to sack him."

In retrospect this would seem to be the first, albeit inadvertent, public admission by the Taoiseach that the option of sacking me was one of the options he was turning over in his own mind. What is strange about Mr. Haughey's behaviour is that, at no stage, either in the morning or the afternoon, did he try to get in contact with me. Yet, already, he seemed to be preparing the ground for something by telling TDs that he could not contact me and that this was intolerable. A number of people were able to get through quite easily while I was in the O'Callaghans home in Athlone, including two ministers, a Senator, my private secretary, and, absurdly, a journalist from the town who wanted to interview Brendan O'Callaghan for a local angle on the big national story. At no stage that morning, or indeed later in the afternoon did I get a call from Mr. Haughey or indeed from any of his personal staff seeking to speak to me. If he had wanted to contact me he could have done so at any stage that day by simply picking up a phone. In fact, my son Brian and Esmonde Smith were representing me in my Dáil office all that day, and were in constant communication with me and everybody else

At the lunch in Iveagh House, Queen Beatrix was to pleasantly observe that, "We realise that today other issues are occupying your mind." Quoting Edmund Burke, she perhaps unwittingly got to the heart of the day's events when she said, "All government is founded on compromise and barter." In the chamber, the Dáil debate on the confidence motion continued with a vengeance. It was to be an extraordinarily bitter debate, the virulence of which had not been seen at Leinster House for some years. All three of the opposition leaders accused Mr. Haughey of ringing Áras an Uachtaráin back in 1982, each one in turn accusing him of being abusive to an army officer on the night in question.

The Labour Party Leader, Dick Spring, was to lead the pack in terms of bitterness with a contribution which many subsequently criticised for its language and content. The key passage, much criticised since, read as follows:

"This debate is not about Brian Lenihan, when it is all boiled down. This debate, essentially, is about the evil spirit that controls one political party in this Republic, and it's about the way in which that spirit has begun to corrupt the entire political system in our country. This is a debate about greed for office, about disregard for truth and about contempt for political standards. It is a debate about the way in which a once great party has been brought to its knees by the grasping acquisitiveness of its leader. It is ultimately a debate about the cancer that is eating away at our body politic - and the virus which caused that cancer, An Taoiseach, Charles J. Haughey."

At one stage, it was being contemplated that I might make a contribution to the Dáil debate but on balance I did not consider it a good idea. Given the virulence and invective in the debate, it was probably just as well that I stayed away. Brian and Esmonde Smith, ensconced in my office in Leinster House, kept an eye on things as they developed there and were kept in regular contact with me. They were, at all stages, able to keep me abreast of events as they unfolded in Dublin. Ann and I left for Dublin around lunchtime with Peg Fogarty travelling with us in the car. Peg is an old family friend and also worked in my private office at the department. It was originally intended that we would go to our home in Castleknock but, when we rang there, my son Paul told us that there were at least half a dozen journalists and photographers camped outside. It was then decided we would spend the final hour or two before the vote at Peg's home in Rathgar. On the way up in the car, I prepared a statement to be read to the parliamentary party later in the afternoon. I decided not to attend because I thought that it might inhibit rather than help discussion. On my journey from Athlone to Dublin, Mary O'Rourke rang through to fill me in on what was happening at her end.

At around half past three the parliamentary party resumed its discussions. Before this, according to Gerald Barry, the political correspondent for the Sunday Tribune, Mr. Haughey "was able to tell Des O'Malley, in phone contact and at meetings, that the problem would be resolved. He would not say how." After lunch, Brian, Deputy Liam Lawlor and Esmonde Smith were busy cross-checking my statement, which I had phoned through to them. In the afternoon, there was to be a discussion between all of them and Mary O'Rourke as to who should read the statement to the meeting. It was first thought that Mary should deliver it, but she felt it might not look too good for a sister to deliver it. Liam Lawlor agreed with her and quickly put in that he could present it as my constituency colleague. Copies of the statement were made and Liam went up to the fifth floor to deliver it.

When the Dublin West TD entered the room, the Taoiseach was putting pressure on deputies, saying he had to meet O'Malley at five o'clock. "He was still trying to create the impression for deputies that there were further meetings and possibilities. This confusion was helped by his speech of the previous day at the airport where he said he would not force his friend of 30 years to resign. That was the impression the bulk of TDs had," says Liam. While he was there, a number of deputies including Charlie McCreevey were saying that a Taoiseach must do what a Taoiseach must do. None of the deputies explicitly spelt out what they meant and perhaps they didn't want to either. At one point there was confusion as deputies asked, did the Taoiseach need a mandate from the parliamentary party to retrieve the Dáil situation and avoid a general election. The answer came from the top table that the Taoiseach did not need such a mandate. However, it is clear that Mr. Haughey wanted some sort of sanction, no matter how muddied, from deputies. He wanted anybody who was unhappy to say so now, rather than blame him later for what they were sanctioning.

It was about twenty to five when Liam Lawlor got to deliver the statement. He stressed from the outset that he was in no position to answer questions, that he was simply conveying the Tánaiste's message to the meeting. Liam was seated just behind those at the top table who included Jim Tunney, as Chairman of the parliamentary party, Mr. Haughey and deputy John Browne from Wexford. The statement read as follows:

"I do not propose to resign as Tánaiste and Minister for Defence. I have carried out my duties as Minister for Defence to the fullest extent of my abilities. I am proud of the improvements I have effected in the arrangements for pay and conditions of service in the Defence Forces.

"I do not wish to delay the deliberations of the parliamentary party for too long but I do want to say a few pertinent things to each and every one of you.

"I am your candidate for the office of President. I am proud to have been chosen by you, after a democratically held vote in this very room, to carry the banner for Fianna Fáil in this important election. This party has a long and proud tradition of service to the Irish people and I am proud to have been associated with that tradition for over 30 years. Your confidence in me as the Fianna Fáil candidate is based on your knowledge and appreciation of my contribution to this party and to public life in Ireland.

"Everybody here, without exception, knows what I stand for - and honesty and integrity are chief among the guiding principles of my public life.

"I would remind you that when called upon to do so - on very many occasions - I helped to maintain the unity and purpose of this party in times of difficulty, and often was subjected to the slings and arrows of ridicule and public criticism for doing so. I have given my all towards preserving the strength and vitality of the Fianna Fáil organisation, not only in my own constituency, but throughout the whole of Ireland. Time after time I have led with others from the front, and not only during election campaigns. I have supported every democratically elected leader of this party, Seán Lemass, Jack Lynch and Charlie Haughey.

"When I give my support I give my all and I have no doubt that that commitment, loyalty and support will now be reciprocated in full by the parliamentary party and the organisation as a whole.

"In conclusion, I want to thank you for the magnificent support which all of you and your supporters have given throughout this campaign. With your continued support I have no doubt that my election to the office of President of Ireland is assured."

After this statement was read a number of deputies spoke, among them Seán Power, Síle De Valera, Noel Dempsey and M.J. Nolan, all indicating that if the choice was to be between sacrificing Brian Lenihan and facing a general election, they were in favour of going to the polls. Seán Power from Kildare put it bluntly when he put it to the Taoiseach that if it was Brian Lenihan's head they were looking for today, what would happen in six months time when they looked for the Taoiseach's head on a plate. Others who apparently did not favour capitulation to the PDs demands included Ned O'Keefe, John Browne, Dick Roche, Seamus Cullimore and Joe Jacob. More speakers were offering. From his position seated behind the top table Liam Lawlor says, "I got the impression that those at the top table were getting quite worried at the level of support for Brian." An element of panic was setting in. Sitting at the front of the meeting, one TD turned around to the rest of the assembled deputies and said it was the Taoiseach's prerogative to take whatever action was necessary to avoid a general election. Time was pressing on and the meeting broke up amid some confusion.

Mr. Haughey went from that meeting to meet with the PD leader Dessie O'Malley. It is not clear what transpired when they met. It may have been a last ditch effort by the Taoiseach to avoid what was now becoming an inevitable choice in his own mind between sacking me or facing a general election. In the meantime, Albert Reynolds and others made their own final attempt to resolve things by seeking to set up a meeting between me and Dessie O'Malley. A room at the Berkeley Court was hastily arranged where it would have been possible to enter and leave without being noticed. The notion was that some face to face meeting between the two of us might break the impasse. The proposal was tentatively put to me down the phone while I was at Peg Fogarty's home in Rathgar. I rejected this proposal believing that it could yield little. The main reason why I did not go ahead with this meeting was that I simply did not trust O'Malley. He would probably have used the encounter to press me again to resign, a course I had firmly decided was not on the cards. There was also the possibility that news of the encounter would end up all over the papers the next day. If the Government had fallen. then this meeting would have been cited as another reason why I was to be blamed for the resulting general election. In any event, I was in no mood for what struck me as a macabre political encounter with my putative executioner. At this stage, the problem was a matter for the Taoiseach and O'Malley to sort out between them.

Fergus Finlay, the Labour Party press officer, has claimed that my removal from Government was just one of a number of options offered to Mr. Haughey. "On the day of the vote of no confidence in the Government, I received a call from a senior member of the PD executive, who is not a member of the Government, with a message for the Leader of the Labour Party. He wanted to make it clear that the PDs had not specifically asked for the sacking of Brian Lenihan. He added that they wanted the Government to put its house in order and suggested a number of ways that this might be achieved. One option was that the whole phone call to the Áras saga might be solved by the setting up, after the Presidential election, of a public inquiry. He stressed that the PDs would vote for the government if they got agreement on this," Finlay told the Irish Independent last year.

Interviewed for this book, Fergus Finlay said the phone call came from Strasbourg on the morning of the no confidence debate. "What was the motive? Perhaps for the record because they believed at that stage that the Government was going to fall and that they would be left carrying the can for bringing it down. The message from Strasbourg was passed from one European colleague to another," says Finlay. Though the latter would not reveal from whom the message came, it would not be improbable to surmise that it came from Pat Cox. He is a member of the European Parliament and a senior member of the PD executive.

The suggestion that there were other options available to Mr. Haughey begs a number of questions. If there were other options why weren't these put to me, to other colleagues and finally to the parliamentary party itself? All three should have been told. The promise of a public inquiry after the election would not have damaged my campaign and would have satisfied the PDs public demand that "credibility" in the government be restored. It must also be asked why Mr. Haughey, if given this alternative course, chose to dismiss me rather than hold a public inquiry into the events of 1982? Surely he, more than anybody else, had nothing to lose by such an inquiry into who exactly phoned Áras an Uachtaráin on the night in question? Had he not already, on that morning of my dismissal, rejected, in the most trenchant and forthright manner, allegations that he in fact had abused an army officer on the phone to the Áras that night? The real truth, of course, may be that the PDs were only suggesting that there were other options in order to absolve themselves from the ultimate blame of either seeking my dismissal or bringing down the government.

The assertion that there were other options open to Mr. Haughey has not only been made by Fergus Finlay. With just two days to polling day, the PD Minister for Energy, Bobby Molloy, told the Irish Independent there had been a "range of options" open to Fianna Fáil other than sacking me. He would not say what these options were. Pushed further on the matter, he then, according to the Irish Independent, resolutely refused to confirm or deny that Brian Lenihan's resignation or sacking was the price the PDs demanded for their support.

Their various pronouncements on the matter, both then and subsequently, have been contradictory in the extreme. It must be noted that none of the PD members of the current government, nor any spokesperson for the PDs, would agree to speak on the record about their role in my dismissal for the purposes of this book.

As the afternoon darkened into evening, I waited in a small house in Rathgar for the call that never came from the Taoiseach. His suggestion to the parliamentary party and others that I was incommunicado was grossly misleading. During my short stay at Rathgar there had been calls from a number of people including ministers. At one point there was even a visit from Senator Edward

Bohan and Michael Dawson. My son Brian rang from Leinster House to say the word was out, Charlie was going to sack me. He and Esmonde Smith then travelled out to Rathgar. In the end I took the initiative and rang the Taoiseach at his office in Leinster House. It was just before six o'clock in the evening with one hour to go in the confidence debate. When he again asked me directly to resign, I replied "No."

"It would have helped your campaign, you know," Mr. Haughey said from Leinster House. "We'll agree to differ on that," I replied. He then explained he would be exercising his constitutional prerogative to dismiss me. The telephone conversation lasted a little over a minute. I left the small room to the left of the hall after replacing the receiver and returned to the adjacent room where my family and a number of friends were. "Well, it's done, the Taoiseach has dismissed me," I told them. It was as if a huge burden had been lifted from all of our backs. The relief was palpable on every face, the pressure of the last few days had told on everybody in that room.

Barely minutes after our conversation, the letter confirming my dismissal arrived out by car. Though I was, according to the Taoiseach, incommunicado, he had no difficulty in delivering the letter to me within double quick time. My private Secretary, Brian Spain, stepped from the state car and told me he had a letter from the Taoiseach. At this stage I was in my own car and ready to go into Leinster House. "I am aware of what's in it and I've already replied," I said. Peg Fogarty took a lift with my old friend from Athlone, John Keane, and was in tears as she was driven into Leinster House. With less than half an hour to go in the confidence debate, I was travelling into the Dáil, and the Government would be saved from a general election. I was dismissed from government, and it was incalculable how all of this would affect my campaign. I only knew that if I had resigned things would have got a lot worse.

The final journey into Leinster House was a difficult one. It is very hard, in an instant, to bid goodbye to years of service as a minister. We had arranged to meet my youngest son Paul near Leinster House. He had travelled from school and still did not know what had happened. We had no idea how he would take it and we didn't want him to hear from someone else while he was waiting around. One of the family jumped out of the car and told him. He took it very calmly and said he was glad that I had kept my dignity. Inside Leinster House the news was still not out that I had been dismissed. As I went down the corridor towards the Visitors bar, a surprised Caroline Erskine from Century radio asked one of the company what was up. She looked slightly incredulous when she was told that the Taoiseach had sacked Brian Lenihan. When I arrived in the Dáil's Visitors bar it was almost as if I were Banquo's ghost. A hushed silence came over the bar. I met the Cathaoirleach of the Seanad, Seán Doherty, at the counter and ordered a mineral water. Journalists standing nearby did not know quite what to do. Many of them were colleagues of my son Conor and he broke the news. I went out to vote confidence in the government. In the hall below the stairs up to the Dáil chamber, Conor was being besieged with questions from journalists wondering how it had all happened. It was now clear that my interests were becoming quite distinct from the Taoiseach's. Esmonde Smith was appointed press spokesman for Brian Lenihan, the former Tánaiste and Presidential candidate.

At around ten to seven Mr. Haughey stood up in the Dáil and made his announcement:

"I regret to have to inform the House that this evening I requested the Tánaiste and Minister for Defence, Deputy Brian Lenihan, to resign as a member of the Government and he failed to comply with my request. Accordingly, I propose to exercise my constitutional prerogative to advice the President to terminate his appointment as a member of the Government."

Shortly after 7 pm the Government won its vote of confidence by 83 votes to 80. The PDs had exacted their price for continued support. The party of "honest government" did not contribute one word to the Dáil debate of confidence in the government. There was not a single clap from the government benches when the vote was announced.

After the vote, I and members of the campaign went up to a room behind the chamber. Some of Mr. Haughey's advisers were urging me to keep up with the campaign schedule. I was due in Castlebar that night and they suggested I should hold a press conference about the sacking there. At this stage it seemed to me that they were trying to shuffle me off the stage. In matters of government, damage limitation starts early on. I decided I was holding a press conference immediately before I left. It would have been wrong to deny the media, who had patiently waited outside, the courtesy of a press conference. I then went up to see Mr. Haughey in his room. He had asked for a meeting. There was a brief exchange of words but there was little left to say. It was a sad and emotional occasion.

Out into the chilly night I went and across the plinth at Leinster House, pursued on all sides by supporters, friends and the pressing cameramen. There were a hundred or so supporters at the gate who had waited all evening. At Setanta House I began a press conference. I read from a statement that I had prepared moments before with Brian and Esmonde Smith. I will not quote it all but it sums up how I felt:

"My refusal to resign was based on the completely honourable view which I hold, in that my considered recollection of the events referred to in the recent controversy nearly nine years ago, is the correct and absolute truth in regard to events at that time as far as I was concerned personally. At no time did I suggest other than that.

"As far as I personally am concerned, I was not involved in any contacts with President Hillery at that particular time or since on that particular constitutional issue. I want to make that quite clear. That is the reason why I refused to resign and I would hope that my refusal to resign adds emphasis to the fact that what I want to see is the truth established. I am perfectly happy with what has eventuated and I will let history decide my veracity and the history of the future has started to unfold just now."

After answering a few questions I stressed that it was full steam ahead in my bid to become President of Ireland. I left by plane for Knock in Mayo, the campaign would go on. From there I went to Castlebar where I addressed a rally attended by over a thousand people.

The last words on that day's events should be left to Neil T. Blaney who, on the vote of confidence in the government, abstained:

"A Cheann Comhairle, might I be given an opportunity of recording my abstention deliberately for the reason that I am sick of the performance that has taken place? It is a disgrace to this house."

Neil Blaney has been a member of Dáil Éireann since 1948.

The Resignation Letter

— AS GIVEN TO BRIAN LENIHAN BY AN TAOISEACH CHARLES HAUGHEY

In my thirty years in politics and as a long-serving Minister I have tried never to be a divisive figure. In difficult times for either the Government or the Fianna Fáil Party, I have always played the role of reconciler — often at considerable personal costs.

I deeply regret in clarifying my recollections of events of over eight years ago, the ensuing controversy seems to have put the Government in danger and heightened the risk of a premature and unnecessary General Election. This would be the last thing I would wish.

From my long Government experience, I agree with the almost universal view that the present Government and its Fianna Fáil predecessor have been among the best since the foundation of the state. In the interests of the Irish people, it is absolutely necessary that nothing should deflect the Government from its work at this stage.

I am sorry for the embarrassment a carelessly inaccurate private interview seems to have caused the Government, the Fianna Fáil party and my family and countless friends through the country.

I see clearly that the Presidential Election and the survival of the Government are separate and distinct and must be kept apart, I wish to do that.

Accordingly, I have today tendered my resignation as Tánaiste and Minister for Defence in order to enable the Government to continue with its successful programme. This decision is mine and mine alone. I have not been subject to pressure from any quarter.

I want the people and not the Dáil to decide who should be their President. I believe I am doing that and that my party, my colleagues and above all the people will agree.

I am more determined than ever to win the Presidential Election. In a lifetime in politics, I have faced more than the normal ups and downs — political and especially personal. I have never shirked a battle, and I will not do so now. I will now be free to concentrate all my energies and efforts on my campaign to be the people's President.

11

SEVEN DAYS

With seven days left in the campaign, I was dismissed from the government. Wednesday, November 7 would finally decide everything. My departure from government was not without sadness. However, the pressure on me and the campaign over the previous week had brought things to breaking-point. The next morning's newspapers were full of the story of my sacking. There were profiles of me and my political life to date. The coverage had all the hallmarks of obituary writing. My old friend, now sadly deceased, John Healy, wrote a two page spread in the Independent about myself, Haughey and Donogh O'Malley in the good old days. John had appeared on The Late Late Show tribute programme back in March and explained that the saddest task he was ever asked to do was to compile my obituary. That was when I was on death's door and about to receive a liver transplant. This time, good professional that he was, John was taking no chances. He began his article with the words, "Brian Lenihan isn't quite finished. I am long enough in this business to know when to write a man's obituary. That time is not yet." While there was sadness the day after the dismissal, it was mixed with a sense of relief. My dismissal from government, I hoped, would bury the Duffy tape issue and the electorate would have a chance to judge the candidates on their individual merits. While it would be unrealistic to expect that the voters would forget the tape issue entirely, it was not unreasonable to expect that public attention would be refocused back to the selection of a President.

On the Thursday morning, my wife and I went into the city centre for a planned walk-about in Henry Street. There were over a thousand people there to greet us. At one point the crowd was blocking one side of O'Connell Street. It proved impossible to meet anyone. There was also a small group of anti-extradition protesters around making noise. The canvass or walk-about never really got anywhere. There were no great political developments that day. There was one thing of note which was never really picked up by the media in the manner that I thought it might be at the time. I told journalists that if I was elected President I would release any record that existed about the controversial affair of the phone calls to Áras an Uachtaráin.

To me this seemed eminently fair. In the period leading up to the Dáil debate of confidence in the government there had been mentions by opposition spokesmen about log books which recorded the phone calls to Áras on a given night. Opposition spokesmen insisted, almost as an article of faith, that there was documentary evidence available to prove who made phone calls on the night in question. It was claimed by opposition TDs that the log books existed. Not unnaturally, they claimed that if these records did exist then the government should release them. In a way I was surprised that the newspapers did not make much of my promise to open up these records if elected President. It was an up-front honest approach. I was all for disclosure and had nothing to hide from in the release of these records. Mrs. Robinson took a different approach saying that she would not be making the telephone records available if elected, saying that the President should not become involved in this party political row. To me it was no party political row, it was my reputation that was on the line. After the election, when Mr. Haughey had taken over the Defence portfolio, I inquired about the log books. I was told by officials that no such record actually existed either in the Áras or in the Department of Defence.

That night I was on Today Tonight, chaired by Olivia O'Leary, in the first and only three-way televised debate between the candidates. I felt I performed well and it made me wonder about the party's strategy of minimising my TV appearances from the outset of the campaign. The original notion was that the other two were so weak as candidates that it would only enhance their status if I appeared too much with them in TV debates.

The precise effect that my dismissal had on the Robinson campaign can be judged from Fergus Finlay's book on their campaign:

"The actual outcome was almost as bad from Mary's point of

view. Instead of the Government collapsing, the debate ended with the Taoiseach announcing that he had dismissed Brian Lenihan from the Cabinet, and the former Tánaiste was immediately photographed being carried shoulder-high across the front of Leinster House to an office across the road, where he gave a fighting press conference announcing that he would carry on to victory. The sight of the sacked Brian Lenihan, surrounded by hundreds of well-wishers and looking younger, fitter, and more determined than she felt, made her begin to regret her decision to stand aloof from the controversy that had surrounded him for the previous week. She began to calculate that by showing her own instinctive human sympathy, she had encouraged others to feel sympathetic too. Now she felt that if the Government and Fianna Fáil could dispense with him, that made him "fair game" for attack.

"As the bus made its way back to Dublin on Thursday, stopping in all the major towns on the way, Mary wrestled with a decision. She now believed that in the debate that night on RTE, she would have to take Brian Lenihan on. She no longer felt like a front-runner, but that she was beginning to falter, and that Lenihan in particular was catching up fast. Physically and mentally, she was exhausted. She had come so far, so close to doing the impossible, and she could feel it slipping away."

There were clearly the elements of a crisis in the Robinson campaign. The worst had been thrown at me and there was still a chance I could make it to the Áras. Her advisers before the programme suggested that she should not go on the attack against me. Their concern seemed to be that she should do nothing to encourage more sympathy for me than I had already got. But all these advisers gathered in the Robinson home had reckoned without one person and that was the ubiquitous Eoghan Harris. Finlay takes up the story again:

"Shortly before the group left for the television studios, the phone rang. It was Eoghan Harris. She took the call, and in his usual rapid-fire fashion told her that the time had come to go for Lenihan bald-headed. Take the gloves off, he told her, and don't pussyfoot around - otherwise you'll let him re-establish some credibility. As an experienced professional, Harris would know that the last piece of advice she received before the programme would stick in Mary's mind. Coming so close to the programme, and allowing her no time to weigh up his advice, it was the worst thing Harris could have done."

It was precisely this advice that she took. Because of the luck of the draw Olivia O'Leary threw her the first question. Mrs. Robinson turned the question around into an attack on me. It was ham-fisted and drawn out but, more importantly from my point of view, it seemed in stark contrast to her earlier pronouncements on the Duffy tape affair. I could not believe my luck, it was almost as if Mary Robinson had finally dropped the mask. Up to this she had been stating she felt sympathy for the position I and my family found ourselves in. She tried in her public statements to remain aloof from the whole business. Three days before the Today Tonight interview she declared she had no intention of "dancing on Brian Lenihan's grave" in this election.

Then, as the interview developed, Austin Currie seemed to be changing tack too. He launched into a strong attack on Mrs. Robinson for her socialist connections. Apart from her embarrassing Hot Press interview at the outset of the campaign, he raised the matter of her links with the Workers Party, a party which Currie solemnly intoned was "not just a socialist party but a revolutionary socialist party". One would have imagined from Currie's tone that it was a crime to be a socialist. Mrs. Robinson denied being a socialist, saying that she refused to be labelled. Currie's attack on the Workers Party struck me as odd. If he did want to do so, this was an occasion, ironically enough, where he could have used his northern origins to his own best advantage. If he had wanted to maximise his impact he should have concentrated more on the Workers Party's connections in the north and its uncertain relationship with the Official IRA which, we are led to believe, does not exist anymore.

Despite Currie's strong attack on Robinson, they both ended the programme by holding out the hope of a mutual transfer pact on vote transfers. Even with my long years in politics, it all struck me as a mite cynical. In a matter of days, both campaigns were to agree a transfer pact. After the programme we all went back to the hospitality room. It is very difficult to tell who had won at this stage. Esmonde Smith and most of the others who were with me that night were pleased with my performance. It is very hard to win on these programmes. Some TV analysts argue that the big "election debates" type programmes do not alter people's opinions but rather just reinforce existing views of the different candidates. It is very important to do well in them as it sets a mood for the rest of the campaign. That night there were just over a million viewers watching the programme which Peter Feeney, Editor of Current Affairs at RTE, describes as "a phenomenal viewership".

The morning papers on the Friday were undecided as to who had won out in the TV debate. All three said different candidates had won. John Waters in the Irish Times gave victory to me saying that, "anyone who tuned into the debate hoping to see Brian the Baptist carrying his head under his oxter would have been sorely disappointed ... There was no sign about him of the savagery of the previous 48 hours, not so much as a bloodstain to connect him with the harsh judgment of his erstwhile master, administered at the impious insistence of Salome O'Malley." The underlying consensus seems to have been that it was too close to call. Austin Currie's performance seemed to have come as a surprise to all of the pundits. His strong performance was hardly surprising. My own instinct afterwards was that the professional politicians had both done well on the night. Peter Feeney, the Editor of Current Affairs in RTE, felt Mrs. Robinson had made a mistake in her attack on me. Her relative inexperience when it comes to high-pressure political interviews showed on the night. It was quite ironic really given her statement at the outset of the campaign that I was avoiding TV debates with her. Up in the hospitality suite after the programme I chatted with Austin and Anita Currie. Mrs. Robinson had left early.

The campaign was beginning to heat up again. Two government ministers intervened in the debate to criticise Mrs. Robinson. The Minister for Social Welfare, Michael Woods, said that her claim that she should not be labelled as a socialist "flies in the face of her own political record and that she is supported in her campaign by the Labour Party and the Workers Party". The Minister for Foreign Affairs, Gerry Collins, issued a statement saying that she had snubbed President Reagan's visit to Ireland in 1984 when she boycotted his address to the joint Houses of the Oireachtas, an action, he said, which associated her with the attitude of the Workers Party at the time. Another statement from Fianna Fáil raised a statement she made back in 1982 where she professed to be a socialist, saying she favoured nationalising the banks and controlling building land. The following day she was denying that she had ever said this. This was untrue and the next day's Irish Times produced the exact quote and when she had said it. She did say it but at this stage the media were relatively well disposed towards her and were not inclined to pursue it much further.

On the Friday, it was on to The Late Late Show where all of the candidates were again to appear but this time along with their spouses. My wife Ann was very nervous before the programme. She had appeared on the programme before but that was her first ever appearance on television. The last few days had taken their toll and she was not in the mood for the appearance. However, she was quite happy to go on as she would only be on for a minute.

The Late Late Show began. Up to the first interval Austin Currie and Mrs. Robinson had made a few side swipes at me over mature recollections. Gay then asked all three of us had we ever done anything illegal or dishonest in our public lives. Austin Currie replied "yes", that he had broken the law during his days campaigning for civil rights in the north and emerged quite well. Mrs. Robinson said she could not remember anything from her public life of that nature and then went on to attack me. At this point I interjected "I dislike this pietistic nonsense" and went on to say "let whoever is without sin cast the first stone". This drew a strong round of applause from the studio audience. Mrs. Robinson seemed ill at ease in the cosy armchair atmosphere of The Late Late. She was trying too hard to score points and mistaking the essentially informal nature of the interview. Her nerves were slightly frayed.

While the commercials played, Currie and I relaxed but Mrs.

Robinson became cross with Gay Byrne in front of the studio audience. She claimed she had been misled about the format of the programme. She had, she said, been led to believe that the appearance on The Late Late was to be an easy going affair concentrating on the more human aspects of the campaign. She complained that the questions were very political and not at all what she had expected. She also insisted that the audience was loaded with political activists. It was an extraordinary outburst and not one calculated to get the audience on her side, whoever they were. Upstairs in the hospitality suites, my own advisers and Austin Currie's were dumbfounded at her attitude which came over on the internal monitors. Gay Byrne himself was clearly stung by her comments and took them as a reflection on his own professional bone fides. When the programme came back on air he summarised her allegations, mentioning her claims about the audience. Gay reiterated that the audience was a normal night's choice of those who had applied months previous to get the chance to sit in on The Late Late Show.

That day, an Irish Press opinion poll had shown that the gap was narrowing between me and Mrs. Robinson. She was at 43% and I was at 39%. On the Saturday, I spent the day campaigning in Mayo and Galway, travelling from Ballyhaunis, through Ballina to Tuam and Galway city. On the Sunday I did some after Mass meetings in West Limerick - Rathkeale, Askeaton, Abbeyfeale and Newcastlewest. There was a tangible feeling coming from around the country that I was beginning to recover. In Dublin, canvassers were reporting that people were impressed with my two television appearances. As I had predicted, with my dismissal now out of the way, attention was beginning to switch back to the central issue of the campaign - who was the best suited to occupy the post of President? The extent of my recovery since the dismissal was remarkable. There was undoubtedly a sympathy factor at work, with people acknowledging that I had paid far too high a price for what was, at worst, a mistaken account of events nearly nine years before. At another level, my refusal to give in to Mr. Haughey's demand that I should resign had proved, once and for all, the nonsense in the charge made by both of my opponents, that because of my loyalty to him over the years, I was unsuitable to hold the office of President. If proof were needed of my political independence it was there on my dismissal day.

However, the campaign was still highly charged and the opinion polls highly volatile. With swings in support like those over the last week or so, anything could make the difference with just four days to polling day. While I was out campaigning, Fianna Fáil decided to change their tactics. They decided to concentrate their fire power on Mrs. Robinson's left-wing credentials. The feeling at headquarters seemed to be that if it had worked in the general election of 1989 then it would also work in 1990. In the general election, the health cuts issue was allowed to run out of control. In the closing week of the campaign, in an effort to shore up support among the middle classes, stress was put on the possibility of a Fine Gael coalition with the left wing parties. By all accounts, it seemed to have worked in parts of middle class south Dublin and Dun Laoghaire, where a late surge in these areas was reported for Fianna Fáil. Fianna Fáil pressed ahead with full page newspaper advertisements which asked the question: "Is the left right for the Park?" It was negative advertising and really missed the whole point of the election. In 1989 there were real issues involved. Pollsters have well demonstrated that, when all is stripped down, most voters cast their vote in general elections on the basis of the economic issues, in other words how they feel a particular party will safeguard their living standards.

But the Presidential election was entirely different. Living standards would not be affected no matter who was put into the Áras. Therefore, any attempt to frighten off voters from voting for a perceived "left winger" would inevitably fall on deaf ears. In fact putting a left winger in the Park, if one were cynical enough, was exactly the right way of silencing the left. The perceived threat posed by a Robinson Presidency just did not shape up when one looked at the elaborately circumscribed nature of the office. Mentioning Mary Robinson's connections with the "Stalinist Workers Party" would only have been effective if mentioned early and constantly during the campaign. As things stood, it looked like a last-minute act of desperation on Fianna Fáil's part.

On Saturday, both the Robinson and Currie campaign managers finally stitched up their transfer pact. Fianna Fáil's last minute advertising ploy, stressing Mrs. Robinson's left wing credential, was also aimed at preventing a transfer exchange on the ground. The theory was that the ultra Fine Gael type voter would not find it in themselves to vote for a left winger or indeed pass on a transfer. One of the main consequences of the Duffy tape affair was a dramatic drop in the level of transfers I was getting from Currie voters. This showed up very clearly in the opinion polls. Transfers were always going to be crucial in the campaign and it did not look good on this front as I faced into the final few days.

Meanwhile, on the Saturday, Padraig Flynn made his by now famous contribution to the Saturday View programme. It was to be a source of great speculation subsequently with some people on the Robinson campaign arguing that it was his comments here that nipped my poll recovery in the bud. There was no doubt that I was bouncing back. My strong performance in the two scheduled TV appearances seemed to have struck a chord. The Labour Party activists in the Robinson camp were frightened that I was making a come-back. How harmful the Padraig Flynn factor was, is impossible to tell. He appeared on the programme from RTE's Castlebar studios and this may have been a disadvantage from the start. Labour's Brendan Howlin, a deputy from Wexford, and Michael McDowell of the PDs were the other guests on the show hosted by Rodney Rice. About half way through the programme Padraig Flynn began to comment on Mary Robinson's campaign. This is the part of the interview which caused the media storm:

"She was pretty well constructed in this campaign by her handlers, the Labour Party and the Workers Party," he said. "Of course, it doesn't always suit if you get labelled a socialist, because that's a very narrow focus in this country - so she has to try and have it both ways. She has to have new clothes and her new look and her new hairdo and she has the new interest in her family, being a mother and all that kind of thing. But none of you know, none of us who knew Mary Robinson very well in previous incarnations ever heard her claiming to be a great wife and mother".

At this point McDowell tried to interrupt the Minister but to no avail. There were also interruptions while he was saying the following:

"Mary Robinson reconstructs herself to fit the fashion of the time, so we have this thing about you can be substituted at will, whether it's the pro-socialist thing, or pro-contraception, or pro-abortion - whatever it is. But at least we should know. Mary Robinson is a socialist, she says it and has admitted it previously. Now she may have changed her mind, and if she has changed her mind, so be it. But at least she should tell us that she has changed her mind, and not be misleading us," continued Padraig Flynn.

After he was finished Michael McDowell attacked the Minister's remarks describing them as "disgusting". It would appear that McDowell's outrage was slightly contrived. Later that day McDowell ran into Mrs. Robinson while she was getting a bite to eat before hitting the trail again. Mrs. Robinson remarked after meeting him "With enemies like Michael, who needs friends". Later that day Padraig Flynn issued a statement in which he said that: "I am happy to state that Mrs. Mary Robinson's family life is exemplary. It was never my intention to suggest otherwise. I deeply regret that anything I said during the lively exchange may have inadvertently conveyed the contrary view."

Mrs. Robinson's initial reaction was to say that it was a case of "mud thrown, ground lost," adding that she could afford to "laugh it off". However she changed her mind, and on Monday she called on me to apologise, saying that "a person must repudiate any given smear in whose name it was being done and on whose behalf it was being done". I pointed out that Mr. Flynn had himself already apologised and that I was not in the business of going around apologising for every remark made on my behalf. I did, though, dissociate myself from any remarks "that could be construed as a personal reflection on any of the other candidates". I also pointed out that since both Mrs. Robinson and Austin Currie had spent the best part of the campaign impugning my integrity maybe I was the one who was due an apology.

Despite the fact that Padraig Flynn had apologised for his remarks, she continued right up to polling day to demand an apology from me, conveniently forgetting the fact that I had already dissociated myself from the remarks.

On Sunday, my campaign found its way back to Dublin again. There was a large rally organised for the National Stadium that evening. It was the first time Mr. Haughey and I had met since my dismissal. When the Taoiseach got up to speak he was well received but there was an undercurrent of booing from the crowd. Some had clearly not forgiven him for my dismissal. Mr. Haughey made his strongest attack to date on Mrs. Robinson's left wing credentials and the role the media had played in the campaign. Charlie was painting it on with a pretty thick brush. He went on to hint at the infiltration of our national institutions by the Workers Party. The crowd began to chant "RTE, RTE". He compared Fine Gael's plot to trap me with "the plot to destroy Parnell by the use of Piggot and his forged letters".

After the week-end it was down to Kerry starting off in Listowel and then stopping in Ballyduff, Causeway, Ballyheigue, Ardfert, Tralee, Castleisland, Farranfore, Milltown and Killorglin before winding up in Killarney. The rally in Killarney was one of the biggest of the campaign with over five thousand people showing up and I was led into the town standing up in a horse-drawn carriage. I could see from familiar faces that they were in from the far flung peninsulas of Dingle, Iveragh and Kenmare.

Tuesday, the eve of polling, was spent quietly canvassing the suburban shopping centres in Dublin. On polling day I cast my vote as usual at the Castleknock polling booth, glad for once that it was all over now. I spent polling day touring the large urban polling booths in the city and county.

At around eleven in the morning on the first day of the count at Dublin's RDS, I became aware that things were not going to work out. The count was then played out into a second day but at this stage the party's tally people at the count knew the transfer rate from Currie would not be high enough. I had headed the poll and received 44% of the total votes cast. Though disappointed that I was going to lose, I was in fact the people's first choice. On the second and final day of the count I appeared at the RDS. As the speeches were being made following Mrs. Robinson's election as Uachtarán na hÉireann, there was no sign of Austin Currie or

Alan Dukes. Along with the Returning Officer, Mr. Tim Sexton, there was just myself, Dick Spring, Mrs. Robinson and the Taoiseach present on the stand. Fine Gael's Jim Mitchell, the party's Director of Elections, was there but declined to come up on the podium and did not speak.

Mitchell had other business to attend to. That evening Deputy Fergus O'Brien put down a motion of "no confidence" in Alan Dukes' leadership of Fine Gael. Dukes was about to become the real political casualty of the Presidential campaign. I made my few remarks of thanks, shook hands with Mary Robinson and in a strange way felt liberated. I was free and no longer a stag at bay.

12

ANALYSIS

As the votes were counted on the morning of Thursday November 8th, it soon became clear that, although I was topping the poll, Mary Robinson would win the election with a heavy transfer of second preferences from Austin Currie. When the first count was completed there was a 64.1 per cent turnout, with a valid poll of 1,574,651 votes. The highest turnouts were in Cork North West (74.3%), Limerick West (70.6%) and Tipperary North (70.2%). The lowest turnouts were in Donegal North East (51.2%), Donegal South West (53.3%) and Dublin South West (55.7%).

The first count result was as follows:

Lenihan	694,484	(44.1%)
Robinson	612,265	(38.9%)
Currie	267,902	(17.0%)

When broken down regionally, I led on the first count in Connaught/Ulster, Leinster and Munster, whereas Robinson led in Dublin. I will analyse the regional results in percentage terms only.

In Connaught/Ulster, the result was Lenihan 49.1%, Robinson 31.3%, and Currie 19.6%. In Dublin, the result was Lenihan 39.0%, Robinson 47.5%, and Currie 13.5%. In Leinster the result was Lenihan 46.9%, Robinson 36.6% and Currie 16.5%. Finally, in Munster, the result was Lenihan 43.6%, Robinson 37.3%, and Currie 19.1%.

In ten constituencies, I obtained over 50% of the first preference vote: Donegal North East, Cavan-Monaghan, Donegal South West, Limerick West, Longford-Westmeath, Roscommon, Louth, Laois-Offaly, Galway East and Kerry South. Robinson won over half the first preference vote in three constituencies: Dun Laoghaire, Dublin South East and Dublin South. Currie's best constituencies were Cork South West (29%), Cork North West (28%) and Roscommon (23%).

The most remarkable aspect of the result was the overwhelming extent to which Currie voters transferred to Robinson. The second count saw Currie's votes distributed as follows:

Lenihan	+ 36,789	(13.7%)
Robinson	+ 205,565	(76.7%)
Non-transferable	25,548	(9.5%)

Thus the final result was

Lenihan	731,273	(47.2%)
Robinson	817,830	(52.8%)

Mrs. Robinson had won by 86,000 votes.

Quite clearly the results indicate a slump in Currie's support compared to the Fine Gael vote in the 1989 general election and, conversely, a massive rise in Robinson's support compared to the combined left-wing vote in the '89 election. My vote at 44.1% is almost exactly the same as the percentage vote Fianna Fáil obtained at the last election: 44.2%. However, it would be wrong to conflate both figures. A constituency-by-constituency analysis clearly demonstrates that many people who did not support Fianna Fáil at the last general election supported me in the presidential election, and conversely many who had voted for Fianna Fáil at the '89 election did not support my candidature for the presidency. It is my contention that a close analysis of the figures shows that in every constituency in the country there were considerable swings to me among voters who did not support Fianna Fáil at the last election, while many erstwhile Fianna Fáil voters did not support my candidature. Some of the swings are due to local factors. For example, the large swings to me in Donegal North East (16.07%) and Roscommon (13.44%) were undoubtedly due in large measure to the fact that independent deputies Neil Blaney and Tom Fox were absent from the race in both constituencies. The swing in Roscommon was also helped by the fact that I represented the area in the Dáil from 1961 to 1973. In Donegal North East, Neil Blaney worked hard for me, and I acknowledge his help and that of his supporters.

The swings against me in the two Mayo constituencies - 4.64% in East Mayo and 7.08% in West Mayo - can be partly explained by the fact that Mrs. Robinson is from Ballina. The swing of 7.19% against me in the Taoiseach's constituency of Dublin North Central, where the vote fell to a respectable 44.5%, is probably due to the fact that Mr. Haughey as Taoiseach gets a strong personal vote in the constituency which he was unable to translate into support for me in the presidential election. However, voting patterns in the election show several trends that are of particular interest.

(i) There was undoubtedly a large swing to me among working class voters in urban areas. This trend is graphically illustrated by the results in Dublin city. In the three most predominantly working class constituencies in Dublin - Dublin North West, Dublin South West and Dublin Central - there were large swings to me compared to the FF vote at the last election. In the North West constituency, which mainly covers Finglas and Ballymun, I obtained 42% of the vote, compared to 35% for FF at the last election. In South West, which covers the greater Tallaght area, I also obtained 42%, compared to 34% at the '89 election. In Dublin Central, which covers the North inner city, the vote went up from 45% to 47% and in Cabra polling stations to 50% and 54%. In my own constituency in Dublin West, I was very pleased to see the vote increasing from just under 40% to 45.6%. While this was, without doubt, due to the fact that I have represented the constituency since 1977, it is interesting to note that the swings were most pronounced in the large housing estates in Ballyfermot, Neilstown and Mulhuddart. For example, in Ballyfermot my vote went up from 31% for Fianna Fáil in 1989 to 51% in 1990.

This same trend is evident in the other urban areas throughout the country. In Cork there was a swing of almost 6% to me in the more working class north city constituency, while a swing of almost 7% against me was recorded in the more middle class south-city constituency. In Louth my vote went up by 7.56% from 43% to over 50%. Here there were big swings to me in the large housing estates of Dundalk and Drogheda.

Waterford intrigued me. Leaving aside the big swings in Donegal North East and Roscommon, which, as I have already pointed out, were largely due to local factors, the swing to me in Waterford was the biggest in the whole country. The vote for Fianna Fáil in the '89 election was 34.8%. In the presidential election I obtained 44.5% in the Waterford constituency. This was an increase of 9.7%. A case study of the presidential election results in Waterford, with full computer analysis, has been conducted by John D. Walsh and Peter Griffin and was produced early this year by Adapt Marketing Ltd. Waterford. It provides a fascinating case study for two reasons. Firstly, the results in Waterford closely mirror the results nationwide. The turnout in Waterford (63.7%) is almost identical to the national turnout (64.1%). The result in Waterford is almost the exact same as the national result: Lenihan 44.5% (44.1% nationwide), Robinson 39.6% (38.9% nationwide) and Currie 15.95 (17% nationwide). The second reason why Waterford is such an interesting subject for a case study is that the constituency offers a good mix of urban and rural, taking in a large urban conurbation with its own city corporation, small outlying towns and rural areas dependent on agriculture.

This case study showed that the largest swings to me in the constituency were in Waterford city, where there was a swing of 12.4% with my vote rising from Fianna Fáil's 28.6% in the '89 election to 41% in the presidential election. In the Waterford County Council area, the vote went up by 3.4% from 43.6% to 47%. Within the different wards in Waterford city the swings are even more compelling. In Wards 1 and 3, the vote went up by 15% and 19% respectively, whereas in Ward 2 the vote went up by only 2.5%. John Walsh has conducted a social class profile based on income group classification towards the end of the case study. This profile is very revealing. In what he classifies as the working class areas, my vote increased by 18.6% compared to the FF vote in the '89 election. In the lower middle class areas, my vote increased by 10.7%. In the middle class areas, my vote went up by

3.5% and finally, in what he classifies as the upper middle class areas, my vote went down by 5.8% compared to the FF vote last time out, and this in a constituency recording a swing of almost 10% in my favour. Interestingly, in the upper middle class areas, Mary Robinson, the candidate of the left, took 57.1% of the votes compared to 27.4% for myself, while in the middle class areas she took 49.4% compared to my 33.7%. In the working class areas, her vote dropped by almost 10% compared to the large combined left-wing vote in those areas at the last general election.

(ii) As is already becoming clear, the second most significant trend in the presidential election is that there was a swing against me among middle class voters who voted for Fianna Fáil in the last general election. This trend was brought out in the detailed case study of the Waterford constituency, which showed Mrs. Robinson attracting huge support in middle class areas. This trend is also illustrated by the results in Dublin. Mrs. Robinson took over 50% of the first preference votes in the three most middle class constituencies in Dublin and indeed in the whole country. In Dublin South East, she took over 51% of the first preference vote, while my vote in the constituency went down by over 3% from the 35% Fianna Fáil vote at the '89 election to 32% in the presidential election. In Dublin South, Robinson again took over 51% of the vote on the first count, while my vote declined by a huge 11.7% to 31.7%. In Dun Laoghaire, Robinson took her largest share of the vote nationwide - 54.6% - while my vote went down on the Fianna Fáil vote by over 4% to just over 28%. These three predominantly middle class Dublin constituencies returned the largest Robinson percentage votes in the country. Conversely they were the three worst Lenihan constituencies in the country. In Northside Dublin's middle class areas, the swing away from Lenihan among FF general election voters was also apparent. This explains the 5.86% swing against me in Dublin North East, and again the 3.4% swing against me in Dublin North.

A surprising feature of the presidential election was the manner in which the Fianna Fáil vote declined in the heartland FF areas in the West and the Midlands. Although I polled extremely well in Limerick West, the strongest Fianna Fáil constituency in the country, taking 52% of the vote, my support was well down on the 60% vote Fianna Fáil got there in the last general election. Again in Clare I polled well, taking just under 50%, but my vote was down on the 55% vote Fianna Fáil got there in '89. The same in East Galway where my vote was down from 59% to 50%. In Laois-Offaly the vote went down by 4% from 54% to 50%, in Meath by 3% from 52% to 49% and in South Kerry from 53.5% to 50%. My vote even went down marginally in my native Longford-West-meath. Despite a huge Lenihan vote in my home town of Athlone, the vote in the constituency as a whole, while still an impressive 53%, was slightly down on the 54% FF vote in the last general election. This was what media commentators were to dub the Ballinamuck factor. Ballinamuck is a rural polling booth in Longford where Robinson came from nowhere to poll as many votes as Lenihan. Ballinamuck soon became a by-word for all those heartland areas which might have been expected to be stronger in their support of Fianna Fáil. The Ballinamuck factor has been largely interpreted as indicating that large numbers of female voters came out to vote for Robinson. Mrs. Robinson's victory speech, in which she spoke of the women of Ireland - *mná na hÉireann* - coming out in their droves to rock the system, did much to reinforce this myth. The simple fact of the matter is that the opinion polls, published immediately before the election, showed both myself and Robinson attracting equal levels of support among female voters. A much more plausible interpreta-tion of the Ballinamuck factor is that it is simply another reflection of a swing against me among certain Fianna Fáil supporters. In many of Fianna Fáil's heartland constituencies, conservative, or middle class Fianna Fáil supporters, switched allegiance to Robin-son, probably due to a disenchantment with me over the Duffy tapes and the dismissal. This was simply another reflection of the swing against me among middle class voters nationally.

This point is brought out by Michael Murphy in his official analysis for the Fianna Fáil party of the Lenihan vote in the presidential election. Murphy concludes his analysis by stating that "if Fianna Fáil's strongest areas had voted for Lenihan as they voted in 1989, the result could have been different ... statistical analysis strongly suggests that the result (of the presidential election) can be explained in terms of a differential swing of middle class voters away from Lenihan and working class voters to him."

(iii) Another trend which cannot escape notice is the extent to which the PD vote came out in support of Robinson. This was particularly evident in those constituencies where the PDs have a strong presence. Thus, in Dessie O'Malley's constituency of Limerick East, where the PDs hold two of the five seats, the Lenihan vote was only up by 2% from 32% to 34%. Here the bulk of the PD vote clearly transferred in Robinson's favour. Again in Bobby Molloy's constituency, Galway West, the Lenihan vote was only up just over 1% on the FF general election figure. Mary Robinson polled unusually well in the West Galway constituency, narrowly beating Lenihan on the first count with both candidates taking 41% of the vote. Again in Cork city, where the PDs have representatives in the two city constituencies, Robinson's strong showing indicates that most of the PD voters in the city backed her in the presidential election.

(iv) A final trend of a purely regional nature, which might be worth noting, is that the Lenihan vote in the presidential election was up on the Fianna Fáil vote in the border counties. While the swing in North Donegal can be explained by Neil Blaney's support, and the swing of 7.56% in Louth was largely reflective of the swings in the large housing estates of Dundalk and Drogheda, these figures must also be assessed in the context of an increase of 3% on the FF vote in both Cavan-Monaghan and Sligo-Leitrim.

Nevertheless, it must be noted that there was a slight fall in the Lenihan vote in South Donegal, where the vote fell from 55% in the general election to 53% in the presidential election. The overall impression that one gets from these figures is that Fianna Fáil strongholds in the border counties held up better than Fianna Fáil strongholds elsewhere in the country. This may have been due to a concern in the border counties about the stance taken by Mrs. Robinson on the Anglo-Irish Agreement back in 1985 and her identification with the arguments advanced against the Agreement by the Unionists at that time. In support of this explanation, it must be noted that some of Robinson's poorest levels of support in the election were recorded in the counties of Monaghan, Cavan, Sligo, Leitrim and Donegal.

It is quite clear from this analysis that my vote in the election was essentially a social democratic vote in the universal meaning of that term. I obtained a considerable vote from the same segment of people who would vote Democrat in the United States, Labour in Britain or Australia, Socialist or Social Democrat in France, Germany, Spain, Austria and the Scandinavian countries.

The paradox is that while Mary Robinson was nominated by parties of the Left, many of her voters were middle-class supporters of Fianna Fáil, Fine Gael and the PDs. She also attracted conservatives, liberal right-wingers, and even reactionary elements, all of whom felt comfortable with her candidature, because they knew well that constitutional restrictions would prevent the emergence of any dangerous left-wing signals from the Presidential office in the event of her election.

Former Government Minister, John Boland, expressed it all very well in his "Politics" column of the Sunday Business Post during the campaign on the 21st October: "What all of this means is that the threat of a Lift-off for the Left will not be taken seriously by this electorate. They perceive Robinson for what she is: a liberal with basically upper middle-class values, and who, if scraped hard enough, would display many conservative beliefs. The sort of person many of them would like to believe themselves to be!"

Eoghan Harris, now working with Fine Gael, and others played cynically to this market. However, Fianna Fáil can learn from the election, and present itself clearly in the future as a party related to where its real strength lies in Irish society.

13

THE LIBERAL ETHIC

On the 24th January 1950 a report appeared in the Irish Times with the headline "Liberal Ethic Condemned by Professor". The report was to stir up something of a controversy. It concerned a public lecture given by the then Chair of Philosophy at University College Galway, the very Reverend Felim O Briain. The report described how the priestly philosopher had declared in his lecture that "the only freedom that would triumph in the absence of the full Christian code was the freedom of the armed man to suppress the liberty of all who differed from his views." Fr. O'Briain expressed concern in his lecture that liberals and socialists were undermining the traditional mores of the Irish people by advancing the cause of birth control. Fr. O'Briain was also concerned about what he saw as a latent anti-clericalism in Ireland that expressed itself in the occasional letter to the Irish Times that complained about the country being "priest-ridden". He linked this form of anti-clericalism to more robust methods used in the Iron Curtain countries.

Before long, letters were penned by serious people anxious to defend and define their concept of liberalism, and over the next two months, letters were to flow through the newspaper's letter-box from up to fifty contributors. In turn Fr. O'Briain developed what he had said in his lecture. What is most remarkable about the controversy is not so much the contents of the letters but rather the response it evoked from the Irish Times itself. In June 1950, the newspaper produced a slim volume entitled "The Liberal Ethic". It contained short introductory notes to the main letters setting out the scope of the debate. The controversy seems to have focused the Irish Times on its own self-image. For many years since the foundation of the state the Irish Times was seen by most in the 26 counties as the mouthpiece of southern Unionism. The paper's writers seemed to find the new state a poor substitute for the link with Britain. To coin a phrase, the Irish Times had lost its empire and had yet to find a role. It is from the 1950s on, that the newspaper began to come to terms with the new State and, in its own way, to identify with it. Liberalism became its guiding philosophy and the letters controversy played no small part in this development. In a real sense the Irish Times has become the house journal of Irish liberalism.

The Liberal Ethic advanced by the Irish Times for forty years is an admirable philosophy of social and political behaviour embracing an ethical and tolerant attitude to the problems of our times. At its roots, liberalism is meant to be tolerant - tolerant of other people's views and ready to accept diversity. I have always found it attractive in its pluralistic approach, and its civilised endeavour to weave diverse strands into the fabric of our ethos. It is, therefore, with some sadness that I am compelled to say that the performance of the Irish Times during the recent presidential election was a radical departure from the liberal ethic that the paper has for so long cherished. It is not so much the opinions expressed in the paper's columns that I call into question as the conduct of events leading to the release of the tape by Mr. Jim Duffy. The conduct of the Irish Times during these events was such that I do hope the paper will make a serious attempt to look at itself and reflect on what has happened. The Irish Times, as a newspaper, prides itself in having an "Ethics Committee" to lay down guidelines for its journalists on how they should carry out their duties. I hope and trust that this book will inspire that committee to ensure the maintenance of the traditional high standards of the newspaper.

Throughout the election campaign, the Irish Times was to present coverage that was very favourable to Mrs. Robinson's candidature. The general thrust of their editorial policy was outlined on the eve of polling when their editorial endorsed Mrs. Robinson's candidature for the Presidency. In an editorial headed "Choosing Between two Irelands", it was stated that the events of 1982 suggested that Mr. Lenihan would not hold, with particular conviction, the view that the President must be seen to be independent of party political interest. The editorial took the view that the untruthful statements made by Mr. Lenihan were the reason why he was no longer the front runner in the presidential race. The editorial then continued:

"To choose Mr. Lenihan would be to elect a man who is widely liked, vastly experienced and, in the culture of his party and his times, a man who has served his public well. But he has shown himself to be enmeshed in a set of attitudes and values from which this State must escape; a set of attitudes and values which ought to be consigned to history. To choose Mrs. Robinson might be to choose a degree of uncertainty, of inconsistency, of challenge. But underneath the multi-layered persona which has been fashioned by her campaign managers there are qualities which have characterised her years in politics, in public life and in the law. She may have shifted ground in the campaign and she may have backpedalled where she has believed herself in danger of running foul of public opinion. Yet, she represents and has committed herself over the years to a vision of a future Ireland which can be open, generous, pluralist and tolerant.

"This is where the choice lies, where two cultures and two Irelands clash. We shall learn something about ourselves as a people when the votes to be cast tomorrow are counted."

The editorial created a stereotype of me as a dishonest politician whose values are somehow rooted in an age where dishonesty was acceptable. The creation of stereotypes of this kind is an intellectually vacuous exercise which I do not pretend to comprehend. This stereotype of me was re-inforced in an article written by Mary Holland the next day where she wrote that a vote for Mrs. Robinson was a vote for change, while a vote for Brian Lenihan, while perhaps inspired by "generous instincts" of sympathy for "his tired, worn face", and for "his wife's distress", was a vote for "a doomed political culture". The Irish Times made it clear that it did not consider me fit to hold the office of President as they did not view me as a person of integrity. I therefore deserved no better than to be consigned to the scrapheap of history. Over the years I have always sought to do what was right by my own lights. I have never abused public office for personal gain. I have been honest and fair in my dealings as a public representative. My record of public service is an open book for all to see. I believe that my record is one that I am entitled to feel proud of. While it is easy to understand the attitude of the Irish Times in the immediate aftermath of the release of the Duffy tape, I cannot be so chari-table about their refusal to accept the truth of what I was saying after I had stood by my convictions and paid the ultimate political price for doing so in being dismissed.

As I have already noted, many of the paper's opinion writers wrote articles which favoured Mary Robinson. In several cases these included actual endorsements of Mrs. Robinson's candida-ture. No writer for the paper came out and endorsed the Fianna Fáil candidate although 44% of the Irish people did. After the election, in December 1990, the Irish Times invited an outside academic and communications expert, Luke Gibbons, to come and appraise them of their coverage during the presidential cam-paign. In seminar sessions with the paper's journalists Mr. Gib-bons, who is a lecturer in Communications in Dublin City Univer-sity, took the clear view that the paper was biased towards Mrs. Robinson during the campaign.

I would like, nonetheless, to emphasise that I do not object to any endorsements of Mrs. Robinson's candidature that were made by the Irish Times. I believe that a newspaper is entitled, through its editorial and opinion columns, to express its own political preferences in whatever manner it deems fit. A newspa-per espousing liberal principles should, of course, be careful to present balanced coverage that is tolerant of different viewpoints. Having said that, it is, at the end of the day, the prerogative of the Irish Times to choose how to express its preferences. If it chooses to endorse a particular candidate I have no objection to make, provided such bias does not extend to inaccurate reporting. At a crucial juncture in the Presidential Election, the Irish Times published information about me which it ought to have known to be untrue. This is an important point concerning the conduct of the Irish Times in the election and it is a point that I intend to return to later in this chapter.

Another matter of controversy, concerning the paper's involvement in the campaign, surfaced in the Irish Times' own letter columns after the campaign was over. This is the question of the extent to which columnists and members of the Irish Times Editorial Staff participated directly or indirectly in the Robinson campaign. In a letter to the Irish Times after the election Mr. Cormac Lucey, who was involved in the Currie campaign and was a member of the key election committee that advised the Fine Gael Director of Elections Jim Mitchell, wrote in complaining that "in the week approaching the vote Nuala O'Faolain and Mary Holland wrote opinion pieces endorsing Mary Robinson's candidacy without stating the fact that they had both been involved in Mary Robinson's campaign during the early stages." Although the letter was published, it was accompanied by a reply from the Editor, Mr. Conor Brady, which was printed at the end of the letter. The reply ran as follows:

"It is not correct to suggest that Mary Holland or Nuala O'Faolain were involved in the campaign to elect President Robinson. They attended one meeting at which she outlined her ideas for the Presidency."

In a later column Ms. O'Faolain was to deny participation in the Robinson campaign. "I wasn't involved in the campaign at all. I went to a meeting in Mrs. Robinson's house back in June sometime. She outlined her view of what the Presidency could be and she explained why she had agreed to run for it ... I wouldn't call going to that meeting campaigning. I'm always going to meetings where people launch campaigns. I recall a Fianna Fáil launch in the Shelbourne ballroom complete with stirring musak ..."

Mr. Lucey, however, was not prepared to accept this, and wrote back to the Irish Times complaining that "by juxtaposing her account of the Robinson meeting with an account of attending an earlier Fianna Fáil campaign launch in the Shelbourne Hotel, Nuala O'Faolain implies that the Robinson meeting was in the nature of an open press conference designed to communicate information to the media".

It may be worthwhile at this point explaining a little more about this meeting which Nuala O'Faolain and Mary Holland, among others, attended in Mrs. Robinson's home back in June. According to Fergus Finlay, the Labour Party Press Officer who was working on the Robinson campaign, the meeting was called so that prominent women from all walks of life could contribute to the campaign. Finlay says that "any journalists who attended, attended as women". The idea for the meeting came from the former RTE producer Eoghan Harris who was involved in the Robinson campaign. The meeting was called "a rapping session". It is an American idea where people bounce ideas around, in effect a sort of brain-storming session. Caroline Erskine, then of Century Radio and Geraldine Kennedy of the Irish Times were among those invited to this meeting. They declined to attend, however, as they were concerned about the status of the meeting. However, other female journalists did attend, including Mary Holland, Nuala O'Faolain, Mary Maher and Mary Cummins, all from the Irish Times.

However, I was very disappointed that the Irish Times chose to be involved in the release of the Duffy tape. Mr. Duffy had of course written an article for the Irish Times on September 27 in which he stated that I was among the telephone callers to the Áras on January 27, 1982. The day after I had denied this on Questions and Answers, Tuesday October 23, Dick Walsh, Political Editor of the Irish Times, spoke to Duffy. We are led to believe that the conversation was to be about some further articles the research student was going to write for the newspaper. Duffy was asked by Walsh about how he knew that Brian Lenihan had rung Áras an Uachtaráin back in 1982. Duffy told him about the tape. Walsh then made a proposal to him. At this stage Duffy was still apparently reluctant to produce the tape and make it public. Emily O'Reilly takes up the story in her book *Candidate*. The relevant passage reads as follows:

"According to Duffy, Walsh then told him that the conversation with Lenihan should be made public knowledge, that the proof that Brian Lenihan had lied should be published. Duffy refused. Walsh said he understood his position but suggested that perhaps the paper might interview him instead, give Duffy an opportunity to say that he knew on the basis of his research that Lenihan had lied. Duffy rang off saying that he would consider it."

Later that afternoon Duffy played the tape to a journalist on the Irish Times staff whom he refused to name. Apparently his objective was to get an impartial assessment of the contents of his interview with me the previous May. Later that evening he played the tape again to the paper's Political Editor, but this time in the presence of Conor Brady, Editor of the Irish Times, and Denis Coughlan, political correspondent for the paper. Emily O'Reilly again takes up the story:

"Duffy then agreed that the Irish Times could run a low-key story, stating that they had corroborative evidence that Lenihan, Sylvester Barrett and Charles Haughey had made phone calls to Áras an Uachtaráin, but not giving any hint as to what this evidence was."

It has been reported that the Editor, Conor Brady, was willing to comply with the young man's request that the story be low-key. He instructed that the physical presentation of the story should not be sensationalised and that the information itself be suitably qualified so that it be obscure to the general reader but quite clear to those involved. He also directed that the story should run below the fold on page one, rather than dramatically across the top of the page.

But low-key it was not. It was a front-page lead article with the headline well above the fold. It was unqualified, direct and to the point. It was packed with sensational detail and was anything but obscure. Duffy must have known that if the article was to appear on the front page of the paper it would be far from obscure. The Irish Times must have known that as soon as the article was published Duffy would have no choice but to release the contents of the tape. All journalists know they have to be prepared to stand over what they write, and if they cannot, they and their newspapers can be faced with expensive libel suits.

This article, published in the Irish Times on Wednesday October 24, was written by Denis Coughlan. The headline ran "Lenihan did make call he now denies". The opening paragraphs of the story ran as follows:

"Fianna Fáil's presidential candidate Mr. Brian Lenihan was one of three members of the party's front bench who telephoned President Hillery in an effort to persuade him not to dissolve the Dáil following the defeat of the Fine Gael Labour Coalition on the 1982 budget.

"Corroborative evidence of Mr. Lenihan's role in the approach which failed to secure a transfer of power without an election became available to the Irish Times last night. The other callers were Mr. Charles Haughey and Mr. Sylvester Barrett, a former minister, subsequently Minister of State, who had been one of Dr. Hillery's parliamentary colleagues in the constituency of Clare. The telephone calls, made after the Government had been defeated by a single vote on the night of January 27th, 1982, followed discussions among members of the Fianna Fáil front bench in their Leinster House offices with Mr. Haughey playing a leading role. The calls were taken by the President in Áras an Uachtaráin where he was in the company of the resigning Taoiseach Dr. Garret Fitzgerald."

At no stage did the Irish Times approach me with their so-called corroborative evidence and look for my reaction to it before rushing into print with it. There were strong imperatives for doing so as the corroborative evidence they were relying on was both flawed and it contradicted what were up to then known facts:

(1) The article stated that myself, Barrett and Haughey not only put through telephone calls to the Áras, but that the calls were taken by the President. Whatever about some people ringing the Áras, it had never been suggested that Dr. Hillery had spoken to anyone. If the Irish Times had carried out the most rudimentary enquiries it could have established that nobody spoke to the President that night back in 1982. Indeed, Irish Times correspondent and former TD, Geraldine Kennedy, refe red two days later in the Irish Times of 27th October to her article of February 7th, 1982, in which she stated, "They (Haughey, Barrett, Lenihan) did not speak to Dr. Hillery". Raymond Smith in his book *Garret : The Enigma* was very specific that "none of those who rang actually got

through to the President personally." Joe Joyce and Peter Murtagh
in *The Boss* stated that the members of Fianna Fáil who attempted
to get through to the President "never succeeded in talking to the
President". It is hard to believe how the Irish Times could have
published such a gross error of fact. Their mistake is further
underlined by the fact that Geraldine Kennedy was, and I understand still is on the staff of the newspaper. In fact, on the Saturday
after the story was published, Ms. Kennedy wrote a piece in the
paper's Saturday column stating that the President, Dr. Hillery,
spoke to nobody that night. However, by the time her piece
appeared the following Saturday, buried inside the paper, the
damage had been done and it really didn't seem to matter
anymore.

(2) The article states that the calls were taken in the Áras by the
President while he was in the company of the resigning Taoiseach
Garret Fitzgerald. Not even Garret Fitzgerald in his many claims
had suggested this. Fitzgerald, in his most audacious claim on
Questions and Answers, went no further than to say that he was in
Áras an Uachtaráin when the calls came through. He never said
anything about being in the President's company when the calls
came through. The President did not take any calls and so Garret
Fitzgerald could not have been in his company when the calls were
taken. Indeed Garret Fitzgerald wasn't even in the precincts of
Áras an Uachtaráin when the calls were made, let alone taken. It
seems quite clear that the Irish Times accepted without question
the claim made by Garret Fitzgerald earlier in the week that he was
in Áras an Uachtaráin when the phone calls came through and
that he knew how many there were. This was an amazing error
which becomes all the more disturbing when set against the welter
of evidence that the President did not in fact speak to anyone on
the night in question.

The inevitable outcome of the Irish Times report published on
Wednesday October 24 was that the paper would have to back up
the story and reveal the source upon which the story was based.
This the Irish Times did, but in quite extraordinary circum-
stances. It called a press conference in Room 525 of the Westbury
Hotel on the following day, Thursday October 26. At this confer-

ence the famous excerpt of the taped interview was played. Jim Duffy was of course present at the conference while the Irish Times was represented by its managing editor, Mr. Eoin McVey and by Mr. Ken Gray, its deputy editor. The room was hired by the Irish Times, the apparatus set up and leading journalists were invited along to listen to what would have been to a newspaper man a major scoop for his next day's paper. Here it was being handed out gratis by the Irish Times to all its competitors! Never before in the annals of the press had an Irish newspaper been so generous to its rivals. I can think of only one explanation for this "generosity". The Irish Times appeared to be more interested in exposing the tape to the full blast of the electronic media than it was in revealing the contents of the tape in its own newspaper columns where the impact may not have been so devastating. Calling a press conference amounted to active and unprecedented participation by a newspaper in an election campaign. Why was this done?

What was most remarkable about the Irish Times press conference was the manner in which it was stage managed. The invited audience was told that the tape, or at least the relevant part of it, was being released because of what Mr. Duffy described as political pressure. It was also revealed that Mr. Duffy was an active member of Fine Gael, certainly from 1984 to 1987. Since he was shielded by the Irish Times from answering any further questions this could not be probed further. Duffy did read a prepared statement in which he made it clear that the reason why he released the tape was to defend what he had written in his Irish Times article on September 27 that I was among the callers to Áras an Uachtaráin in 1982. He stated that "I have received no denial concerning the information published in that article and I stand over the accuracy of its contents".

This makes it quite clear that Duffy, with the help of the Irish Times, was using for journalistic purposes, information that had been gathered for academic purposes. Was the Irish Times not aware that a breach of academic ethics was involved? If the Irish Times was so aware, then it was using confidential information for a purpose for which it was not intended.

By far the most unacceptable aspect to the Irish Times press conference was the manner in which the tape was stopped short. This meant that the assembled media did not have the opportunity of hearing that part of the tape where I stress that the interview was confidential. This follows very shortly after the end of the excerpt that they and Duffy disclosed. As I have already pointed out in an earlier chapter, the fuller transcript of the tape shows beyond all doubt that Mr. Duffy agreed that the interview was confidential. It is also absolutely certain that my concerns about this question of confidentiality related to the complete interview and not just to the events of 1982. No amount of partial presentation by either Mr. Duffy or the Irish Times can cover up the fact that the interview was conducted on any basis other than that of strict confidentiality. The Irish Times was quite clearly aware of this at the time of the release of the tape and chose not to disclose this vital information to the media at the press conference. Why?

Over a long time, I shared many of the views advanced by the Irish Times over the years, and have regarded people like Douglas Gageby as quite outstanding in their positive contribution to our national life. Recent events in the election have therefore disappointed me as they represent a serious departure by the Irish Times management from their high liberal standards. The essence of liberalism is a generous stimulation and acknowledgement of many points of view, recognising the various manifestations of the human spirit. The sort of aggressive liberalism that has debased an admirable ethic into a cult which is at variance with many values in our society does not represent the Liberal Ethic. It is in fact the very negation of true liberalism.

The one-sided support given to one candidate in the Presidential election was illiberal in its very bias. Moreover, the manner in which the presentation of the Duffy tape was organised was highly questionable by ordinary standards. By the standards of the Irish Times it was low to behold.

14

LOOKING AHEAD

I had entered into politics in the fifties to serve my country and its people. It was a time of great change and other young men like me were drawn to Fianna Fáil as a party interested in progressive change. Men like Neil Blaney, Kevin Boland, Paddy Hillery, Sean Flanagan, Eoin Ryan, George Colley, Donogh O'Malley, Jack Lynch and Charlie Haughey. We were taking over from an older generation of leaders. However, we were lucky enough to be led by a wise man, Seán Lemass, who recognised the need for change and acted upon it. He was older than us but in a way even more radical. Things did happen and Ireland began to shake off the sluggish economic performance of the past and achieve growth rates similar to other developing western nations. The sixties were a marvellous time to be in politics and the achievements are there to be seen today.

I steered the Succession Act through the Dáil and with it gave statutory recognition to a woman's right to a share of her deceased husband's estate. It was and remains a major step in equality legislation, from now on husband and wife would enjoy equal entitlements under the law. There were other achievements too. The one I am particularly proud of is the relaxation of Ireland's censorship laws in relation to authors and writers. It is hard to believe now in the 1990s but some of our greatest literary works were forbidden fruit under the law. The extent of that pernicious censorship is well set out by the American writer Paul Blanshard in his book, *The Irish and Catholic Power* (1953):

"Like Spain's Inquisition under Torquemada the Irish Book Censorship is not so much famous as infamous. It is probably the best-known feature of the Irish clerical republic. At one time or another the censorship has victimised almost every distinguished writer of fiction in the non-Irish world and it has brought under its blight Ireland's greatest poets, dramatists and scholars."

How real that censorship was, is brought home by the case of

John McGahern just two years before my legislation was enacted in 1967. Then aged 35 and a school teacher in the west of Ireland, he found his second novel, *The Dark,* censored by the official censoring authorities. It developed into a major controversy when his teaching contract was not renewed. He left to live in England and write in exile. I discussed the matter with the recently deceased writer, Seán O'Faoláin, and I set about changing our censorship laws in relation to both works of literature and the cinema. The immediate effect of my legislation was to un-ban between five and six thousand books. Among the authors whose books had been banned were Samuel Beckett, James Joyce, George Bernard Shaw, Seán O'Casey and Brendan Behan. Almost every conceivable international writer of repute had also suffered at the hands of the Irish censor. I'm glad to say that this piece of reforming legislation still stands.

Lemass was great to work with. He let his young ministers get on with their own tasks. Earlier, between 1954-57, Lemass had set about transforming the Fianna Fáil organisation on every front. In the autumn of 1956, George Colley and I had the privilege of proposing and seconding a major address by Lemass in Clery's Ballroom on full employment. When Fianna Fáil came into government in March 1957 this paper was subsumed into the first Economic Development Programme which Dr. Whittaker was preparing as Secretary of the Department of Finance. With Lemass as Taoiseach and Whittaker as Secretary of Finance things started to hum from 1959 onwards, and the appropriate legislation and administrative actions were taken to stimulate investment and rev up the economic machine. In those years, I and other young people went around the country changing the party, shaking it up. Noel Browne, the former Health minister in the Inter Party Government, had then joined Fianna Fáil and worked with me on the national executive. We were both part of an education sub-committee of that body with, among others, Eoin Ryan and Michael Yeats, that was working on new policies to reform the educational system with emphasis on equality of opportunity. The substance of that committee's work was to be the basis of subsequent education policy.

The seventies were entirely different. The years of progress continued for the most part with the country firmly implanted in the European Community. However, from 1969 onwards, things had changed, "changed utterly", and the Northern scene affected the whole political landscape, – adding a new dimension of turmoil to affairs North and South. The upheaval of the Arms Trial left its mark on the party and created bitternesses that were to last long. My instinct then was to back Lynch wholeheartedly through the crisis and the years that followed. It was a difficult decision with many of my personal friends on the other side. My support for Lynch was based on a pragmatic desire to keep the party intact and on a principled rejection of personality politics no matter who the personalities were. Later in 1979, the envies created by personality politics of one kind or another were to surface again when Charlie Haughey became leader of Fianna Fáil.

Then, through the eighties, with Mr. Haughey at the helm – these were difficult years as the party attempted, over a series of votes challenging the leadership, to tear itself apart. It was only fitfully that the political establishment began to tackle the problems created by the country's huge debt, high public spending and high personal taxation. In Anglo-Irish relations, the Dublin Castle summit between Mr. Haughey and Mrs. Thatcher ushered in a new era of understanding between the British and Irish governments. The relationship between our two countries will never be an easy one, but the process begun there is widely acknowledged to have gone a fair distance in normalising the relationship in some way.

Back in government again in 1987, and given the Foreign Affairs portfolio, I was determined on one thing - we would operate the Anglo-Irish Agreement despite our public opposition to it when it was signed. Ray MacSharry, as Minister for Finance, was equally determined to get to grips with the country's financial problems. The changes brought in by that government brought a new style of politics to this country. A greater degree of realism entered into public debate. The current coalition government with the PDs has continued that progress and that must be maintained. It is important to note though, that the changes started in 1987 were carried out by a single party Fianna Fáil government. This applies in particular to the new consensus achieved with the social partners in our country. The notion, sometimes prominent in the media, that progress towards a social consensus has been achieved solely because of the current coalition government, is flawed.

Mr. Haughey presided over the first programme in 1987, and the new Programme for Economic and Social Progress is now underway for the rest of the decade. The idea of the social partners participating outside parliament with the Government in economic and social planning is a unique European concept which makes great common-sense, and we have now adapted it successfully to Irish circumstances. It marks a big improvement on the old British concepts of parliamentary sovereignty, and free collective bargaining. It is a national approach involving the community as a whole, and by implication rejects any narrow, sectional or confrontational approach to our nation's development. Again this accords with the principle of economic and social cohesion which is written into the European Community's laws.

The problems confronting Fianna Fáil at the moment are not unlike those confronted by Lemass in the sixties. He, too, found himself in the invidious position of being unable to form a majority government but it did not take too long for him to change that, and Jack Lynch, as his successor, got an over-all majority in 1969. The party Lemass inherited was also, to some extent, fossilised both by its own success and a perception that it stood for some rather out-of-date values in Irish life. Today Fianna Fáil needs to become more in tune with the times. Too often over the last few years, the party's supporters have been unsure of where we stand on the issues of the day. It now needs to harness idealistic beliefs to its strong performance in government and sensible management of the economy. The current coalition government satisfies a need for stable government but Fianna Fáil, as distinct from the government, must look to the longer term. It must face that challenge now rather than limp into the next century a mass party, misunderstood by the masses.

If there has been any benefit from the Presidential election, it has been that it has shaken Fianna Fáil out of its torpor of recent years. It is easy to become complacent and go to the country simply on the party's record in government. Fianna Fáil needs a stronger policy base to fit the needs of a changing Ireland. At a practical level, this must mean a party organisation that is rejuvenated and also functions independent of the party's work in government.

It is not right that a great national party should take for granted its place in the national life. Irish history is littered with examples of parties, great and small, that were swept away by the tide of events. The virtual disappearance of the Irish Parliamentary party in 1918 is but one obvious example. It had spent years in the doldrums following the Parnellite split. Sinn Féin itself, in its turn, was to be split and, for all practical purposes, it was to vote itself out of politics, in the normal sense of that word. More women are needed in political life. In a real sense, a new Lemass is required for the future, be it man or woman, who will pick out the winners and put them into government. It is only when something is tried that it can be seen to work. The election of Mary Robinson has helped in that respect.

The most pernicious problem in Ireland today is family break-down, and all the consequences that flow from it for children, spouses and the community at large. I won't go into the appalling statistics and results that are there for all to see, if we wish to see.

Minister for Justice, Ray Burke, is preparing a White Paper on this matter. We must proceed as a Party with courage and judgement. There is a judicial separation system now in operation, and we should move on to a legal concept of marriage dissolution based on judicially determined criteria of irretrievable break-down.

We should deal with the problem as a social imperative, and there are precedents and examples in mainland Europe that can be examined and adapted to our circumstnces. We must not go about it in a divisive or a confrontational manner. We can succeed on a consensus basis, embracing a sensitive recognition of all aspects – the children, the parents, financial and property factors, welfare and other considerations.

A special Family Court system with related counselling and mediation services should be established. The Labour Court, Labour Relations Commission, conciliation proceedures and industrial relations legislation provide a framework model for what could be done in the area of marital relations and the family.

Fianna Fáil, if it is to survive, rather than just muddle along, must be at the vanguard of such change in our national life. Part of its problem is one of perception. To a large extent the media and intelligentsia have connived to present the Party as an unnecessary growth on the body politic. A negative stereotype has been constructed around Fianna Fáil which is not in tune with reality on the ground. Like many stereotypes, it suits a number of Fianna Fáil's antagonists ranging from secularist zealots to the cultural snob.

That, and a number of other reasons, is why the current Coalition arrangement with the PDs is wrong for Fianna Fáil. The PDs are a party who are perception-led and, to this extent, they are more like the marketing arm of a multinational company than a real political party. Their association in government has helped to build yet another stereotype of Fianna Fáil as a party of the right. The PDs are an opportunistic party of the ideological right. The image of Fianna Fáil as a party of the right is far removed from the reason it was originally founded, and the current reality of where it draws it support. Part of the problem with Irish politics is too much opportunism and too little principle. I am not so naive as to pretend that opportunism can be eliminated from the human condition. However, a balance of principle, policy and reality does need to be restored to our political life. We have mapped out a successful national consensus on economic and social progress for the next ten years. In the future, what is needed is an understanding based on a partnership of parties that reflect that prevailing reality.

Fianna Fáil and the Labour Party have occupied the centre left ground in Irish politics since the 1920s. The recent Presidential election did not change but re-enforced this essential truth. That social-republican ethos was personified by Pearse and Connolly in the 1916 Easter Rebellion, whose 75th anniversary we celebrate this year. There was a shared understanding between Labour and Fianna Fáil in the 1930s when De Valera was Taoiseach. That understanding must be re-cast for modern times to ensure future stability in the political system. It would be a stability based on the principled support of people sharing similar social and national values. Putting it bluntly, the current Coalition government is of short-term value only. The PDs do not share the same values or view of Irish life that Fianna Fáil does. Fianna Fáil is a national party with pronounced support among small farmers and workers. The Labour Party on the other hand has its association with the trade union movement, who is the major player in the Programme for Economic and Social Progress. So, ironically as it happens, the social and economic agenda for the nineties has been set out but the political arrangements that should reflect that have yet to be fixed.

Idealism of one kind or another is the petrol of politics and it is largely in short supply today. This may be one reason why young people find politics so meaningless, why party memberships are falling at a time of economic and social improvement. If the balance of reality is restored to the party political scene, then I am certain that young people will respond. That means the political balance of forces must reflect the social forces in our national life. Fianna Fáil should be clearly identified as the party of social democracy and the only other party that occupies some of that ground is the Labour Party. Other parties who lay claim to that ground are pretenders in their claim. This means that in the future, government on a secure basis can be achieved either by Fianna Fáil on its own, or in an understanding with the Labour Party.

There is an element of dishonesty in the system of election in this country. It is not proportional representation that is at fault here but rather our own particular form of it. The multi-seat arrangement encourages a rather shabby competition between deputies of different parties and between deputies from the same party. The quality of candidate that tends to emerge from this type of election is not always the best, though, as with everything in life, there are plenty of exceptions. Single seat constituencies would cut out much of the unnecessary and sterile competition between deputies, which in my view is valuable time wasted. I would retain the transferable vote so that a candidate under 50% would be dependent on transfers. That very need for transfers also makes a representative far more responsive to the wider needs of the community he or she serves. At any rate, the single seat without the transferable vote, as in Britain, is manifestly unjust and unsuited to our circumstances. At a national level, the single seat transferable vote might lead to a more rational system of party alliances and pre-election transfer arrangements. Proportional representation in a single seat constituency operates well in Australia. We should send an all-party committee to examine the situation there so that we can give serious consideration to its adoption here.

Apart from the purely political lessons to be learnt from the Presidential election, there are some ethical questions that remain to be answered. Aristotle and the Greeks based their whole political philosophy around ethics and the pursuit of good. For them the whole idea of politics was impossible, if not incomprehensible, unless grounded in an intuitive sense of ethics. For them, ethics incorporated the virtues of truth, judgment, courage and finally loyalty, or constancy as they called it. It makes for bad politics, to my mind at least, when these virtues are held in disdain. Yet, from the outset of the campaign, both of my opponents set out to destroy my credibility by holding up my loyalty as evidence that I was in some way unsuited to occupy the post of President. It began on the Rodney Rice programme and continued right through to Dr. Fitzgerald's ambiguous role on the Questions and Answers programme. It was hardly a surprise to learn, at the start of the campaign, that Dr. Fitzgerald was having fresh doubts about Alan Dukes' leadership of Fine Gael, despite the fact that it was he who virtually put Dukes there in the first place. Loyalty has not always been Dr. Fitzgerald's strong point.

In 1979 Dr. Fitzgerald plumbed a new depth in Irish political rhetoric when he spoke of the incoming Taoiseach as being a man of "flawed pedigree". It was typical of his many utterances, in that he failed to spell out what he meant by this insinuation. The only other person I have seen deploy this style of argument against Mr. Haughey in the past is his coalition partner Dessie O'Malley. He was unable to serve in government a few years ago because he had grave reservations about him. He seemed to hint that it was something to do with his time in government with him, and the period of the Arms Trial. It is worth noting that when it comes to Mr. Haughey, a number of politicians are prepared to overstep the normal limits of democratic civility. The Presidential election was no exception in this regard. The Labour leader, Dick Spring, used words like evil spirit, cancer and virus when referring to Mr. Haughey in the Dáil. The philosopher, Eric Vogelin, has made a justifiable critique of the use of similar hate-language by the German Nazis where they dehumanised opponents by depicting them as devils or causes of medical diseases. It would be nice to think that maybe the Presidential election will bring this kind of language to an end.

Throughout my political career I have tried to avoid making personalised or vituperative attacks on opponents. This style of politics serves nothing, and only demeans the very democracy that we cherish. During the Presidential election I don't think I made a personalised remark about either Austin Currie or Mary Robinson. On the night of my dismissal, a journalist asked me did I feel let down or betrayed. My reply then was simple, "I do not use pejorative terms like that. That word is not in my language." I have found, from a lifetime in politics, that bitterness does not get one too far. Naturally, I did not like being dismissed from government when, by my lights, I had done nothing wrong as Tánaiste and Minister for Defence. I know now how difficult, but ultimately rewarding, it will be to climb right back.

Reading back over the Dáil debate for Wednesday, 31 October 1990, one is struck by the virulence of the contributions of deputies from the floor. There seemed to be no grey area between truth and lies. It is all there in that Dáil debate in black and white with each speaker apparently possessing a unique insight into the truth. The election itself was something of a cathartic event bringing political debate to a new level of hypocrisy and humbug. What brought Dáil Éireann to that pass, the night of my dismissal, was in many ways a remarkable conjunction of events where, in the last two weeks of the election campaign, truth, honesty and ethical behaviour were jettisoned on the altar of political opportunism. Lorna Reid, a journalist with the Irish Independent, was to write it thus:

"No one doubted that we were watching the last act of a squalid political mugging."

Firstly, there is the whole role of Dr. Fitzgerald and Fine Gael in the Presidential election. It was unfortunate in the extreme that leading members of that party were to view the election from the outset as but a political scene setter for their own internal leadership battle. It was hardly the right approach to an election for the highest office in the land. Jim Mitchell openly boasted that he and others in Fine Gael had set out to entrap me on the Questions and Answers programme. Later, perhaps regretting his boast, he backtracked a bit and stated that Fine Gael had not known of the contents of the Duffy tape before their release by the Irish Times. There is an inconsistency here. The day after the programme, they told journalists they would produce evidence within 24 hours that my denial on the programme was untrue, in other words that I had rung Áras an Uachtaráin back in 1982. As things turned out, despite their best efforts, they did not. But the Irish Times did. What was the Fine Gael proof, but the very same that the Irish Times produced - the Duffy tape. This suggests that they had access to this evidence, or at the very least, had intimate knowledge of its contents.

Then, there is the behaviour of Jim Duffy, the MA student. It is not necessary here to recount again his strong connections with Fine Gael. It is enough to conclude that his consent to release a portion of his interview with me was a flagrant breach of the ethics of academic research. This is not just my conclusion but that of Dr. Tom Garvin, the Head of the Department of Political Science at UCD. Speaking on RTE radio in January of this year, he was to say of the young research student: "Unfortunately, he (Duffy) is applying the ethics of journalism rather than the ethics of academic research to his use of the tape."

One of my deepest regrets arising out of this whole business is the damage that has been done to academic research in Ireland. Politicians are no longer likely to trust History and Politics scholars seeking assistance in their chosen areas of research. I would not like to see this happen. I would therefore suggest that politicians and academics should get together to devise appropriate guidelines to govern interviews of this kind in the future. Strict rules should be enforced by the academic institutions for breaches of such guidelines. I would like to contribute to this process in whatever way I can.

A question mark must be placed over the Irish Times' use of the "corroborative evidence" which they claimed was contained in the tape. At no stage before playing the tape to the assembled media did they offer me the opportunity to either contradict or correct the contents of that portion, which they released. In the portion of the interview where I discussed the events of 1982, I asked Jim Duffy was he going to go public on this aspect of our conversation and he replied: "No, No, No." At their press conference, the Irish Times stopped the tape before it reached these vital words. Quite apart from that, the Irish Times presented their "corroborative evidence" at a press conference. It seems odd in the extreme that a newspaper, sitting on what was undoubtedly a scoop of kinds, should choose to present it at a press conference rather than in their own newspaper. It was almost as if the Irish Times was becoming an active rather than a passive participant in the election campaign.

The next link in the chain is the performance of the PDs. Their response to the release of the tape was strange for a party who were not even involved in the Presidential campaign. They had chosen to be neutral when it began, but were in reality pursuing a hidden agenda of sometimes covert support for Mrs. Robinson throughout. The controversy unleashed by the release of the tape was to see the PDs adopt the position of moral righteousness in the whole affair. For public consumption they were concerned with the credibility of the government, their fashionable euphemism for political expediency of the most deplorable kind. They had a clear choice between the truth and continuing in government. They chose to sacrifice the truth on the altar of their own calculated political opportunism.

Mr. Haughey's dismissal of me was the final link in the chain of events that occurred in the last two weeks of the campaign. In dismissing me he succumbed to the political blackmail of the PDs. It was a failure of nerve and political leadership on his part. Moreover he, above all others, was aware of the circumstances and happenings at the front bench meeting on January 27th, 1982. He chaired the meeting, he made the moves.

After the Presidential election, units of the Fianna Fáil organisation sought to nominate me to run for the position of president of Fianna Fáil. The office has traditionally incorporated both the leadership of the party and the organisation. Never in the history of the party has the person elected as leader by the parliamentary party not held the post of Uachtarán Fianna Fáil. The two posts have always been occupied by the same person. However, this does not rule out the possibility that members of the organisation can nominate somebody else to run for the Presidency of their organisation. This option has not been exercised in the past but it is there if people think it fit.

My own instinct when faced with this encouragement to stand was to resist that pressure. I felt it would be divisive and unnecessary with the distinct possibility that it would detract from the successful operation of a good government. That said, there were sound political reasons outlined why I should have run. When parties are in government, it is important to draw a symbolic line between the leadership of the party and the leadership of the state. The need for a strong party structure, independent of government, is underlined further when the party is a participant in a coalition government. Quite a few continental parties make a distinction between their party leadership and their party's nominee for Prime Minister or executive President as the case may be. However, I knew that such a contest within Fianna Fáil at that particular time would be depicted as a leadership challenge and would present voters with the spectacle of Fianna Fáil fighting with itself again. At a deeper more philosophical level, it struck me as a return to what I have most resisted in my political career - personality politics. There is a proper time and place for all things.

Over the last few months I have advocated a re-alignment of Fianna Fáil along more social democratic lines. In newspaper interviews, in my recent Ard Fheis speech, and again here in this book, I have set out my reasons for believing this. My views on this subject are nothing new. Many years ago, when a Senator in the 1970s, I outlined the same view and have tried with relative consistency to articulate it since.

In health and mind I am still a relatively young man. Years of involvement in politics at the highest level have not, in the immortal words of Patrick Kavanagh, "flung a ditch on my vision of beauty, love and truth." I have written this book in order to clear the air on certain matters, and to create a strong belief in the vocation of politics based on the will of the people, and expressed through political parties that represent their aspirations in a meaningful way. I stood for the office of President in order to be an active, working President with the experience to manage the office properly and sensitively. However, the electorate decided otherwise. I intend to respect their decision by devoting my energies to the real politics of giving leadership to the people in the positive direction of national affairs over the next decade.

Appendix A

THE OPINION POLLS

For the ease of the reader and the purposes of convenience I have refrained from cluttering the analysis here with references to myself in the first person.

The first opinion polls of the campaign indicated that Lenihan would be elected President by a decisive margin, and the only question was whether Lenihan would be elected on the first count or on transfers from Currie. An Irish Times/MRBI poll published on Wednesday, October 10 showed Brian Lenihan receiving 49 per cent, Mary Robinson 32 per cent and Austin Currie 19 per cent. When asked what their current intentions were in relation to second preferences, Lenihan voters opted for Robinson over Currie (by 52 to 30 per cent), Robinson voters opted for Lenihan over Currie (by 42 to 38 per cent), and Currie voters opted for Robinson over Lenihan (by 58 to 35 per cent).

The poll indicated a considerable amount of cross party voting. Lenihan secured the support of 73 per cent of Fianna Fáil voters, while both Currie and Robinson failed to win the support of the majority of Fine Gael and Labour voters respectively. Robinson was getting strong support from Fine Gael and PD voters. Among middle class voters Robinson led the field, taking 42 per cent as against 40 per cent for Lenihan and 18 per cent for Currie. Among working class voters Lenihan was the clear favourite, taking 56 per cent as against 29 per cent for Robinson and 15 per cent for Currie. Among farmers Lenihan led with 50 per cent, followed by Currie at 27 per cent and Robinson at 23 per cent. The poll was conducted on Friday 5 and Saturday 6 October.

In an opinion poll carried out by the IMS over nine days between October 1 and October 9, and published in the Sunday Independent on October 14, Lenihan was shown to have the support of 51 per cent of voters, with Robinson at 33 per cent and Currie at 16 per cent. The poll made similar findings to the Irish Times/MRBI poll in relation to the destination of second preferences. Lenihan's votes favoured Robinson over Currie by 50 per cent to 20 per cent, Robinson's favoured Lenihan over Currie by 43 to 33 percent, and Currie's favoured Robinson over Lenihan 49 to 32 per cent.

The poll also found that Robinson was attracting strong middle class support and that many Fine Gael voters intended to vote for her (37 per cent as against only 39 per cent for Currie). Among PD voters she was taking 57 per cent, among Labour voters 74 per cent, and among Workers' Party voters 59 per cent.

After that there were no surveys until just after the release of the taped interview with Mr. Duffy. The IMS conducted a poll for the Sunday Independent on October 28. The poll was conducted in the Greater Dublin area only, and was carried out in the immediate aftermath of the release of the tapes on the evening of Thursday October 25 and all day Friday October 26. The poll showed Mary Robinson taking 51 per cent in the Greater Dublin area, with Brian Lenihan taking 32 per cent and Austin Currie 17 per cent. These figures compared with 46 per cent for Lenihan in Dublin only two weeks previously, 40 per cent for Robinson and 14 per cent for Currie. The poll also showed a dramatic slippage in second preferences going Lenihan's way. Robinson's supporters now indicated that they would transfer to Currie over Lenihan by 53 to 24 per cent, while Currie's supporters now indicated that they would transfer to Robinson over Lenihan by more than a three to one margin (66 to 21 per cent).

A breakdown of Mary Robinson's support in this Dublin poll showed her to be backed by 56 per cent of women and 46 per cent of men. She had above average support among those aged between 25 and 49. Among middle class voters she took a massive 62 per cent of those polled. By contrast, support for Brian Lenihan among middle class Dubliners collapsed in the poll, with just 20 per cent supporting him. However, he retained above average backing among Dublin's working class.

Those polled were also asked whether they felt he should withdraw from the presidential election. 43 per cent said he should withdraw, while 41 per cent said he should continue. 16 per cent expressed no opinion.

This was followed up a few days later with a nationwide IMS poll published in both the Irish Independent and the Star on Wednesday, October 31. The poll had been carried out between Saturday, October 27 and Monday, October 29. The poll showed Mary Robinson taking 52 per cent of the vote, Brian Lenihan 31 per cent, and Austin Currie 17 per cent. Of those who stated that they were previously going to vote for Lenihan, only 65 per cent of them still intended to do so. The remainder were breaking heavily in Robinson's favour. Of Lenihan's supporters, 90 per cent described themselves as Fianna Fáil supporters.

The collapse in Lenihan's support clearly did not favour Currie, who was even outpolled by Robinson among Fine Gael voters (54 per cent of Fine Gael voters were voting for her, as against 41 per cent for Currie). Robinson's support in this poll went right across the board among all social groups but was particularly strong among middle class voters. She did better among women (57 per cent) than among men (46 per cent) and was stronger in urban areas (57 per cent) than rural areas (45 per cent). However, her support went right across the country - in Connaught-Ulster for example she took 52 per cent of those polled. Only two social groups preferred Lenihan over Robinson - those aged over 65 (42 per cent as against 36 per cent) and the farmers where Lenihan took 36 per cent and Robinson 35 per cent.

The poll, however, did not show a reversal of fortune for Fianna Fáil, with the party only registering a minuscule drop in its support. The state of the parties was

Fianna Fáil	49%
Fine Gael	26%
Labour	11%
PDs	7%
Workers' Party	4%
Greens	2%

There was, however, a significant drop in the satisfaction rating for Mr. Haughey's performance as Taoiseach. Mr. Haughey's rating dropped from the 57 per cent satisfied – 33 per cent dissatisfied rating of the IMS poll, taken three weeks previously, to a rating of 48 per cent satisfied – 45 per cent dissatisfied.

The most telling aspect of the poll was to be found in the statistics concerning whether Brian Lenihan was believed by the public in his denials of ringing the Áras and speaking to the President. 57 per cent believed that the truth was in the taped interview with political science student Jim Duffy, in which Lenihan said that he had "got through" to President Hillery. Only 18 per cent believed that he was telling the truth in saying, after the playing of the tape, that he never phoned or got through. 40 per cent of Fianna Fáil voters said that they did not believe his version of events, as against 29 per cent who did. TCD Politics lecturers, Michael Gallagher and Michael Marsh, who analysed the poll for the Irish Independent, said that "the sad fact for Mr. Lenihan is that his current version of events is just not believed by any group within Irish society - the old and the young, the farmers and the workers, urban and rural dwellers, men and women - the response is the same." Chris Glennon, political correspondent for the paper, said the poll had torn the heart out of Lenihan's campaign. The Editorial stated that the findings of the poll pointed only to one conclusion: "Brian Lenihan has no chance of being elected President of Ireland." All of this, however, was to change after my dismissal.

In the final poll of the campaign, published in the Irish Times on the eve of polling, Tuesday November 6, Brian Lenihan and Mary Robinson were running neck and neck, each securing 43 per cent of the popular vote, with Austin Currie taking the remaining 14 per cent when the "don't knows" were excluded. However, when candidate support was analysed by those who state that they will definitely vote, the revised figures were Lenihan 45 per cent, Robinson 42 per cent, and Currie 13 per cent. Either way the poll predicted that the outcome of the election would be determined by Currie's transfers, which was in fact what happened when the votes were counted.

This poll was conducted by the MRBI on Friday 2nd and Saturday 3rd November, in the immediate aftermath of the dismissal and after the Today Tonight television debate and the appearance of the candidates and their spouses on The Late Late Show.

The poll showed that after the political drama of the previous fortnight, Lenihan's support was down seven percentage points in Leinster and Munster, five points in Dublin and three points in Connaught/Ulster. His middle class support nationwide remained virtually unchanged at 39 per cent, while his support amongst farmers dropped nine points to 41 per cent, and amongst working class voters a fall of ten points to 46 per cent was charted. He nevertheless remained the favoured choice of working class and farming voters.

Robinson's middle class support rose from 42 per cent to 48 per cent; in the working class from 29 per cent to 42 per cent; and amongst farmers from 23 per cent to 36 per cent. Currie lost support in all three categories, and most emphatically among middle class voters. Amongst urban voters Robinson took 49 per cent of the vote against 41 per cent for Lenihan, with Currie taking only 10 per cent. Amongst rural voters Lenihan led with 45 per cent, with Robinson taking 34 per cent and Currie a noticeably better 21 per cent. Regionally, the poll showed Robinson leading in Munster and Dublin, and Lenihan leading in Leinster and Connaught/Ulster.

On transfers, the poll showed Robinson taking 70 per cent of Currie's transfers, as against 58 per cent in the MRBI poll taken four weeks previously. Lenihan's transfers from Currie had declined from the last MRBI poll in early October from 35 per cent to 20 per cent.

Amongst Fianna Fáil voters, 76 per cent stated that they would vote for Lenihan, 19 per cent for Robinson and 4 per cent for Currie. Amongst Fine Gael voters, Robinson was actually out-polling Currie, taking 54 per cent as against 42 for Currie and 4 per cent for Lenihan. The poll also showed Robinson taking the support of the vast bulk of Labour, Workers Party and PD voters.

The poll did not show, as is commonly assumed, that Robinson was attracting a significant level of support among female voters. Both Lenihan and Currie made an identical impact among women voters. However, there does seem to have been an age factor in her vote, with younger people under 34 supporting Robinson over Lenihan by 47 to 39 per cent.

Jack Jones of the MRBI said the poll showed that the campaign had been the most volatile in the history of the state. He warned it was not possible to provide reliable indications of the likely outcome due to the very considerable evidence of volatility to date. He concluded that the campaign was still in a state of flux, with the final days likely to be the most critical and decisive of the whole campaign.

Appendix B

THE ROLE OF THE PRESIDENT UNDER THE CONSTITUTION

The creation of the office of President, in the words of the late John Kelly, "is one of the most conspicuous innovations of the 1937 Constitution". Under the Constitution the President takes precedence over all other persons in the State. The President holds office for seven years and is eligible for re-election to that office once, but only once. A President may be impeached for stated misbehaviour. Article 12.10 lays down a special impeachment procedure whereby a charge is preferred and investigated by the two Houses of the Oireachtas. Apart from the impeachment procedure, the President is not answerable to either House of the Oireachtas or to any court for the exercise and performance of the powers and functions of his office.

Candidates for the office of President must be over 35 years of age. There are only three ways whereby a candidate may be nominated for the office.

(1) Former or retiring Presidents may become candidates on their own nomination.

(2) A candidate may be nominated by twenty members of the Oireachtas.

(3) A candidate may be nominated by four county councils, including county boroughs.

Obviously, where only one candidate is nominated to the office it is unnecessary to proceed to a ballot for his election. This has happened on five occasions: in 1938 when Dr. Douglas Hyde was elected the first President of Ireland, in 1952 when Seán T. O'Kelly was elected to his second term of office as President, in 1974 when Cearbhall Ó Dálaigh was elected President, and in 1976 and 1983 when Dr. Patrick Hillery was elected to his two terms of office as President. There have been five contested elections: in 1945 when Seán T. O'Kelly was elected to his first term of office, in 1959 and 1966 when Eamon De Valera was elected to his two terms of office, in 1973 when Erskine Childers was elected the fourth President, and again in 1990 with the election of Mary Robinson.

The role of the President is primarily ceremonial. The President appoints the Taoiseach on the nomination of the Dáil, and the other members of the Government and the Attorney General on the nomination of the Taoiseach. On the advice of the Taoiseach, the President accepts the resignation or terminates the appointment of members of the Government and the Attorney General, and summons and dissolves Dáil Éireann. On the advice of the Government, the President appoints the judges of the Supreme Court, the High Court and all other courts established in pursuance of the Constitution. The President signs and promulgates laws made by the Oireachtas. The supreme command of the Defence Forces is vested in the President to be exercised on the advice of the Government. The right of pardon and the power to commute or remit punishment imposed by any court exercising criminal jurisdiction are vested in the President, again to be exercised on the advice of the Government.

The Constitution imposes two important restrictions on the President.

(1) The President may only leave the State during his term of office with the consent of the Government.

(2) There are restrictions on the President's right of expression. Under Article 13.7 the President may, after consultation with the Council of State, communicate with the Houses of the Oireachtas by message or address on any matter of national or public importance, or may address a message to the Nation at any time on any such matter. Every such message or address must, however, have received the approval of the Government. The late Professor John Kelly takes the view that the law does not impose total silence on the President except for whatever the Government may approve.

"In as much as the President has ... important, independent and politically sensitive functions ... the ordinary democratic axioms imply that he must submit to criticism for his exercise of them. The same axioms, and those of justice, equally require that he should be free to answer criticism. In such a context Article

13.7 scarcely comes into play; nor could it be said that "message to the Nation" is a phrase which fits it."

In the Dáil debate on the draft Constitution in 1937 De Valera seems to have taken a much more restrictive view of the President's freedom to contribute to public debate. When it was put to De Valera that the President should be able to explain a refusal to dissolve the Dáil or to submit a Bill to referendum, he disagreed strongly. It was clear that De Valera wished to avoid any possible clash between the President and the Government, saying that "you would immediately have two authorities, and you cannot have that". This issue surfaced during the by now famous Donegan affair in 1976. On that occasion, President Cearbhall Ó Dálaigh was abusively criticised by the then Minister for Defence, Paddy Donegan, for exercising his power under Article 26 of the Constitution to refer the Emergency Powers Bill to the Supreme Court for a decision on whether the Bill was repugnant to the Constitution. President Ó Dálaigh resigned over the issue to protect the independence of the office of President. He argued that since the President was not free to speak publicly without the consent of the Government, he should be immune from criticism in the exercise of his functions as President. It is interesting to note that Ó Dálaigh did not respond to the criticism made of him by Donegan until after he had resigned as President.

At this stage, it is worth listing the independent powers which the President does enjoy under the Constitution.

(1) The President may, in his absolute discretion, appoint up to seven persons whom he may think fit to be members of the Council of State (Articles 31 and 32). The Council of State also consists of seven ex-officio members and every former President, Taoiseach and Chief Justice who is able and willing to act as a member of the Council. The function of the Council of State is to aid and counsel the President on all matters on which the President may consult the Council, in relation to the exercise and performance by him of such of his powers and functions as are expressed by the Constitution to be exercisable and performable after consultation with the Council of State.

(2) The President may in his absolute discretion refuse to

dissolve Dáil Éireann on the advice of a Taoiseach who has ceased to retain the support of a majority in Dáil Éireann (Article 13.2.1). The wording of this provision is uncertain. When has a Taoiseach "ceased to retain the support of a majority in Dáil Éireann"? Does this require a defeat on a vote of confidence in the Government or defeat on a major issue such as a budget? Or has a Taoiseach ceased to retain majority support before any defeat in a Dáil vote when, on a head count of Dáil deputies, the government can no longer count on the support of over half the Dáil deputies? It is important to note that should the President exercise this power to refuse a dissolution, his role is limited to his decision to refuse to dissolve the Dáil. The Constitution does not accord the President any role in the formation of a new Government. Once the President has made his decision, the Taoiseach requesting a dissolution must resign and the Dáil must elect a new Taoiseach.

This power to refuse a dissolution is potentially an extremely important one. Given the apolitical nature of the office of President, it is presumably a power which the framers of the Constitution did not envisage would be exercised, save in the most exceptional of circumstances. A wise and prudent President would be very slow to refuse a request for a dissolution from the Taoiseach of the day and indeed this has been the practice of President Hillery over the last few years when Taoisigh, who have ceased to retain the support of a majority of the Dáil, have made requests for a dissolution.

(3) The President may at any time, after consultation with the Council of State, convene a meeting of either or both of the Houses of the Oireachtas (Article 13.2.3). According to Mr. McDunphy, secretary to the first President, Dr. Douglas Hyde, the purpose of this provision is to prevent the undesirable non-use of powers by the authorities in whom they are normally vested. Thus, if the Dáil were in recess at a time of crisis, and the appropriate authorities failed to re-convene the Dáil to discuss the crisis and respond to it, the President could intervene to convene a meeting of the Dáil and/or Seanad. The only occasion upon which this power has been exercised was in 1969 when President De Valera convened a joint meeting of the Houses of the Oireachtas for

rather different reasons - to mark the fiftieth anniversary of the foundation of Dáil Éireann.

(4) Under Article 26 the President may, after consultation with the Council of State, refer any bill (subject to certain exceptions) to the Supreme Court for a decision on the question as to whether such a bill is repugnant to the Constitution. It is this power to refer bills to the supreme Court that has been most frequently invoked by Presidents down the years. Even here, however, there is an argument that the President should be cautious about exercising his powers, as Article 34.3.4 confers a permanent immunity on any Act which has successfully passed an Article 26 reference. This is not the case with legislation subjected to the ordinary processes of judicial review which, notwithstanding any prior judicial decision upholding its constitutionality, may be challenged at some point in the future.

(5) The President enjoys several powers which relate to the protection of the Seanad:

Where a bill is passed in accordance with Article 23.1 of the Constitution without the consent of the Seanad, then Article 27 provides that a majority of the members of the Seanad and not less than one third of the members of the Dáil may petition the President to decline to sign and promulgate the bill as a law, on the grounds that the bill contains a proposal of such national importance that the will of the people thereon ought to be ascertained. The President must pronounce his decision after consultation with the Council of State, and if he decides that the will of the people ought to be ascertained, he must decline to sign the bill until the proposal shall have been approved by the people at a referendum within eighteen months, or by a resolution of Dáil Éireann within eighteen months after a dissolution and reassembly of the Dáil.

Under Article 21 the Seanad is given a much more limited role in relation to the enactment of money bills than in the case of other legislation. It is the Ceann Comhairle of the Dáil who certifies that a certain bill is a money bill. Under Article 22, the Seanad, by a resolution passed at a sitting at which not less than thirty members are present, may request the President to refer the question whether the bill is a money bill to a Committee of Privileges. If the President, after consultation with the Council of State, decides to accede to the request he shall, again after consultation with the Council of State, appoint a Committee of Privileges consisting of an equal number of members of Dáil Éireann and Seanad Éireann and a Chairman who shall be a judge of the Supreme Court.

Under Article 24 the consent of the President is necessary to an abridgment of the time for the consideration by the Seanad of a bill which has been passed by the Dáil and is, in the opinion of the Government, urgent and immediately necessary for the preservation of public peace and security or by reason of the existence of a public emergency, whether domestic or international.

None of these powers have ever been exercised. It is not difficult to see why. Of the sixty members of the Seanad, eleven are nominated by the Taoiseach. This ensures a virtually in-built Government majority in the Seanad. Therefore, there is never likely to be a political conflict between the Dáil and the Seanad, which would appear to make the President's powers in relation to the protection of the rights of the Seanad fairly redundant.

(6) One final aspect of the President's role, which should be noted, is that the Taoiseach is under a constitutional obligation to keep the President generally informed on matters of domestic and international policy (Article 28.5.2). This provision could be interpreted to give the President a consultative role in relation to the development of government policy. How it works out in practice must, in the final analysis, depend on the nature of the President's relationship with the Taoiseach of the day.

Oifig an Taoisigh
Office of the Taoiseach

31 October 1990

Mr Brian Lenihan, T.D.,
Tánaiste and Minister for Defence.

A Thánaiste, a Aire,

I am writing to request you, pursuant to Article 28.9.4° of the Constitution, for reasons which I deem to be sufficient, to resign as a member of the Government.

I should like you to know that, in the event of failure to comply with this request, I shall with great regret be compelled to advise the President to terminate your appointment as a member of the Government.

Yours sincerely,

Taoiseach

Oifig an Taoisigh. Tithe an Rialtais. Baile Átha Cliath 2.
Office of the Taoiseach. Government Buildings, Dublin 2.

239

Index